Taste of Home

GIRLS NIGHT IN

T0270149

TASTE OF HOME BOOKS • RDA ENTHUSIAST BRANDS, LLC • MILWAUKEE, WI

© 2024 RDA Enthusiast Brands, LLC.
1610 N. 2nd St., Suite 102, Milwaukee WI 53212-3906
All rights reserved. Taste of Home is a registered
trademark of RDA Enthusiast Brands, LLC.

Visit us at **tasteofhome.com** for other Taste of
Home books and products.

International Standard Book Number:
979-8-88977-053-4

Chief Content Officer: Jason Burhmester
Content Director: Mark Hagen
Creative Director: Raeann Thompson
Associate Creative Director: Jami Geittmann
Senior Editor: Christine Rukavena
Editor: Hazel Wheaton
Senior Art Director: Courtney Lovetere
Manager, Production Design: Satyandra Raghav
Senior Print Publication Designer: Jogesh Antony
Project Coordinator: Sierra Schuler
Production Artist: Nithya Venkatakrishnan
Deputy Editor, Copy Desk: Ann M. Walter
Copy Editor: Suchismita Ukil
Contributing Copy Editor: Nancy J. Stohs

Cover Photography:
Photographer: Mark Derse
Set Stylist: Melissa Franco
Food Stylists: Sue Draheim

Pictured on front cover: Brie in Puff Pastry,
p. 30; Marinated Almond-Stuffed Olives, p. 31;
Original Burrata Toast, p. 26; Strawberry Riesling
Wine Spritzer, p. 59; Raspberry Chipotle Chicken
Pinwheels, p. 39

Pattern: oxygen/Getty Images

Pictured on back cover: Honey Champagne
Fondue, p. 167; Mini Blueberry Bundt Cakes, p. 118;
Strawberry Shortcake Salad, p. 86; Cotton Candy
Champagne Cocktails, p. 181; French Fry Fest
Board, p. 66; Caramelized Ham & Swiss Buns,
p. 113; Individual Pizza Crusts, p. 195; Mexican
Steak Fajitas, p. 217; No-Bake Oreo Pie, p. 123;
Layered Fresh Fruit Salad, p. 82

Printed in China
1 3 5 7 9 10 8 6 4 2

CONTENTS

IT'S A GREAT NIGHT TO STAY IN!

Sometimes the best nights with friends aren't spent out on the town, but staying in instead. Who doesn't love keeping the party at home and binge-watching TV, playing games or simply just hanging out? It's all good! And while your besties could likely make a frozen pizza memorable, why not treat them to something with a little more panache ... where the food is as fun as the company?

Girls' Night In helps you step up your hosting game, with more than 400 recipes ideal for easy entertaining—emphasis on easy. Check out these snacks, appetizers, small-plate dinners, charcuterie boards, sweets and desserts. They all serve up delicious fun while keeping prep work to a minimum. See how effortless it is to impress the gang without spending a fortune or wasting the night away in the kitchen.

You'll even find simple suggestions for wine pairings as well the secrets behind no-fuss cocktails and mocktails.

Need an excuse for a party? You'll find 24 themed menus inside. Whether you're planning an evening of wine and tapas or a totally awesome '80s party, hosting special get-togethers is a snap.

Because the recipes are chosen for their flavor and convenience, you'll want to savor them all the time—with or without company. Just look for the *#GIRLDINNER* tag for advice on creating sensational meals for one.

So raise a glass to (and with) your best friends! It's time for sipping and sharing, munching and memory making. For brunches, showers, dinner parties, movie nights and more, your place will be the most popular spot in town.

WHAT IS "GIRL DINNER," ANYWAY?

For everything from mac-and-cheese dinners to grazing on a charcuterie plate, we've got you covered on the trend that took the internet by storm.

It all started when TikTok user Olivia Maher, aka @liviemaher, posted a video showing off her evening meal—a glass of red wine, pieces of bread, butter, cheese, grapes and pickles. "I call this girl dinner," she explained, "or medieval peasant."

Her post struck a chord with a world full of overworked, time-crunched, budget-strapped women. Maher's original TikTok racked up millions of views, and thousands of users posted their own in response.

The many different women posting their videos showed a huge variety of girl dinners—with the common thread being low-maintenance meals made up of random food items. The plates are sometimes harmonious, sometimes nonsensical but almost always *pretty*.

The initial inspiration for girl dinners seems to be a pared-down take on the charcuterie board: A random assembly of fridge and pantry findings to serve one. Maher's "medieval peasant" quip isn't far off—the ultra-traditional British "ploughman's lunch" is almost exactly what Maher originally posted, only with a good ale standing in for the red wine.

The main theme is "appetizers for dinner." Instead of starting a meal with a small plate, why not simply combine a few to create a meal? Girl dinners can also consist of favorite side dishes or servings of go-to comfort foods.

The trend was so popular Popeyes even offered its own "girl dinner," comprised of classic sides—mashed potatoes, mac and cheese, Cajun fries, coleslaw, biscuits and red beans with rice.

The upshot is that a girl dinner is whatever you want it to be. It's the easy meal you turn to after a tiring day when you just want to stay home. It relies on carefree satisfaction with your kitchen's contents. It turns the idea of a traditional dinner—full of preparation and labor—on its head. It's an act of self-care and indulgence ... and fun.

Why not enjoy the tasty apps you serve friends on your own? Because "nights in" are sometimes just for one, this book offers tips for transforming recipes into perfect, easy, single-serve meals. Simply look for the *#GIRLDINNER* tag scattered throughout the book. The hints cover how to prepare tasty bites in advance, what to pair them with or how to add a healthy twist. Then get cozy and settle in for a girl dinner you'll want to enjoy time and again.

COOKBOOK CLUBS: A NEW KIND OF POTLUCK

For a modern take on old-school potlucks, try starting a cookbook club! The trend, featured on *Good Morning America* and other news shows, is like a crowd-sourced version of *Julie & Julia*. In that book (then film), a single ambitious newbie cooked her way through every single recipe in Julia Child's epic *Mastering the Art of French Cooking*. (Yes, even the aspic.) Cookbook clubs are founded on the firm belief that everything is better when shared with friends. And maybe with less aspic.

Start with a small group of friends, and choose a cookbook to work from—one that people will have fun with. (Maybe even the book you're holding right now?) Everyone will need to make something from the book, so the recipes should be appealing and accessible. Ask members to claim their recipes so there's no overlap. Then set the day, time and place, and enjoy! You can make it a regular event, inviting more to join as your club gets off the ground. Rotate hosting duties and choose new books to keep it fresh—what a great reason to have a party!

CAN I GET YOU A DRINK?

Keep an eye out for these icons—we offer suggestions for the perfect beverage to accompany specific dishes throughout this book. If it's a cocktail (the glass on the left), we'll direct you to a recipe so you can make it at home.

FOOD & DRINK

FRUITY
HORSERADISH
CREAM CHEESE
P. 27

APPETIZERS & SMALL PLATES

Tasty and easy to create, finger food and nibbly bits are the heart of any good party. They can be as casual or as elegant as you wish, and it's fun to come up with an array of apps to suit the season and the occasion!

SUN-DRIED TOMATO PESTO
Layer a Ritz cracker with mascarpone cheese, sun-dried tomato pesto and a micro basil leaf.

PEAR & CHEDDAR
Dab apple butter on a water cracker and top with aged white cheddar, pear slice and sliced toasted almonds.

WISE CRACKERS

The snappy snack base gets elevated with tasty toppers that make guests say, "Ooh...good one!"

SMOKED TROUT
Top a salt-and-pepper cracker with creme fraiche, capers, smoked trout and minced red onion.

CRAB & AVOCADO
Slather a sourdough cracker with cream cheese, then top with a peeled grapefruit slice, lump crabmeat and an avocado slice.

MEDITERRANEAN
Hummus, halved green and black olives, thinly sliced garlic, crumbled feta, and a drizzle of olive oil top a hearty sourdough cracker.

BUFFALO
Top a Ritz cracker with crumbled blue cheese, shredded chicken, Buffalo sauce and julienned celery.

SPICY PORK
Pile queso fresco, shredded pork, salsa and a jalapeno slice on a multi-seed cracker.

SPAM
Load up a crispy rice cracker with hoisin sauce, seared Spam, shredded nori and spicy chili crisp.

BISCOFF
Biscoff cookie butter, sliced strawberry, shaved white chocolate and Biscoff cookie crumbles are irresistible on a water cracker.

PASTRAMI
Try honey mustard, Swiss cheese, sauerkraut, pastrami and a cornichon half on a hearty nut-and-seed cracker.

SWEET ONION PIMIENTO CHEESE DEVILED EGGS

For my mother's 92nd birthday, we had deviled eggs topped with pimientos as part of the spread. They're timeless and always in good taste.
—Linda Foreman, Locust Grove, OK

TAKES: 15 min. • **MAKES:** 1 dozen

- 6 hard-boiled large eggs
- ¼ cup finely shredded sharp cheddar cheese
- 2 Tbsp. mayonnaise
- 4 tsp. diced pimientos, drained
- 2 tsp. finely chopped sweet onion
- 1 tsp. Dijon mustard
- 1 small garlic clove, minced
- ¼ tsp. salt
- ⅛ tsp. pepper
   Additional diced pimientos and finely shredded sharp cheddar cheese

Cut eggs lengthwise in half. Remove yolks, reserving whites. In a bowl, mash yolks. Stir in cheese, mayonnaise, pimientos, onion, mustard, garlic, salt and pepper. Spoon or pipe mixture into egg whites. Sprinkle with additional pimientos and cheese. Refrigerate, covered, until serving.

1 STUFFED EGG HALF 67 cal., 5g fat (2g sat. fat), 96mg chol., 128mg sod., 1g carb. (0 sugars, 0 fiber), 4g pro.

TEST KITCHEN TIPS

- To cut calories, replace the mayo with the same amount of plain Greek yogurt.

- To quickly peel fresh garlic, gently crush the clove with the flat side of a large knife blade to loosen the peel.

MINI CHICKEN EMPANADAS

MINI CHICKEN EMPANADAS

Refrigerated pie crust makes quick work of assembling these bite-sized appetizers loaded with chicken and cheese. I've made them several times since receiving the recipe from a friend.
—Betty Fulks, Onia, AR

PREP: 30 min. • **BAKE:** 15 min./batch
MAKES: about 2½ dozen

- 1 cup finely chopped cooked chicken
- ⅔ cup shredded Colby-Monterey Jack cheese
- 3 Tbsp. cream cheese, softened
- 4 tsp. chopped sweet red pepper
- 2 tsp. chopped seeded jalapeno pepper
- 1 tsp. ground cumin
- ½ tsp. salt
- ⅛ tsp. pepper
- 2 sheets refrigerated pie crust
   Optional: Egg wash and salsa verde

1. Preheat oven to 400°. In a small bowl, combine the first 8 ingredients. On a lightly floured surface, roll each crust into a 15-in. circle. Cut out circles with a floured 3-in. round biscuit cutter.
2. Place about 1 tsp. filling on 1 half of each circle. Moisten edges with water. Fold crust over filling. Press edges with a fork to seal.
3. Transfer to greased baking sheets. If desired, brush with egg wash. Bake until golden brown, 12-15 minutes. Remove to wire racks. Serve warm, with salsa if desired.

NOTE Wear disposable gloves when cutting hot peppers; the oils can burn skin. Avoid touching your face.

1 EMPANADA 81 cal., 5g fat (2g sat. fat), 10mg chol., 108mg sod., 7g carb. (1g sugars, 0 fiber), 2g pro. **DIABETIC EXCHANGES** 1 fat, ½ starch.

GRILLED
SHRIMP-STUFFED
MUSHROOMS

GRILLED SHRIMP-STUFFED MUSHROOMS

I love this recipe because it's fast and easy. The mushrooms can also be cooked on an indoor grill or grill pan.
—Patti Duncan, Colorado Springs, CO

TAKES: 30 min. • **MAKES:** 1 dozen

- 6 uncooked shrimp (16-20 per lb.), peeled and deveined, tails removed
- 6 bacon strips
- 12 baby portobello mushrooms, stems removed
- 2 Tbsp. barbecue sauce

1. Cut shrimp and bacon strips in half. Place 1 piece of shrimp on each mushroom cap. Wrap each mushroom with a piece of bacon; secure with a toothpick.
2. Grill, covered, over indirect medium heat or broil 4 in. from heat until bacon is crisp and mushrooms are tender, 10-15 minutes, turning occasionally. Brush with barbecue sauce; grill 5 minutes longer. Discard toothpicks before serving.

1 STUFFED MUSHROOM 77 cal., 6g fat (2g sat. fat), 25mg chol., 137mg sod., 2g carb. (1g sugars, 0 fiber), 4g pro.

HAWAIIAN EGG ROLLS

An avid cook, I am constantly trying to come up with recipes for leftovers. This one gives a whole new twist to extra ham. These egg rolls freeze well; I thaw as many as needed and bake them. My children love them!

—*Terri Wheeler, Vadnais Heights, MN*

TAKES: 25 min. • **MAKES:** 7 egg rolls

- 10 fresh spinach leaves, julienned
- ½ tsp. ground ginger
- 2 Tbsp. olive oil
- ½ lb. fully cooked ham, coarsely ground (about 2 cups)
- 4 water chestnuts, chopped
- ¼ cup crushed pineapple, undrained
- 2 Tbsp. chopped green onion
- 1 Tbsp. soy sauce
- 7 egg roll wrappers
  Canola oil for frying
  Sweet-and-sour sauce

1. In a large saucepan, saute spinach and ginger in olive oil for 1-2 minutes. In a large bowl, combine ham, water chestnuts, pineapple, green onion and soy sauce. Stir in the spinach mixture.
2. Place 3 Tbsp. of the ham mixture in the center of each egg roll wrapper. Fold bottom corner over filling; fold sides over filling toward center. Moisten remaining corner with water; roll up tightly to seal.
3. In an electric skillet, heat 1 in. canola oil to 375°. Fry egg rolls until golden brown, about 2 minutes on each side. Drain on paper towels. Serve with sweet-and-sour sauce.
1 EGG ROLL 311 cal., 20g fat (4g sat. fat), 21mg chol., 743mg sod., 22g carb. (2g sugars, 1g fiber), 10g pro.

TRADITIONAL SCONES

TRADITIONAL SCONES

Making scones is simple; I learned to make them when my wife and I hosted an English tea. These are light and tasty.

—*Chuck Hinz, Parma, OH*

PREP: 20 min. • **BAKE:** 25 min.
MAKES: 1 dozen

- 2 cups all-purpose flour
- 2 Tbsp. sugar
- 3 tsp. baking powder
- ⅛ tsp. baking soda
- 6 Tbsp. cold butter, cubed
- 1 large egg
- ½ cup buttermilk
  Jam of your choice, optional

1. Preheat oven to 350°. In a large bowl, combine flour, sugar, baking powder and baking soda. Cut in butter until mixture resembles coarse crumbs. In a small bowl, whisk egg and buttermilk until blended; add to the crumb mixture just until moistened.
2. Turn out dough onto a lightly floured surface; gently knead 10 times. Divide in half; pat each portion into a 5-in. circle. Cut each circle into 6 wedges.
3. Separate the wedges and place 1 in. apart on an ungreased baking sheet. Bake until golden brown, 25-30 minutes. Serve warm, with jam if desired.
NOTE To substitute for each cup of buttermilk, use 1 Tbsp. white vinegar or lemon juice plus enough milk to measure 1 cup. Stir, then let stand 5 min. Or, use 1 cup plain yogurt or 1¾ tsp. cream of tartar plus 1 cup milk.
1 SCONE 144 cal., 6g fat (4g sat. fat), 33mg chol., 170mg sod., 19g carb. (3g sugars, 1g fiber), 3g pro.

CUCUMBER CANAPES

CHEESE-STUFFED CHERRY TOMATOES

We grow plenty of tomatoes, so my husband and I often pick enough cherry tomatoes for these easy-to-fix appetizers. This is one of our favorite recipes, and it's impossible to eat just one.
—*Mary Lou Robison, Greensboro, NC*

PREP: 15 min. + chilling • **MAKES:** 1 dozen

- 1   pint cherry tomatoes
- 1   pkg. (4 oz.) crumbled feta cheese
- ½   cup finely chopped red onion
- ½   cup olive oil
- ¼   cup red wine vinegar
- 1   Tbsp. dried oregano
      Salt and pepper to taste

1. Cut a thin slice off the top of each tomato. Scoop out and discard pulp. Invert tomatoes onto paper towels to drain. Combine cheese and onion; spoon into tomatoes.
2. In a small bowl, whisk oil, vinegar, oregano, salt and pepper. Spoon over tomatoes. Refrigerate, covered, for 30 minutes or until ready to serve.
1 TOMATO 111 cal., 11g fat (2g sat. fat), 5mg chol., 93mg sod., 2g carb. (1g sugars, 1g fiber), 2g pro.

CUCUMBER CANAPES

I always get requests for the recipe whenever I serve these delicate finger sandwiches with a creamy herb spread and bright red and green garnishes.
—*Nadine Whittaker, South Plymouth, MA*

PREP: 20 min. + chilling • **MAKES:** 2 dozen

- 1   cup mayonnaise
- 3   oz. cream cheese, softened
- 1   Tbsp. grated onion
- 1   Tbsp. minced chives
- ½   tsp. cider vinegar
- ½   tsp. Worcestershire sauce
- 1   garlic clove, minced
- ¼   tsp. paprika
- ⅛   tsp. curry powder
- ⅛   tsp. each dried oregano, thyme, basil, parsley flakes and dill weed

- 1   loaf (1 lb.) white or rye bread
- 2   medium cucumbers, scored and thinly sliced
      Diced pimientos and additional dill weed

1. In a blender or food processor, combine mayonnaise, cream cheese, onion, chives, vinegar, Worcestershire sauce, garlic and seasonings. Cover and process until blended. Refrigerate, covered, for 24 hours.
2. Using a 2½-in. biscuit cutter, cut out circles from bread slices. Spread the mayonnaise mixture over bread; top with cucumber slices. Garnish with pimientos and dill.
1 CANAPE 120 cal., 9g fat (2g sat. fat), 7mg chol., 134mg sod., 8g carb. (1g sugars, 1g fiber), 2g pro.

CHIPOTLE GUACAMOLE

My guacamole is so good because it has just a hint of smoke from chipotle peppers. Stir them in or put a dollop in the center of the dip so people who aren't into peppers can scoop around them.
—Gayle Sullivan, Salem, MA

PREP: 15 min. + chilling • **MAKES:** 3 cups

- 4 medium ripe avocados, peeled and pitted
- 1 small tomato, seeded and chopped
- ⅓ cup finely chopped red onion
- 3 garlic cloves, minced
- 2 Tbsp. lemon juice
- 2 Tbsp. olive oil
- ¼ tsp. salt
- 1 to 2 Tbsp. minced fresh cilantro, optional
- 1 finely chopped chipotle pepper in adobo sauce plus 1 tsp. adobo sauce
  Tortilla chips

Mash avocados. Stir in next 6 ingredients and, if desired, cilantro. Dollop chipotle pepper and adobo sauce over center of the guacamole. Refrigerate for 1 hour. Serve with chips.
¼ CUP 103 cal., 9g fat (1g sat. fat), 0 chol., 70mg sod., 5g carb. (1g sugars, 3g fiber), 1g pro.

LEMONY BACON-ARTICHOKE DIP

Move over, spinach artichoke dip—bacon adds much more flavor! You might want to double this fabulous recipe because there are never any leftovers.
—Heidi Jobe, Carrollton, GA

PREP: 20 min. • **BAKE:** 25 min.
MAKES: 12 servings (3 cups)

- 5 thick-sliced bacon strips, chopped
- 1 can (14 oz.) water-packed quartered artichoke hearts, drained and chopped
- 2 garlic cloves, minced
- 2 pkg. (8 oz. each) reduced-fat cream cheese
- ⅓ cup sour cream
- ½ tsp. onion salt
- ¼ tsp. salt
- ⅛ tsp. pepper
- 2 Tbsp. lemon juice
- ½ cup grated Parmesan cheese
  Pita bread wedges, toasted
  Assorted vegetables, optional

1. Preheat oven to 400°. In a large skillet, cook bacon over medium heat until crisp, stirring occasionally. Remove with a slotted spoon; drain on paper towels. Discard drippings, reserving 2 tsp. in pan. Add artichoke hearts and garlic to drippings; cook and stir 1 minute.
2. In a large bowl, beat cream cheese, sour cream, onion salt, salt and pepper until smooth. Beat in lemon juice. Fold in the artichoke mixture and half the bacon.
3. Transfer to a greased 2-qt. baking dish. Sprinkle with the remaining bacon; top with Parmesan cheese. Bake, uncovered, until golden brown, 25-30 minutes. Serve with pita wedges and, if desired, assorted vegetables.
¼ CUP 166 cal., 13g fat (8g sat. fat), 39mg chol., 535mg sod., 4g carb. (2g sugars, 0 fiber), 8g pro.

HAM & CHEESE BUNDLES

My family looks forward to these rich and delicious egg bundles. They're perfect for holidays, brunches and birthdays.
—Cindy Bride, Bloomfield, IA

PREP: 35 min. • **BAKE:** 15 min.
MAKES: 12 servings

- 15 sheets phyllo dough (14x9 in.)
- ¾ cup butter, melted
- 4 oz. cream cheese, cut into 12 pieces
- 12 large eggs
- ½ tsp. salt
- ½ tsp. pepper
- ½ cup cubed fully cooked ham
- ½ cup shredded provolone cheese
- 2 Tbsp. seasoned bread crumbs
- 2 Tbsp. minced fresh chives

1. Preheat oven to 400°. Place 1 sheet of phyllo dough on a work surface; brush with butter. Layer with 4 additional phyllo sheets, brushing each layer. (Keep remaining phyllo covered with a damp towel to keep it from drying out.) Cut layered sheets crosswise in half, then lengthwise in half. Cover stacks to keep them from drying; repeat with remaining phyllo and butter.
2. Place each stack in a greased muffin cup. Fill each with a piece of cream cheese. Carefully break 1 egg into each cup. Sprinkle with salt and pepper; top with ham, cheese, bread crumbs and chives. Bring phyllo together above filling; pinch to seal and form bundles.
3. Bake until golden brown, 15-18 minutes. Serve warm.
1 BUNDLE 273 cal., 21g fat (12g sat. fat), 233mg chol., 478mg sod., 10g carb. (1g sugars, 0 fiber), 11g pro.

HAM &
CHEESE
BUNDLES

ROCK THAT GUAC

Grab some tortilla chips and get ready to dunk into these sweet and savory spins on the classic, creamy avocado snack.

MAKE THIS **MANGO & HABANERO GUACAMOLE,** P. 220

RADISH + MANDARIN ORANGE

Radishes are often dismissed as a simple salad garnish, but their crisp bite is a welcome addition here. For balance, pair radish's peppery crunch with the soft, sweet tang of mandarin oranges.

Basic Guacamole

In a bowl, mash 3 ripe avocados until almost smooth. Stir in 2-3 Tbsp. fresh lime juice and ½-1 tsp. kosher salt. Let stand 10 minutes to allow flavors to blend. Then get to topping!

GRILLED CHICKEN + CHERRY TOMATO

Chicken breasts hot off the grill and cherry tomatoes plucked from your garden turn a simple snack into a gourmet meal.

BASIL + TOASTED PINE NUTS

For a pesto-inspired take, top guac off with toasted pine nuts and fresh basil ribbons. You can also substitute lemon juice for the traditional lime.

CAJUN SHRIMP + RED PEPPER

Here's a way to not only spice up your guac but also make it dinnerworthy: Top it with a Louisiana classic and a handful of crunchy chopped red pepper.

MANGO + HABANERO

For the ultimate sweet-spicy combo, pair mango with fresh habanero chile peppers. You can control the guac's heat by adjusting how much of the peppers' seeds and ribs you stir into the dip.

BLACK BEAN + CORN

Bright colors and contrasting textures make this combination especially delightful. For extra flavor, start by grilling fresh ears of corn on the cob.

BLUE CHEESE + TOASTED ALMONDS

The crumbly tang of blue cheese paired with the sweet, toasty crunch of almonds is a mind-blowing duo when it's stirred into cool, creamy avocado.

JICAMA + PINEAPPLE

If you're a fan of chunky guac, this combo is for you. Crunchy diced jicama and juicy chopped pineapple make for seriously satisfying bites. To add some smoky flavor, toss the pineapple on the grill for a few minutes before chopping.

BACON + COTIJA CHEESE

Bacon adds crisp, rich texture while Cotija cheese makes things extra creamy. If you're feeling bold, go with applewood smoked bacon for more complex flavor.

APPLE + WHITE ONION

A little bit sweet, a little bit sharp, this matchup is unexpectedly delicious on your guac. Depending on the type of apple you use, this can taste fruity, sugary or tart.

HOW TO MAKE A PINEAPPLE BOWL

Pineapples add a sweet touch to any party. Here's how to create a fun serving bowl using this tropical fruit.

Step 1: Using a large knife, cut a pineapple in half lengthwise.

Step 2: Using a small serrated knife, cut around the edge of the pineapple, leaving a ¾-in.shell.

Step 3: Remove the center core by cutting down both sides of the core at a slight angle; discard core.

Step 4. Cut away fruit on both sides of the removed core. Place dip inside the pineapple shell. Slice removed fruit and serve alongside dip or salsa.

PINEAPPLE SALSA

This mouthwatering salsa features fresh pineapple and cilantro. Besides serving it with chips, you can spoon it over grilled chicken or fish for a jazzed-up meal.
—*Suzi LaPar, Wahiawa, HI*

- -

TAKES: 20 min. • **MAKES:** 3½ cups

   2   cups diced fresh pineapple
   2   medium tomatoes, seeded and
       chopped
   ¾   cup chopped sweet onion
   ¼   cup minced fresh cilantro
   1   jalapeno pepper, seeded and
       chopped
   1   Tbsp. olive oil
   1   tsp. ground coriander
   ¾   tsp. ground cumin
   ½   tsp. salt
   ½   tsp. minced garlic
       Tortilla chips

In a large bowl, combine the first 10 ingredients. Refrigerated, covered, until serving. Serve with tortilla chips.
NOTE Wear disposable gloves when cutting hot peppers; the oils can burn skin. Avoid touching your face.
¼ CUP 29 cal., 1g fat (0 sat. fat) 0 chol., 87mg sod., 5g carb. (4g sugars, 1g fiber), 0 pro.

GORGONZOLA TOMATOES ON ENDIVE

This simple yet elegant appetizer takes advantage of a timesaving ingredient — bottled salad dressing. You'd never guess!
—*Kimberly Gremli, Islip, NY*

- -

TAKES: 25 min. • **MAKES:** 20 appetizers

  20   leaves Belgian endive (about
       2 heads)
   2   medium tomatoes, seeded and
       finely chopped
   3   green onions, thinly sliced
   ½   cup crumbled Gorgonzola cheese
   ½   cup chopped walnuts, toasted
   ⅓   cup balsamic vinaigrette

Arrange endive on a serving platter. In each leaf, layer the tomatoes, green onions, cheese and walnuts. Drizzle with vinaigrette. Chill until serving.
1 APPETIZER 49 cal., 4g fat (1g sat. fat), 3mg chol., 84mg sod., 4g carb. (1g sugars, 2g fiber), 2g pro. **DIABETIC EXCHANGES** 1 fat.

PROSCIUTTO & MELON (PROSCIUTTO E MELONE)

You need only a handful of ingredients and a few minutes to pull this classic appetizer together. Serve it to guests, or whip it up as a summer snack for yourself when melons are in season.
—Taste of Home *Test Kitchen*

- -

TAKES: 15 min. • **MAKES:** 1 dozen

   ½   medium cantaloupe or honeydew
       melon
  12   thin slices prosciutto
   2   Tbsp. honey or balsamic glaze
       Fresh basil leaves

Remove and discard rind and seeds from melon. Cut melon into 6 slices. Cut each slice crosswise in half. Wrap each piece with 1 slice prosciutto; place on a serving platter. Drizzle with honey or glaze; garnish with basil.
1 PIECE 49 cal., 2g fat (1g sat. fat), 13mg chol., 279mg sod., 5g carb. (5g sugars, 0 fiber), 4g pro.

COPYCAT BLOOMIN' ONION

2. For onion, in a shallow bowl, combine flour and seasonings. In an electric skillet or deep fryer, heat oil to 375°. In another shallow bowl, whisk egg and milk. With a sharp knife, slice ½ in. off the top of the onion; peel onion. Cut into 16 wedges to within ½ in. of root end. Gently spread onion petals apart.

3. Hold onion over dry ingredients. Spoon the flour mixture over and around onion petals; shake off excess. Hold onion over egg mixture. Spoon over and around the onion petals; allowing excess to drip off. Again, hold onion over dry ingredients. Spoon flour mixture over and around onion petals; shake off excess.

4. Fry onion, cut-side down, 3 minutes. Flip; fry until golden brown, about 3 minutes longer. Drain on paper towels; sprinkle with additional salt. Serve with sauce.

1 SERVING 442 cal., 31g fat (4g sat. fat), 59mg chol., 1203mg sod., 35g carb. (7g sugars, 2g fiber), 7g pro.

TEST KICHEN TIPS

What kind of onion should I use? We recommend using a large sweet onion, like a Vidalia or a Walla Walla. These types of onions have a mild flavor with a touch of sweetness, making them perfect for this recipe.

What do I serve with a blooming onion? Serve with the sauce outlined in this recipe, or enjoy it with other dips like queso, ranch, barbecue or your favorite aioli.

How do I store the leftovers? Like most fried foods, bloomin' onions are best eaten fresh, but leftovers can be stored in an airtight container. Reheat them in the air fryer for 3 to 4 minutes to get back some of the crispiness.

COPYCAT BLOOMIN' ONION

No one can resist the crunchy goodness of a bloomin' onion. Plus, the dipping sauce makes this an irresistible replica of the famous restaurant version.
—Taste of Home *Test Kitchen*

PREP: 30 min. + chilling • **COOK:** 5 min.
MAKES: 4 servings

- ½ cup mayonnaise
- 2 Tbsp. prepared horseradish
- 2 tsp. ketchup
- ¼ tsp. garlic powder
- ¼ tsp. smoked paprika
- ⅛ tsp. salt
- ⅛ tsp. dried oregano
  Dash cayenne pepper
  Dash pepper

ONION
- 1 cup all-purpose flour
- 1½ tsp. salt
- 1 tsp. garlic powder
- 1 tsp. onion powder
- ½ tsp. paprika
- ½ tsp. dried oregano
- ½ tsp. dried thyme, optional
- ½ tsp. pepper
- ¼ tsp. cayenne pepper
  Oil for deep-fat frying
- 1 large egg, lightly beaten
- ½ cup 2% milk
- 1 large sweet onion

1. To make the sauce, combine the first 9 ingredients. Refrigerate, covered, for at least 2 hours before serving.

TERRIFIC TOMATO TART

Fresh, colorful tomatoes, feta cheese and prepared pesto perfectly complement this appetizer's crispy phyllo dough crust.
—*Diane Halferty, Corpus Christi, TX*

PREP: 15 min. • **BAKE:** 20 min.
MAKES: 8 servings

12 sheets phyllo dough (14x9 in.)
 2 Tbsp. olive oil
 2 Tbsp. dry bread crumbs
 2 Tbsp. prepared pesto
 ¾ cup crumbled feta cheese
 1 medium tomato, cut into ¼-in. slices
 1 large yellow tomato, cut into ¼-in. slices
 ¼ tsp. pepper
 5 to 6 fresh basil leaves, thinly sliced

1. Preheat oven to 400°. Place 1 sheet of phyllo dough on a baking sheet lined with parchment. (Keep remaining phyllo covered with a damp towel to prevent it from drying out.) Brush with ½ tsp. oil and sprinkle with ½ tsp. bread crumbs. Repeat layers, being careful to brush oil all the way to edges.

2. Fold each side ¾ in. toward center to form a rim. Spread with pesto; sprinkle with half the feta cheese. Alternately arrange red and yellow tomato slices over the cheese. Sprinkle with pepper and the remaining feta.

3. Bake until crust is golden brown and crispy, 20-25 minutes. Cool on a wire rack for 5 minutes. Remove parchment before cutting. Garnish with basil.

1 PIECE 135 cal., 7g fat (2g sat. fat), 7mg chol., 221mg sod., 13g carb. (1g sugars, 1g fiber), 5g pro.

TERRIFIC TOMATO TART

BENEDICTINE SPREAD

TOMATILLO SALSA

Dare to deviate from tomato salsa—
try this tomatillo-based version for a
deliciously addictive change of pace.
It's fantastic on its own with tortilla
chips or served as a condiment
alongside a variety of meats.
—*Lori Kostecki, Wausau, WI*

TAKES: 20 min. • **MAKES:** 2¼ cups

- 8 tomatillos, husked
- 1 medium tomato, quartered
- 1 small onion, cut into chunks
- 1 jalapeno pepper, seeded
- 3 Tbsp. fresh cilantro leaves
- 3 garlic cloves, peeled
- 1 Tbsp. lime juice
- ½ tsp. salt
- ¼ tsp. ground cumin
- ⅛ tsp. pepper
   Tortilla chips

1. In a large saucepan, bring 4 cups
water to a boil. Add tomatillos. Reduce
heat; simmer, uncovered, for 5 minutes.
Drain.
2. Place the tomatillos, tomato, onion,
jalapeno, cilantro, garlic, lime juice and
seasonings in a food processor. Cover
and process until blended. Serve with
chips.
NOTE Wear disposable gloves when
cutting hot peppers; the oils can burn
skin. Avoid touching your face.
¼ CUP 19 cal., 0 fat (0 sat. fat), 0 chol.,
133mg sod., 4g carb. (2g sugars, 1g fiber),
1g pro. **DIABETIC EXCHANGES** free food.

BENEDICTINE SPREAD

This version of the famous traditional
Kentucky cucumber spread comes from
our Test Kitchen. Serve it as an appetizer
dip or sandwich filling.
—*Taste of Home Test Kitchen*

TAKES: 15 min. • **MAKES:** 1¾ cups

- 1 pkg. (8 oz.) cream cheese, softened
- 1 Tbsp. mayonnaise
- ¼ tsp. salt
- ⅛ tsp. white pepper
- ⅛ tsp. dill weed
- 1 drop green food coloring, optional
- ¾ cup finely chopped peeled
    cucumber, patted dry
- ¼ cup finely chopped onion
    Optional: Snack rye bread, pita
    bread wedges and assorted fresh
    vegetables

In a small bowl, combine cream cheese,
mayonnaise, salt, white pepper, dill
and, if desired, food coloring; beat until
smooth. Stir in cucumber and onion.
Refrigerate, covered, until serving. Serve
with snack rye bread, pita bread wedges
or vegetables as desired.
2 TBSP. 65 cal., 6g fat (3g sat. fat), 17mg
chol., 98mg sod., 1g carb. (1g sugars,
0 fiber), 1g pro.

JUST THE JUICE?

Benedictine spread was originally
made with only the juice from
cucumbers and onions, not
the chopped vegetables. As
it was used as a spread on
cucumber sandwiches, the added
cucumbers were unnecessary.

ROASTED CHERRY TOMATO BURRATA TOAST

Toss ½ cup cherry tomatoes with ½ tsp. olive oil. Place on a rimmed baking sheet. Roast at 400° until tomatoes begin to burst, about 10 minutes. Spread tomatoes over burrata; sprinkle with salt and pepper.

A LOTTA BURRATA

This rich, creamy spreadable cheese is our new favorite base for a quick and tasty open-faced sandwich.

ORIGINAL BURRATA TOAST

Spread toast with extra virgin olive oil. Spread burrata over toast. Sprinkle with salt and pepper. If desired, drizzle with additional olive oil.

HOT HONEY LEMON BURRATA TOAST

Drizzle burrata with 2 tsp. hot honey. Sprinkle with ½ tsp. grated lemon zest, salt and pepper.

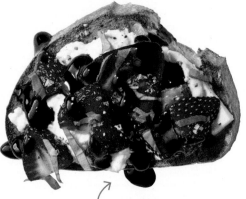

APRICOT ALMOND BURRATA TOAST

Top burrata with 2 tsp. apricot preserves. Sprinkle with 2 tsp. toasted sliced almonds, salt and pepper.

STRAWBERRY BASIL BURRATA TOAST

Top burrata with 2 sliced fresh strawberries. Drizzle with 1 tsp. balsamic glaze. Sprinkle with chopped fresh basil, salt and pepper.

AVOCADO BURRATA TOAST

Top burrata with ¼ medium ripe sliced avocado. Drizzle with additional 1 tsp. olive oil; sprinkle with salt and pepper.

FRUITY HORSERADISH CREAM CHEESE

SPICY EDAMAME

Edamame (pronounced eh-duh-MAH-may) are young soybeans in their pods. While they're great with sushi when you're eating out, they are also easy to make at home. They're a tasty addition to soups, salads and sandwiches, and are great as a standalone snack. They're fun to serve at parties, with smaller bowls set out to catch the empty pods.
—Taste of Home *Test Kitchen*

TAKES: 20 min. • **MAKES:** 6 servings

- 1   pkg. (16 oz.) frozen edamame pods
- 2   tsp. kosher salt
- ¾   tsp. ground ginger
- ½   tsp. garlic powder
- ¼   tsp. crushed red pepper flakes

Place edamame in a large saucepan and cover with water. Bring to a boil. Cook, covered, until tender, 4-5 minutes; drain. Transfer to a large bowl. Add the seasonings; toss to coat.
1 SERVING 52 cal., 2g fat (0 sat. fat), 0 chol., 642mg sod., 5g carb. (1g sugars, 2g fiber), 4g pro.

FRUITY HORSERADISH CREAM CHEESE

Typically called a Jezebel sauce, this sweet, fruity topping has an underlying bite from horseradish. It pairs well with cream cheese, but you could also try it over grilled pork and chicken.
—Rita Reifenstein, Evans City, PA

TAKES: 10 min. • **MAKES:** 1⅓ cups

- 1   pkg. (8 oz.) fat-free cream cheese
- ⅓   cup apple jelly, warmed
- 1   Tbsp. prepared horseradish
- 1½ tsp. ground mustard
- ⅓   cup apricot spreadable fruit
     Assorted crackers

Place cream cheese on a serving plate. In a small microwave-safe bowl, heat jelly until warmed. Stir in horseradish and mustard until blended. Stir in spreadable fruit. Spoon sauce over cream cheese. Serve with crackers. Refrigerate leftovers.
2 TBSP. 73 cal., 0 fat (0 sat. fat), 2mg chol., 128mg sod., 14g carb. (11g sugars, 0 fiber), 3g pro. **DIABETIC EXCHANGES** 1 starch.

RAINBOW QUICHE

MINI ZUCCHINI PIZZAS

This simple recipe makes a fun, quick and easy party appetizer—but you don't have to save it for company! It's also the perfect, low-carb way to satisfy your pizza cravings on busy nights.
—Taste of Home *Test Kitchen*

- -

TAKES: 20 min. • **MAKES:** about 2 dozen

- 1   large zucchini (about 11 oz.), cut diagonally into ¼-in. slices
- ⅛   tsp. salt
- ⅛   tsp. pepper
- ⅓   cup pizza sauce
- ¾   cup shredded part-skim mozzarella cheese
- ½   cup miniature pepperoni slices
     Minced fresh basil

1. Preheat broiler. Arrange zucchini in a single layer on a greased baking sheet. Broil 3-4 in. from heat just until crisp-tender, 1-2 minutes per side.
2. Sprinkle zucchini with salt and pepper; top with sauce, cheese and pepperoni. Broil until cheese is melted, about 1 minute. Sprinkle with basil.
1 MINI PIZZA 29 cal., 2g fat (1g sat. fat), 5mg chol., 108mg sod., 1g carb. (1g sugars, 0 fiber), 2g pro.

#GIRLDINNER

These little mini pizzas make a great super-fast (and healthy!) dinner for one, since you never have to make more than you want to eat in a sitting. Slice just as many zucchini slices as you want, then cover the cut end of the zucchini before placing it in an airtight container in the crisper drawer in the fridge.

RAINBOW QUICHE

With plenty of veggies and a creamy egg-cheese filling, this tasty quiche gets great reviews every time I make it!
—*Lilith Fury, Adena, OH*

- -

PREP: 30 min. • **BAKE:** 40 min. + standing
MAKES: 8 servings

- 1   sheet refrigerated pie crust
- 2   Tbsp. butter
- 1   small onion, finely chopped
- 1   cup sliced fresh mushrooms
- 1   cup small fresh broccoli florets
- ½   cup finely chopped sweet orange pepper
- ½   cup finely chopped sweet red pepper
- 3   large eggs, lightly beaten
- 1⅓   cups half-and-half cream
- ¾   tsp. salt
- ½   tsp. pepper
- 1   cup shredded Mexican cheese blend, divided
- 1   cup fresh baby spinach

1. Preheat oven to 425°. Unroll pie crust onto a lightly floured surface; roll to a 12-in. circle. Transfer to a 9-in. deep-dish pie plate; trim and flute edge. Refrigerate while preparing filling.
2. In a large skillet, heat butter over medium-high heat; saute onion, mushrooms, broccoli and peppers until the mushrooms are lightly browned, 6-8 minutes. Cool slightly.
3. Whisk together eggs, cream, salt and pepper. Sprinkle ½ cup cheese over crust; top with spinach and vegetable mixture. Sprinkle with remaining ½ cup cheese. Pour in the egg mixture.
4. Bake quiche on a lower oven rack for 15 minutes. Reduce oven setting to 350°; bake until a knife inserted in the center comes out clean, 25-30 minutes longer. (Cover edge loosely with foil if necessary to prevent overbrowning.) Let stand 10 minutes before cutting.
1 PIECE 295 cal., 20g fat (10g sat. fat), 115mg chol., 482mg sod., 18g carb. (4g sugars, 1g fiber), 9g pro.

SOUTHWEST
FISH TACOS

PAIRS
WITH

CLASSIC
MARGARITA, P. 56

SOUTHWEST FISH TACOS

These fish tacos are an adaptation of a dish I was served in Bermuda. They're quick because there's so little prep work involved. It's an easy recipe to scale up or down—if you like, serve the filling up in mini tortillas, street-taco style, for a great party appetizer.
—*Jennifer Reid, Farmington, ME*

TAKES: 20 min. • **MAKES:** 4 servings

1½ lbs. sole or cod fillets, cut into 1-in. strips
1 Tbsp. taco seasoning
3 Tbsp. butter, cubed
1 pkg. (10 oz.) angel hair coleslaw mix
½ cup minced fresh cilantro
½ cup mayonnaise
1 Tbsp. lime juice
1 tsp. sugar
¼ tsp. salt
¼ tsp. pepper
8 corn tortillas or taco shells, warmed
    Lime wedges

1. Sprinkle fish with taco seasoning. In a large skillet, heat butter over medium heat; add fish. Cook until fish just begins to flake easily with a fork, 3-4 minutes on each side.
2. Meanwhile, in a small bowl, combine coleslaw, cilantro, mayonnaise, lime juice, sugar, salt and pepper.
3. Place fish in tortillas. Top with coleslaw mixture; serve with lime wedges.

2 TACOS 510 cal., 37g fat (11g sat. fat), 109mg chol., 1170mg sod., 20g carb. (4g sugars, 3g fiber), 23g pro.

BRIE IN PUFF PASTRY

9 WAYS TO KEEP FOOD WARM FOR A PARTY

If you don't have chafing dishes, how do you keep everything warm for a house full of guests?

A **200° oven** is perfect for keeping food warm. Or, make your dishes ahead of time and reheat them in a 350° oven.

Some ovens have specific settings for their **oven drawer**, but it will always be warm if the oven is hot.

If you made a dish in the **slow cooker**, just select the "Keep Warm" setting once it's finished cooking . You can also transfer other dishes to the slow cooker to keep them warm.

Fire up one of the burners of the **grill** on the lowest heat possible and use it to keep dishes warm.

If you don't have a **double boiler**, make one by bringing water to a simmer in sauce pot or skillet. Place a bowl over the pan and let the steam keep it warm.

The thick walls of an **insulated cooler** will keep food warm for about 30 minutes.

A **toaster oven** is perfect for small items like rolls or dessert. The top often gets hot while it's on, so store a dish on top and take advantage of the carryover heat.

Wrap an **electric blanket** around your pots and pans to keep your food toasty and warm while you finish the rest of the meal.

It's weird, but it totally works! Set the **dishwasher** to the dry cycle. Place the food on the top rack and turn the dishwasher on.

BRIE IN PUFF PASTRY

This rich, stylish appetizer adds an elegant touch to any get-together. Feel free to mix it up with your favorite flavor of jam, such as cherry, date or plum, and add a thin layer of sliced almonds before wrapping up the Brie!
—*Marion Lowery, Medford, OR*

TAKES: 30 min. • **MAKES:** 10 servings

- 1 sheet frozen puff pastry, thawed
- ¼ cup apricot preserves
- 1 round (16 oz.) Brie cheese
- 1 large egg
- 1 Tbsp. water
  Assorted dippers

1. Preheat oven to 400°. Roll puff pastry into a 14-in. square. Spread preserves into a 4½-in. circle in the center of the pastry; place cheese over preserves. Fold pastry around cheese; trim excess dough. Pinch edges to seal. Place seam side down on ungreased baking sheet. Beat egg and water; brush over pastry.
2. Bake until crust is puffed and golden brown, 20-25 minutes. Serve warm with crackers, bread or fruit.
1 WEDGE 298 cal., 20g fat (10g sat. fat), 64mg chol., 377mg sod., 19g carb. (4g sugars, 2g fiber), 12g pro.

SMOKED
GOUDA &
ROAST BEEF
PINWHEELS

MARINATED ALMOND-STUFFED OLIVES

Marinated stuffed olives go over so well with company that I try to keep a batch of them in the fridge at all times.
—*Larissa Delk, Columbia, TN*

PREP: 15 min. + marinating
MAKES: 8 cups

- 1 cup blanched almonds, toasted
- 3 cans (6 oz. each) pitted ripe olives, drained
- 3 jars (7 oz. each) pimiento-stuffed olives, undrained
- ½ cup white balsamic vinegar
- ½ cup dry red wine
- ½ cup canola oil
- 1 medium garlic clove, minced
- ½ tsp. sugar
- 1 tsp. dried oregano
- 1 tsp. pepper
- ½ tsp. dill weed
- ½ tsp. dried basil
- ½ tsp. dried parsley flakes

1. Insert an almond into each ripe olive; place in a large bowl. Add pimiento-stuffed olives with olive juice.
2. Whisk vinegar, wine, oil, garlic, sugar and seasonings. Pour mixture over olives. Refrigerate, covered, 8 hours or overnight, stirring occasionally. Transfer to a serving bowl.
¼ CUP 78 cal., 7g fat (0 sat. fat), 0 chol., 455mg sod., 3g carb. (0 sugars, 1g fiber), 1g pro.

SMOKED GOUDA & ROAST BEEF PINWHEELS

Our local deli makes terrific roast beef sandwiches. This pinwheel appetizer re-creates the taste. My family says the pinwheels have so many flavors for such a little treat!
—*Pamela Shank, Parkersburg, WV*

PREP: 20 min. • **BAKE:** 15 min./batch
MAKES: 4 dozen

- ¾ lb. sliced deli roast beef, finely chopped
- 1 pkg. (10 oz.) frozen chopped spinach, thawed and squeezed dry
- 1 pkg. (6½ oz.) garlic-herb spreadable cheese
- 1 cup shredded smoked Gouda cheese
- ¼ cup finely chopped red onion
- 2 tubes (8 oz. each) refrigerated crescent rolls

1. Preheat oven to 375°. In a small bowl, mix the first 5 ingredients until blended. On a lightly floured surface, unroll 1 tube crescent dough into 1 long rectangle; press perforations to seal.
2. Spread half the roast beef mixture over the dough. Roll up jelly-roll style, starting with a long side; pinch seam to seal. Using a serrated knife, cut roll crosswise into twenty-four ½-in. slices. Place slices on parchment-lined baking sheets, cut side down. Repeat with remaining crescent dough and roast beef mixture.
3. Bake 12-14 minutes or until golden brown. Serve warm.
1 APPETIZER 71 cal., 5g fat (2g sat. fat), 11mg chol., 160mg sod., 4g carb. (1g sugars, 0 fiber), 3g pro.

BLUE-RIBBON
BEEF NACHOS

BLUE-RIBBON BEEF NACHOS

Chili powder and sassy salsa season a zesty mixture of ground beef and refried beans sprinkled with green onions, tomatoes and ripe olives.
—*Diane Hixon, Niceville, FL*

TAKES: 20 min. • **MAKES:** 6 servings

1 lb. ground beef
1 small onion, chopped
1 can (16 oz.) refried beans
1 jar (16 oz.) salsa
1 can (6 oz.) ripe olives, chopped
½ cup shredded cheddar cheese
1 green onion, chopped
2 Tbsp. chili powder
1 tsp. salt
Tortilla chips
Optional: Sliced ripe olives, chopped green onions and diced tomatoes

In a large skillet, cook beef and onion over medium heat until the meat is no longer pink, breaking beef into crumbles; drain. Stir in the next 7 ingredients; heat through. Serve over tortilla chips. Top with olives, onions and tomatoes if desired.

1 SERVING 294 cal., 14g fat (6g sat. fat), 53mg chol., 1353mg sod., 19g carb. (5g sugars, 9g fiber), 20g pro.

TEST KITCHEN TIPS

Help! My nachos are soggy! Prevent soggy nachos by adding heavy, wet toppings, like salsa or sour cream, right before you eat, or serve them on the side. Using real cheese instead of processed, liquid cheese helps too.

What toppings should I put on nachos? We recommend a dollop of homemade guacamole (p. 18) or sour cream. For heat, add a few jalapeno slices; for more adventurous ideas, see pp. 34-35.

MOJITO-STYLE YELLOW TOMATO SALSA

MOJITO-STYLE YELLOW TOMATO SALSA

With grilled tomatoes, crunchy peppers and a sprinkle of mint, this fresh salsa is good on just about everything. Try it in fish tacos, on tortilla chips or by the spoonful!
—*Patterson Watkins, Philadelphia, PA*

PREP: 20 min. • **GRILL:** 10 min. + chilling
MAKES: 4 cups

2 lbs. large yellow tomatoes, halved
1 Tbsp. olive oil
2 garlic cloves, minced
1 tsp. chopped shallot
¾ tsp. salt, divided
3 medium limes
2 tsp. coarse sugar
12 fresh mint leaves
¼ cup chopped Cubanelle or banana peppers

1. Grill tomatoes, uncovered, on an oiled rack over high heat or broil 3-4 in. from the heat until skin is slightly charred, 3-4 minutes on each side. Cool to room temperature. Combine oil, garlic, shallot and ¼ tsp. salt. When tomatoes are cool enough to handle, finely chop; stir in garlic mixture until well combined.
2. Finely grate zest of each lime; set aside. Peel limes and discard white membranes; section limes. In a food processor, pulse lime sections, sugar, mint and remaining ½ tsp. salt until finely chopped. Combine with tomatoes; add peppers and lime zest. Mix well.
3. Refrigerate at least 1 hour. Serve with chips or grilled meats.

NOTE Wear disposable gloves when cutting hot peppers; the oils can burn skin. Avoid touching your face.

¼ CUP 23 cal., 1g fat (0 sat. fat), 0 chol., 161mg sod., 4g carb. (1g sugars, 1g fiber), 1g pro. **DIABETIC EXCHANGES** 1 vegetable.

NACHO AVERAGE NACHOS

Up your game with these delicious twists on a classic.

BUFFALO WING NACHOS

I like to use spicy Buffalo sauce, shredded chicken and celery and then finish it off with blue cheese and a drizzle of ranch dressing.
—MARINA CASTLE KELLEY, CANYON COUNTRY, CA

BLACK BEAN NACHOS

We go meatless with corn, black beans, onions, black olives and cheddar cheese.
——BECKY CLINE CARVER, NORTH ROYALTON, OH

GRINDER NACHOS

In our house, it's Italian sausage, mushrooms, onions, pizza sauce (just a little), scamorza cheese and pickled pepper rings.
—BARBARA RANKIN, DES MOINES, IA

CHORIZO NACHOS

We love chorizo, queso, jalapeno and guacamole!
—A.J. LIVELY, CONROE, TX

PULLED PORK BBQ NACHOS

Our go-to nachos are Tex-Mex style: Pulled pork BBQ, coleslaw, BBQ sauce, pickled red onions, nacho cheese and sour cream. Boom!
—DAVE REED III, CHARLOTTE, NC

WALNUT & FIG GOAT CHEESE LOG

Here's a simple spread that calls for only a handful of ingredients. The honey is optional, but I think the little touch of sweetness nicely complements the tang of the goat cheese.
—*Ana-Marie Correll, Hollister, CA*

- -

PREP: 10 min. + chilling • **MAKES:** 1⅓ cups

 2 logs (4 oz. each) fresh goat cheese
 8 dried figs, finely chopped
 ½ cup finely chopped walnuts, toasted, divided
 ¾ tsp. pepper
 1 Tbsp. honey, optional
    Assorted crackers

In a small bowl, crumble cheese. Stir in figs, ¼ cup walnuts, pepper and, if desired, honey. Shape mixture into a log about 6 in. long. Roll log in the remaining ¼ cup walnuts. Refrigerate 4 hours or overnight. Serve with crackers.
2 TBSP. 93 cal., 7g fat (2g sat. fat), 15mg chol., 92mg sod., 6g carb. (3g sugars, 1g fiber), 3g pro.

MUSTARD PRETZEL DIP

MUSTARD PRETZEL DIP

This flavorful dip is addictive, so be careful! It's delicious served with pita chips, crackers and fresh veggies.
—*Iola Egle, Bella Vista, AR*

- -

PREP: 10 min. + chilling • **MAKES:** 3½ cups

 1 cup sour cream
 1 cup mayonnaise
 1 cup prepared mustard
 ½ cup sugar
 ¼ cup dried minced onion
 1 envelope (1 oz.) ranch salad dressing mix
 1 Tbsp. prepared horseradish
    Sourdough pretzel nuggets

In a large bowl, combine the first 7 ingredients. Cover and refrigerate for at least 30 minutes. Serve with pretzels. Refrigerate leftovers.
2 TBSP. 95 cal., 8g fat (2g sat. fat), 2mg chol., 342mg sod., 6g carb. (4g sugars, 0 fiber), 1g pro.

HOW MUCH FOOD?

On average, each guest will have about 6 appetizers at a dinner party; this number should double if it's a cocktail party. Stock up on bulk items like nuts, pretzels and olives that guests can munch on when they arrive and that can fill in any shortfall without attracting attention.

SAUSAGE
WONTON
STARS

SAUSAGE WONTON STARS

These fancy-looking appetizers are ideal when entertaining large groups. The cute crunchy cups are stuffed with a cheesy pork sausage filling that everyone enjoys. We keep a few in the freezer so we can reheat them for late-night snacking.
—*Mary Thomas, North Lewisburg, OH*

TAKES: 30 min. • **MAKES:** 4 dozen

- 1 pkg. (12 oz.) wonton wrappers
- 1 lb. bulk pork sausage
- 2 cups shredded Colby cheese
- ½ medium green pepper, chopped
- ½ medium sweet red pepper, chopped
- 2 bunches green onions, sliced
- ½ cup ranch salad dressing

1. Preheat oven to 350°. Lightly press wonton wrappers onto the bottoms and up the sides of greased miniature muffin cups. Bake until edges are browned, about 5 minutes.
2. In a large skillet, cook sausage over medium heat until no longer pink, breaking it into crumbles; drain. Stir in cheese, peppers, onions and salad dressing. Spoon a rounded Tbsp. into each wonton cup. Bake until heated through, 6-7 minutes.

1 APPETIZER 69 cal., 5g fat (2g sat. fat), 10mg chol., 143mg sod., 4g carb. (0 sugars, 0 fiber), 3g pro.

ASPARAGUS WITH FRESH BASIL SAUCE

Add zip to your party with an easy asparagus dip that can also double as a flavorful sandwich spread.
—*Janie Colle, Hutchinson, KS*

- -

TAKES: 15 min. • **MAKES:** 12 servings

- ¾ cup reduced-fat mayonnaise
- 2 Tbsp. prepared pesto
- 1 Tbsp. grated Parmesan cheese
- 1 Tbsp. minced fresh basil
- 1 tsp. lemon juice
- 1 garlic clove, minced
- 1½ lbs. fresh asparagus, trimmed

1. In a small bowl, mix first 6 ingredients until blended; refrigerate until serving.
2. In a Dutch oven, bring 12 cups water to a boil. Add asparagus in batches; cook, uncovered, until crisp-tender, 2-3 minutes. Remove and immediately drop into ice water. Drain and pat dry. Serve with sauce.
1 SERVING 72 cal., 6g fat (1g sat. fat), 6mg chol., 149mg sod., 3g carb. (1g sugars, 1g fiber), 1g pro. **DIABETIC EXCHANGES** 1½ fat.

EASY COCONUT SHRIMP

EASY COCONUT SHRIMP

Guests are always impressed when I serve these restaurant-quality shrimp. A selection of sauces served alongside adds the perfect touch.
—*Tacy Holliday, Germantown, MD*

- -

TAKES: 25 min. • **MAKES:** about 2 dozen

- 1¼ cups all-purpose flour
- ¼ tsp. seafood seasoning
- 1 large egg, beaten
- ¾ cup pineapple juice
- 1 pkg. (14 oz.) sweetened shredded coconut
- 1 lb. uncooked shrimp (25-30 per lb.), peeled and deveined
  Oil for deep-fat frying
  Optional: Apricot preserves, sweet-and-sour sauce, plum sauce or Dijon mustard

1. In a bowl, combine flour, seasoning, egg and pineapple juice until smooth. Place coconut in a shallow bowl. Dip shrimp into the batter, then coat with the coconut.
2. In an electric skillet or deep-fat fryer, heat oil to 375°. Fry shrimp, a few at a time, until golden brown, about 1½ minutes, turning occasionally. Drain on paper towels. Serve with dipping sauce or mustard if desired.
1 SHRIMP 171 cal., 11g fat (6g sat. fat), 31mg chol., 76mg sod., 14g carb. (8g sugars, 1g fiber), 5g pro.

RASPBERRY
CHIPOTLE
CHICKEN
PINWHEELS

4. In a small saucepan, melt raspberry jam. Drizzle jam over warm pinwheels. Serve immediately.

1 PINWHEEL 106 cal., 6g fat (2g sat. fat), 10mg chol., 140mg sod., 10g carb. (2g sugars, 1g fiber), 3g pro.

ITALIAN SAUSAGE BRUSCHETTA

Sometimes I garnish each slice of this bruschetta with a sprig of fresh basil.
—*Teresa Ralston, New Albany, OH*

TAKES: 20 min. • **MAKES:** 2 dozen

- 1 lb. bulk Italian sausage
- 8 oz. mascarpone cheese, softened
- 3 Tbsp. prepared pesto
- 24 slices French bread baguette (½ in. thick)
- ⅓ cup olive oil
- ¾ cup finely chopped seeded plum tomatoes
- 3 Tbsp. chopped fresh parsley
- 3 Tbsp. shredded Parmesan cheese

1. In a large skillet, cook sausage over medium heat 6-8 minutes or until no longer pink, breaking into crumbles; drain. In a small bowl, combine the mascarpone cheese and pesto.
2. Preheat broiler. Place the bread on ungreased baking sheets. Brush bread with oil on both sides. Broil 3-4 in. from the heat until golden brown, 30-45 seconds on each side. Spread with the mascarpone mixture. Top each slice with sausage, tomatoes, parsley and Parmesan cheese. Serve warm.

1 APPETIZER 143 cal., 12g fat (4g sat. fat), 24mg chol., 196mg sod., 5g carb. (0 sugars, 0 fiber), 4g pro.

RASPBERRY CHIPOTLE CHICKEN PINWHEELS

I love the flavor profile of raspberry and chipotle together, so I came up with these delicious puff pastry appetizers for a get-together. They were a hit! These pinwheels also make a fantastic dinner served alongside a simple salad with balsamic dressing.
—*Noelle Myers, Grand Forks, ND*

PREP: 20 min. • **BAKE:** 25 min.
MAKES: 3 dozen

- 1 pkg. (8 oz.) cream cheese, softened
- 1 pkg. (10 oz.) frozen chopped spinach, thawed and squeezed dry
- 2 chipotle peppers in adobo sauce, chopped, seeds removed
- 1 Tbsp. adobo sauce
- 3 green onions, chopped
- ¼ tsp. ground cinnamon
- 1 pkg. (17 oz.) frozen puff pastry, thawed
- 12 slices deli chicken
- ⅓ cup seedless raspberry jam

1. Preheat oven to 400°. In a small bowl, combine the cream cheese, spinach, chipotle peppers, adobo sauce, green onions and cinnamon.
2. On a lightly floured surface, unfold puff pastry. Spread the cream cheese mixture to within ½ in. of edges. Layer 6 slices of roast chicken over mixture. Roll up jelly-roll style; pinch ends to seal. Cut crosswise into eighteen ½-in. slices. Place cut side down on greased baking sheets. Repeat with second sheet of puff pastry.
3. Bake 20-25 minutes or until pastry is puffed and golden brown.

BUFFALO WING DIP

MARINATED PORK KABOBS

This recipe was originally for lamb, but I adapted it to pork and adjusted the spices. It's always requested when the grill comes out for the season.
—Bobbie Jo Miller, Fallon, NV

- -

PREP: 15 min. + marinating
GRILL: 15 min. • **MAKES:** 8 servings

    2   cups plain yogurt
    2   Tbsp. lemon juice
    4   garlic cloves, minced
   ½   tsp. ground cumin
   ¼   tsp. ground coriander
    2   lbs. pork tenderloin, cut into
        1½-in. cubes
    8   small white onions, halved
    8   cherry tomatoes
    1   medium sweet red pepper,
        cut into 1½-in. pieces
    1   medium green pepper, cut into
        1½-in. pieces
        Salt and pepper to taste

1. In a shallow dish, combine yogurt, lemon juice, garlic, cumin and coriander. Add pork and turn to coat; cover and refrigerate 6 hours or overnight.
2. Alternate threading pork, onions, tomatoes and peppers on 8 metal or soaked wooden skewers. Sprinkle with salt and pepper. Grill, covered, over medium heat until meat juices run clear, 15-20 minutes, turning occasionally.
1 KABOB 190 cal., 5g fat (2g sat. fat), 67mg chol., 63mg sod., 11g carb. (7g sugars, 2g fiber), 25g pro. **DIABETIC EXCHANGES** 3 lean meat, 1 vegetable, ½ fat.

BUFFALO WING DIP

All the signature flavors of Buffalo chicken wings are waiting to be scooped up in this warm dip. We love it with tortilla chips or celery sticks, but it can be served with crackers or pita chips, too.
—Lisa Delmont, Lititz, PA

- -

PREP: 15 min. • **BAKE:** 25 min.
MAKES: 24 servings

    2   pkg. (8 oz. each) cream cheese,
        softened
    1   bottle (5 oz.) Louisiana-style
        hot sauce
    2   cups chopped cooked chicken breast
    2   cups shredded cheddar cheese,
        divided
    1   cup crumbled blue cheese
   ¾   cup chopped celery
        Tortilla chips and celery sticks

1. Preheat oven to 350°. In a large mixing bowl, beat cream cheese and hot sauce until smooth. Stir in chicken, 1 cup cheddar cheese, blue cheese and celery. Transfer to a greased 2-qt. baking dish. Sprinkle with the remaining 1 cup cheddar cheese.
2. Bake, uncovered, until heated through, 25-30 minutes. If desired, top with additional blue cheese crumbles and chopped celery. Serve with tortilla chips and celery sticks.
¼ CUP 143 cal., 12g fat (7g sat. fat), 42mg chol., 232mg sod., 2g carb. (1g sugars, 0 fiber), 8g pro.

MARINATED
PORK
KABOBS

MAI TAI
P. 51

COCKTAILS & MOCKTAILS

When it's time to serve up drinks to your friends, turn your kitchen into a mixologist's dream. Whether you're serving classic cocktails, new inventions or alcohol-free "mocktails," treat your guests to something special.

BLOODY MARY BAR

Set a buffet of fixin's and let guests jazz up their own bloody.

- Put out an assortment of flavored salts and seasonings to rim the glasses.

- Set the bar high with add-ons such as beef sticks, bacon, cheese, deviled eggs or even soft pretzels.

- Include a bottle of hot pepper sauce for those who like a little extra heat.

- Don't forget the sudsy beer chasers!

UNCLE MERLE'S BLOODY MARY

I had a good friend who was not related to me, but everyone called him Uncle Merle. He gave me this recipe and made me promise not to give it to anyone until he passed away. Uncle Merle is gone now, but his recipe lives on.
—Ronald Roth, Three Rivers, MI

TAKES: 10 min. • **MAKES:** 5 servings

- 4 cups tomato juice
- 1 Tbsp. white vinegar
- 1½ tsp. sugar
- 1½ tsp. Worcestershire sauce
- 1 tsp. beef bouillon granules
- ½ tsp. salt
- ¼ tsp. onion powder
- ¼ tsp. celery salt
- ¼ tsp. pepper
- ⅛ tsp. garlic powder
- 1 drop hot pepper sauce
  Dash ground cinnamon, optional
  Ice cubes
- 7½ oz. vodka
  Optional garnish: Celery ribs, cooked shrimp, cherry tomatoes, jalapeno peppers, string cheese, lemon wedges, cooked bacon, beef snack sticks, cucumber spears, olives, cubed cheese, Old Bay seasoning and celery salt

In a pitcher, mix the first 11 ingredients until blended. If desired, stir in cinnamon. For each serving, pour ¾ cup mixture over ice; stir in 1½ Tbsp. of vodka. Garnish as desired.
1 CUP 119 cal., 1g fat (0 sat. fat), 0 chol., 961mg sod., 9g carb. (7g sugars, 1g fiber), 2g pro.

RASPBERRY CHAMPAGNE COCKTAIL

When eating out, I often ordered a fizzy, fruity beverage. Then I decided to make my own at home, giving mimosas a raspberry touch.
—Hillary Tedesco, Crofton, MD

TAKES: 5 min. • **MAKES:** 1 serving

- 1 oz. raspberry liqueur
- ⅔ cup chilled champagne
  Fresh raspberries

Place raspberry liqueur in a champagne flute; top with champagne. Top with raspberries.
¾ CUP 211 cal., 0 fat (0 sat. fat), 0 chol., 0 sod., 13g carb. (11g sugars, 0 fiber), 0 pro.

SOUR CHERRY SHANDY

A shandy is beer mixed with a non-alcoholic drink like fruit juice or lemonade. Shandies come in all different flavors, but we love this one made with tart cherry juice.
—Taste of Home Test Kitchen

TAKES: 5 min. • **MAKES:** 1 serving

- ½ cup tart cherry juice
- 2 Tbsp. simple syrup
- 1½ cups beer, chilled

Combine cherry juice and simple syrup in a chilled pint glass; stir until blended. Top with chilled beer.
2 CUPS 327 cal., 0 fat (0 sat. fat), 0 chol., 17mg sod., 57g carb. (53g sugars, 0 fiber), 1g pro.

QUICK WHITE SANGRIA

Using white instead of red wine makes my version of sangria a bit lighter than the usual, yet with the same wonderful sweetness. Frozen fruit allows me to serve this refreshing sipper any time of year.
—Sharon Tipton, Casselberry, FL

TAKES: 15 min. • **MAKES:** 8 servings

- ¼ cup sugar
- ¼ cup brandy
- 1 cup sliced peeled fresh or frozen peaches, thawed
- 1 cup sliced fresh or frozen sliced strawberries, thawed
- 1 medium lemon, sliced
- 1 medium lime, sliced
- 1 bottle (750 ml) dry white wine, chilled
- 1 can (12 oz.) lemon-lime soda, chilled
  Ice cubes

In a pitcher, mix sugar and brandy until the sugar is dissolved. Add the next 6 ingredients; stir gently to combine. Serve over ice.
¾ CUP 147 cal., 0 fat (0 sat. fat), 0 chol., 9mg sod., 17g carb. (14g sugars, 1g fiber), 0 pro.

CLASSIC MIMOSA

FLAWLESSLY OPEN A CHAMPAGNE BOTTLE

Here are foolproof steps to opening a bottle of bubbly without worrying about cork-related injuries to either your friends or your ceiling!

STEP 1: If there's a pull tab on the foil cover, pull on it to cut through and remove the foil. Or use a paring knife to cut the metal foil right below the lip of the bottle.

STEP 2: Gently twist the "O" ring of the wire cage until it comes loose. You can leave the wire cage over the cork or carefully remove it and set aside.

STEP 3: Cover the top of the bottle with a kitchen towel. Place one hand on top of the bottle with your thumb firmly on the cork. Rotate the bottle while holding the cork. The cork should begin spinning slightly, and you should hear a gentle hiss. Gently twist the cork to remove it from the bottle.

CHAMPAGNE WISHES

When bubbles beckon, these mimosa makeovers keep the celebration sparkling!

GINGER MULE MIMOSA

BLUE LAGOON MIMOSA

BEERMOSA

POMEGRANATE MIMOSA

TEQUILA SUNRISE MIMOSA

APPLE CIDER MIMOSA
Pour 2 oz. spiced apple cider into a champagne flute or wine glass; top with 3 oz. champagne.

BEERMOSA
Pour 2 oz. orange juice into a champagne flute or wine glass; top with 3 oz. Belgian-style white beer.

BLUE LAGOON MIMOSA
Pour 2 oz. lemonade and ½ oz. blue curacao into a champagne flute or wine glass; top with 3 oz. champagne.

CLASSIC MIMOSA
Pour 2 oz. orange juice into a wine glass or champagne flute; top with 3 oz. champagne.

GINGER MULE MIMOSA
Pour 1 oz. ginger liqueur and ½ oz. lime juice into a champagne flute or wine glass; top with 4 oz. champagne.

HAWAIIAN MIMOSA
Pour 2 oz. pineapple juice and 1 oz. coconut rum into a champagne flute or wine glass; top with 2 oz. champagne.

PEACH MELBA BELLINI
Pour 2 oz. peach nectar and 1 oz. raspberry liqueur into a champagne flute or wine glass; top with 2 oz. champagne.

PEPPERMINT MIMOSA
Pour ½ oz. peppermint schnapps into a champagne flute or wine glass; top with 4½ oz. champagne.

POMEGRANATE MIMOSA
Pour 1 oz. pomegranate juice and 1 oz. pomegranate liqueur into a champagne flute or wine glass; top with 3 oz. champagne.

TEQUILA SUNRISE MIMOSA
Pour 2 oz. orange juice and 1 oz. tequila into a champagne flute or wine glass; top with 2 oz. champagne. Slowly pour ½ oz. grenadine on top.

*To make nonalcoholic mimosas, swap in any dry sparkling white grape juice for the champagne; use nonalcoholic white ale in the Beermosa.

BLACKBERRY BALSAMIC MANHATTAN

I sampled this twist on one of my favorite cocktails while visiting the Elk Store Winery & Distillery in Fredericksburg, Texas. The bartender kindly shared his recipe so I could make it at home.
—Susan Stetzel, Gainesville, NY

- -

TAKES: 10 min. • **MAKES:** 1 serving

- 5 fresh blackberries
    Ice cubes
- 2½ oz. bourbon
- 1 oz. sweet vermouth
- 1 tsp. simple syrup
- ½ tsp. aged balsamic vinegar
- 2 dashes bitters
    Optional garnish: Rosemary sprigs, fresh berries, orange wedges

In a shaker, muddle blackberries. Fill shaker three-fourths full with ice. Add next 5 ingredients; stir until well-chilled, 20-30 seconds. Strain into a coupe or cocktail glass, or an ice-filled rocks glass. Garnish as desired.
1 SERVING 232 cal., 0 fat (0 sat. fat), 0 chol., 3mg sod., 10g carb. (6g sugars, 0 fiber), 0 pro.

CHERRY LIMEADE

CHERRY LIMEADE

My guests always enjoy this refreshing cherry-topped drink. It's just right on a hot southern summer afternoon.
—Awynne Thurstenson, Siloam Springs, AR

- -

TAKES: 10 min. • **MAKES:** 8 servings

- ¾ cup lime juice
- 1 cup sugar
- ½ cup maraschino cherry juice
- 2 liters lime carbonated water, chilled
    Ice cubes
- 8 maraschino cherries with stems
- 8 lime slices

1. In a large pitcher, combine lime juice and sugar. Cover and refrigerate.
2. Just before serving, stir cherry juice, carbonated water and some ice cubes into lime juice mixture. Garnish with maraschino cherries and lime slices.
1 CUP 142 cal., 0 fat (0 sat. fat), 0 chol., 2mg sod., 39g carb. (31g sugars, 2g fiber), 0 pro.

CHAMPAGNE COCKTAIL

This amber drink is a champagne twist on the traditional old-fashioned. Try it with extra-dry champagne.
—Taste of Home Test Kitchen

- -

TAKES: 5 min. • **MAKES:** 1 serving

- 1 sugar cube or ½ tsp. sugar
- 6 dashes bitters
- ½ oz. brandy
- ½ cup chilled champagne
    Optional garnishes: Fresh rosemary sprig and fresh or frozen cranberries

Place sugar in a champagne flute or cocktail glass; sprinkle with bitters. Add brandy; top with champagne. If desired, top with rosemary and cranberries.
1 SERVING 130 cal., 0 fat (0 sat. fat), 0 chol., 0 sod., 5g carb. (2g sugars, 0 fiber), 0 pro.

NUTTY HAWAIIAN

PERFECT LEMON MARTINI

This combo of tart lemon and sweet liqueur will tingle your taste buds.
—*Marilee Anker, Chatsworth, CA*

- -

TAKES: 5 min. • **MAKES:** 1 serving

- 1 lemon slice
- Sugar
- Ice cubes
- 2 oz. vodka
- 1½ oz. limoncello
- ½ oz. lemon juice

1. Using the lemon slice, moisten rim of a chilled cocktail glass; set lemon aside. Sprinkle sugar on a plate; hold the glass upside down and dip rim into sugar. Discard remaining sugar on plate.
2. Fill a shaker three-fourths full with ice. Add vodka, limoncello and lemon juice; cover and shake until condensation forms on the outside of the shaker, 10-15 seconds. Strain into the prepared glass. Garnish with the lemon slice.
1 SERVING 286 cal., 0 fat (0 sat. fat), 0 chol., 1mg sod., 18g carb. (17g sugars, 0 fiber), 0 pro.

NUTTY HAWAIIAN

I came up with this tropical cocktail on a whim one day. Later, when my husband and I went to Key West, Florida, I asked the bartender at an open bar to make it. He loved it so much he asked if he could use it, and of course I said yes!
—*Tracy Davidheiser, Reading, PA*

- -

TAKES: 5 min. • **MAKES:** 2 servings

- Ice cubes
- 2 oz. Southern Comfort
- 2 oz. coconut rum
- 1½ oz. amaretto
- 2 cans (6 oz. each) unsweetened pineapple juice
- Maraschino cherries

Fill a shaker three-fourths full with ice. Add Southern Comfort, rum, amaretto and juice. Cover; shake for 10-15 seconds or until condensation forms on outside of shaker. Strain into chilled glasses filled with ice. Top with cherries.
1 CUP 299 cal., 0 fat (0 sat. fat), 0 chol., 6mg sod., 30g carb. (25g sugars, 0 fiber), 1g pro.

THE QUICK CHILL

To chill a cocktail glass quickly, fill it with ice while you mix the drink, then dump out the ice cubes and pour. Or wrap a wet paper towel around the glass and stick it in the freezer for 3-5 minutes.

THE ESSENTIAL SUMMER BAR

If your idea of a great summer day is sipping a cocktail with friends, make sure the bar's ready when you are. Don't worry if you're missing a few items—basics go a long way.

THE BASICS
Classic summer spirits:
Rum • Bourbon or whiskey • Gin • Vodka • Tequila

BUILD ON THE BASE
A few secondary options will help you customize your cocktails. Bitters and flavored liqueurs are used in small quantities, so a single bottle will log a lot of miles.
Bitters (classic Angostura) • Orange liqueur (Cointreau or Grand Marnier) • Elderflower liqueur (St-Germain) • Ginger liqueur (Domaine de Canton)

FROM THE FARMERS MARKET
Fresh produce for garnishes and muddling:
Celery • Tomato • Citrus • Seasonal stone fruits and berries • Herbs

MIXERS
Nonalcoholic liquid ingredients added to cocktails:
Club soda • Tonic water • Colas and ginger ale • Juice • Simple syrups

THE TOOL KIT
An initial investment in a few key items will pay you back for years:
Cocktail shaker and strainer • Muddler (or a wooden spoon) • Ice cube trays • Paring knife • Bottle/wine opener • Peeler • Hand-held citrus press • Straws

SIPPING PRETTY
Add these colorful ice cubes to drinks to make them extra special. Just fill an ice tray with water and pop in fresh herbs, citrus or berries, then freeze.

BERRIES
Blueberries • Raspberries • Strawberries

HERBS
Basil • Mint

CITRUS
Lemon • Lime • Orange

SIDECAR

MAI TAI

This party favorite has been around for quite some time. It's not overly fruity and features a good blend of sweet and sour. For a splash of color, garnish with strawberries and lime.
—Taste of Home *Test Kitchen*

- -

TAKES: 5 min. • **MAKES:** 1 serving

  1½ to 2 cups ice cubes
   2 oz. light rum
  ¾ oz. Triple Sec
  ½ oz. lemon juice
  1½ tsp. lime juice
  1½ tsp. amaretto
      Optional garnish: Lime slice, lime twist, edible flowers and fresh pineapple

Fill a shaker three-fourths full with ice. Place remaining ice in a rocks glass; set aside. Add the rum, Triple Sec, juices and amaretto to shaker; cover and shake for 10-15 seconds or until condensation forms on outside of shaker. Strain into prepared glass. Garnish as desired.
⅔ CUP 241 cal., 0 fat (0 sat. fat), 0 chol., 7mg sod., 15g carb. (13g sugars, 0 fiber), 0 pro.

SIDECAR

Welcome summer with this tart citrus delight. Treat yourself to this sunny drink.
—Taste of Home *Test Kitchen*

- -

TAKES: 5 min. • **MAKES:** 1 serving

    Ice cubes
  1 oz. brandy
  ⅔ oz. (4 tsp.) Triple Sec
  1½ to 3 tsp. lemon juice
    Lemon twist, optional

Fill a shaker three-fourths full with ice. Add brandy, Triple Sec and lemon juice. Cover and shake for 15-20 seconds or until condensation forms on the outside of the shaker. Strain into a chilled cocktail glass. Garnish as desired.
1 SERVING 137 cal., 0 fat (0 sat. fat), 0 chol., 2mg sod., 10g carb. (8g sugars, 0 fiber), 0 pro.

SPARKLING BERRY PUNCH

I often serve this refreshing cranberry beverage at Christmastime, but it's a lovely choice for any special occasion. Add a few cranberries to each glass for extra flair.
—Kay Curtis, Guthrie, OK

- -

TAKES: 10 min. • **MAKES:** about 2 qt.

  6 cups cranberry juice, chilled
  2 cans (12 oz. each) ginger ale, chilled
  ¼ tsp. almond extract
    Ice cubes

Combine first 3 ingredients in a punch bowl or pitcher. Serve immediately in chilled glasses over ice.
1 CUP 102 cal., 0 fat (0 sat. fat), 0 chol., 7mg sod., 27g carb. (27g sugars, 0 fiber), 1g pro.

HOT BUTTERED RUM

A friend gave me this recipe more than 30 years ago; I think of her every winter when I stir up a batch. It freezes well, so feel free to make it ahead of time.
—*Joyce Moynihan, Lakeville, MN*

TAKES: 15 min.
MAKES: 7 servings (3½ cups mix)

- 1 cup butter, softened
- ½ cup confectioners' sugar
- ½ cup packed brown sugar
- 2 cups vanilla ice cream, softened
- 1 tsp. ground cinnamon
- 1 tsp. ground nutmeg

EACH SERVING
- ½ cup boiling water
- 1 to 3 Tbsp. rum
  Additional nutmeg

1. Cream butter and sugars until light and fluffy, 5-7 minutes. Beat in the ice cream, cinnamon and nutmeg. Cover and store in the freezer.
2. For each serving, place ½ cup butter mixture in a mug, add boiling water and stir to dissolve. Stir in rum. Sprinkle with additional nutmeg.
1 CUP 428 cal., 30g fat (19g sat. fat), 85mg chol., 221mg sod., 33g carb. (30g sugars, 0 fiber), 2g pro.

FIRESIDE GLOGG

An aromatic blend of spices flavors this superb Scandinavian beverage. It is served warmed, and its sweet, fruity taste will warm you to your toes.
—*Sue Brown, West Bend, WI*

PREP: 25 min. • **COOK:** 40 min.
MAKES: 8 servings

- 4 cups port wine or apple cider, divided
- 3 cups fresh or frozen cranberries, thawed
- ¼ cup packed brown sugar
- 4 orange zest strips (3 in.)
- 3 cinnamon sticks (3 in.)
- 5 slices fresh peeled gingerroot
- 5 cardamom pods
- 5 whole cloves
- 4 cups apple cider or juice
- ½ cup blanched almonds
- ½ cup raisins

1. In a large saucepan, combine 3 cups wine, cranberries, brown sugar, orange zest, cinnamon sticks, ginger slices, cardamom and cloves. Cook over medium heat until berries pop, about 15 minutes. Mash slightly and cook 10 minutes longer.
2. Strain and discard pulp, orange zest and spices. Return mixture to pan; stir in cider, almonds, raisins and remaining 1 cup wine. Bring to a boil. Reduce heat; simmer, uncovered, for 15 minutes. Serve warm.
¾ CUP 229 cal., 5g fat (0 sat. fat), 0 chol., 22mg sod., 39g carb. (29g sugars, 3g fiber), 2g pro.

BRANDY OLD-FASHIONED SWEET

Here in Wisconsin, we make this old-fashioned fave with brandy instead of whiskey and soda instead of water. The results: a milder, sweeter cocktail.
—*Taste of Home Test Kitchen*

TAKES: 10 min. • **MAKES:** 1 serving

- 1 orange slice
- 1 maraschino cherry
- 1½ oz. maraschino cherry juice
- 1 tsp. bitters
- ¼ to ⅓ cup ice cubes
- 1½ oz. brandy
- 2 tsp. water
- 1 tsp. orange juice
- 3 oz. lemon-lime soda

In a rocks glass, muddle orange slice, cherry, cherry juice and bitters. Add ice. Pour in brandy, water, orange juice and soda.
1 SERVING 277 cal., 0 fat (0 sat. fat), 0 chol., 18mg sod., 36g carb. (17g sugars, 0 fiber), 0 pro.

TEST KITCHEN TIPS

Should I use brandy or bourbon?
While brandy is the classic Wisconsin choice, bourbon or rye whiskey are also delicious options.

What bitters should I use?
Angostura bitters are the traditional choice, but craft bitters are flooding the market. Try orange, cherry or smoked cinnamon for an updated twist.

What can I use for a garnish?
Classic old-fashioned recipes aways include cherries—you can upgrade to Luxardo cherries if you'd like. The typical garnish is a speared cherry with an orange slice, but a cinnamon stick is another classic complement.

BRANDY OLD-FASHIONED SWEET

MULLED WINE

This mulled wine is soothing and satisfying with a delightful blend of spices warmed to perfection. Chilling the wine mixture overnight allows the flavors to blend, so don't omit this essential step.
—Taste of Home *Test Kitchen*

PREP: 15 min. • **COOK:** 30 min. + chilling
MAKES: 5 servings

- 1   bottle (750 ml) fruity red wine
- 1   cup brandy
- 1   cup sugar
- 1   medium orange, sliced
- 1   medium lemon, sliced
- ⅛ tsp. ground nutmeg
- 2   cinnamon sticks (3 in.)
- ½ tsp. whole allspice
- ½ tsp. aniseed
- ½ tsp. whole peppercorns
- 3   whole cloves
  Optional garnish: Orange slices, star anise and additional cinnamon sticks

1. In a large saucepan, combine the first 6 ingredients. Place cinnamon sticks, allspice, aniseed, peppercorns and cloves on a double thickness of cheesecloth. Gather corners of cloth to enclose spices; tie securely with string. Place in pan.
2. Bring to a boil, stirring occasionally. Reduce heat; simmer gently, covered, 20 minutes. Transfer to a covered container; cool slightly. Refrigerate, covered, overnight.
3. Strain the wine mixture into a large saucepan, discarding fruit and the spice bag; reheat. Serve warm. Garnish, if desired, with orange slices, star anise and additional cinnamon sticks.
¾ CUP 379 cal., 0 fat (0 sat. fat), 0 chol., 10mg sod., 46g carb. (41g sugars, 0 fiber), 0 pro.

SPARKLING COCONUT GRAPE JUICE

SPARKLING COCONUT GRAPE JUICE

This refreshing mix of lime, coconut and grape is a nice change of pace from lemonade and party punch. Add a splash of gin if you're feeling bold!
—Shelly Bevington, Hermiston, OR

TAKES: 5 min. • **MAKES:** 6 servings

- 4   cups white grape juice
- 2   tsp. lime juice
  Ice cubes
- 2   cups coconut-flavored sparkling water, chilled
  Optional garnish: Lime wedges or slices

In a pitcher, combine grape juice and lime juice. Fill 6 tall glasses with ice. Pour juice mixture evenly into glasses; top off with sparkling water. Stir to combine. Garnish with lime wedges if desired.
1 CUP 94 cal., 0 fat (0 sat. fat), 0 chol., 13mg sod., 24g carb. (21g sugars, 0 fiber), 0 pro.

CRAN & CHERRY PUNCH

This crimson-colored beverage is wonderful for Christmas and looks festive in a glass punch bowl.
—*Lori Daniels, Beverly, WV*

- -

PREP: 15 min. + freezing • **MAKES:** 3½ qt.

- ⅓ cup fresh or frozen cranberries
- 2 lemon slices, cut into 6 wedges
- 1 pkg. (3 oz.) cherry gelatin
- 1 cup boiling water
- 3 cups cold water
- 6 cups cranberry juice, chilled
- ¾ cup thawed lemonade concentrate
- 1 liter ginger ale, chilled

1. Place several cranberries and a piece of lemon in each compartment of an ice cube tray; fill with water and freeze.
2. In a punch bowl or large container, dissolve gelatin in boiling water. Stir in the cold water, cranberry juice and lemonade concentrate. Just before serving, stir in ginger ale. Serve over cranberry-lemon ice cubes.
¾ CUP 99 cal., 0 fat (0 sat. fat), 0 chol., 17mg sod., 25g carb. (24g sugars, 0 fiber), 1g pro. **DIABETIC EXCHANGES** 1 starch, ½ fruit.

REFRESHING BEER MARGARITAS

I'm always surprised when people say they didn't know this drink existed. It's an ideal summertime cocktail, and it's easy to double or even triple the recipe for larger get-togethers.
—*Arianne Barnett, Kansas City, MO*

- -

TAKES: 5 min. • **MAKES:** 6 servings

- Lime slices and kosher salt, optional
- 2 bottles (12 oz. each) beer
- 1 can (12 oz.) frozen limeade concentrate, thawed
- ¾ cup tequila
- ¼ cup sweet and sour mix
- Ice cubes
- Lime slices

1. If desired, use lime slices to moisten the rims of 6 margarita or cocktail glasses. Sprinkle salt on a plate; hold each glass upside down and dip rims into salt. Discard remaining salt.
2. In a pitcher, combine the beer, limeade concentrate, tequila and sweet and sour mix. Serve in prepared glasses over ice. Garnish with lime slices.
¾ CUP 244 cal., 0 fat (0 sat. fat), 0 chol., 8mg sod., 37g carb. (33g sugars, 0 fiber), 1g pro.

TEST KITCHEN TIP

When choosing a beer, stay away from heavy, flavorful brews like stouts, porters or brown ales. You're looking for a beer that will complement, not overpower, the flavors in the cocktail. Try a lager (a Mexican-style lager is ideal!) or a light ale. And as with all recipes, choose a beer that you'd actually want to drink on its own!

MAKE IT A MOCKTAIL!

Whether you're avoiding alcohol altogether at your party, or you're planning for a few non-drinkers in your crowd, treat the mocktails with as much thought as you'd put into regular cocktails.

A range of drink ingredients is key—different juices and sodas offer guests a chance to mix and match. Club soda adds effervescence and a subtle mineral flavor to drinks without the extra sugar that comes with soda.

Stock your "bar" with fresh ingredients. Muddled fruit (berries or citrus) and herbs (mint, basil, rosemary) makes everything feel a bit fancier—and taste delicious! Try zingier ingredients such as slices of fresh ginger, jalapeno or serrano peppers. And of course, save some fresh fruit and herb sprigs for garnish.

Simple syrups add sweetness and flavor, and a splash of cider vinegar can stand in for bitters.

To make basic syrup, just boil a 1:1 ratio of water and sugar in a saucepan for five minutes, until the sugar dissolves. For flavored syrup, add fruit, fresh herbs or whole spices to the mix. Once it's done boiling, let it cool and then strain the syrup into a decorative bottle. Add a pretty label, and guests can choose their own sweetener.

MARGARITA MANIA

Whether you love 'em on the rocks or blended to perfection, these tart and tangy refreshers turn any smiley, sunny day into a fiesta.

To make salted rims, moisten rim of cocktail glass with lime wedge. Sprinkle kosher salt on a plate; dip rim in salt. Fill glass with ice.

CLASSIC MARGARITA

CARIBBEAN MARGARITA

GRAPEFRUIT SUNSET MARGARITA

MELON MARGARITA

AMARETTO MARGARITA

Shaken Margarita
Pour ingredients into a cocktail shaker. Fill with ice; cover and shake until frost forms on the outside of the shaker, 15-20 seconds. Strain into prepared glass. Garnish if desired.

CLASSIC MARGARITA
1½ oz. blanco tequila; 1 oz. Triple Sec; ½ oz. freshly squeezed lime juice. **Garnish:** Lime wedge.

MELON MARGARITA
1½ oz. blanco tequila; 1½ oz. melon liqueur; ½ oz. freshly squeezed lime juice. **Garnish:** Honeydew melon balls.

CARIBBEAN MARGARITA
1½ oz. blanco tequila; 1 oz. blue curacao; ½ oz. freshly squeezed lime juice. **Garnish:** Starfruit slice.

AMARETTO MARGARITA
1½ oz. blanco tequila; 1 oz. Triple Sec; ½ oz. freshly squeezed lime juice; ½ oz. amaretto. **Garnish:** Maraschino cherry.

GRAPEFRUIT SUNSET MARGARITA
1½ oz. blanco tequila; 1 oz. Triple Sec; 1 oz. ruby red grapefruit juice. **Garnish:** 1 tsp. grenadine syrup; grapefruit slice.

BLUEBERRY-MINT FROZEN MARGARITA

STRAWBERRY-BASIL FROZEN MARGARITA

FROZEN COCONUT MARGARITA

RASPBERRY GINGER FROZEN MARGARITA

SRIRACHA-MANGO FROZEN MARGARITA

HOW TO MAKE A PITCHER OF MARGARITAS

If you and your friends enjoy margaritas when warm weather rolls around, making a whole pitcher at once is easier than making them glass by glass.

High-quality ingredients are a must. Invest in a decent bottle of tequila Blanco and orange liqueur. And always use fresh-squeezed lime juice; bottled will make your margarita taste bitter.

Rely on the 3-2-1 ratio (3 parts tequila, 2 parts orange liqueur, 1 part lime juice), no matter what size batch you're mixing. The measurements for each size batch are in the chart below.

Salt the rims of the glasses (see instructions, opposite page). You'll need ¼ cup salt for 12 glasses. Fill each glass about halfway with crushed or cubed ice.

In a large pitcher, combine the tequila, orange liqueur and lime juice. Add ice and stir with a large spoon until the cocktail is chilled and the outside of the pitcher has formed condensation.

For sweeter margaritas, add simple syrup—use about ¼ cup for a 12-serving batch, so 1 tsp. per serving. For flavored margaritas, add flavorings like fruit puree, fruit juice or other ingredients.

Then, simply divide the pitcher of margaritas among the prepared glasses and enjoy! To keep the ice cubes in the pitcher from splashing into the glasses, use a spoon to hold them back.

Frozen Margarita
Prepare glass as desired. Pour ingredients into a blender; cover and process until smooth. Pour into glass. Garnish if desired.

RASPBERRY-GINGER FROZEN MARGARITA

*1 cup frozen unsweetened raspberries; 1½ oz. blanco tequila; 1 oz. ginger liqueur; 1 oz. raspberry liqueur; ½ oz. freshly squeezed lime juice. **Garnish:** Sugared rim; strawberry; crystallized ginger slice.*

BLUEBERRY-MINT FROZEN MARGARITA

*1 cup frozen unsweetened blueberries; 1½ oz. blanco tequila; 1 oz. Triple Sec; ½ oz. freshly squeezed lime juice; 4 fresh mint leaves. **Garnish:** Sugared rim; mint sprig.*

FROZEN COCONUT MARGARITA

*1 cup crushed ice; 2 oz. cream of coconut; 1½ oz. blanco tequila; 1 oz. Triple Sec; ½ oz. freshly squeezed lime juice. **Garnish:** Chopped toasted shredded coconut on rim; toasted coconut slices.*

SRIRACHA-MANGO FROZEN MARGARITA

*1 cup frozen mango chunks; 1½ oz. blanco tequila; 1 oz. mango nectar; ½ oz. freshly squeezed lime juice; ½ tsp. Sriracha chili sauce. **Garnish:** Sugared rim; mango slice.*

STRAWBERRY-BASIL FROZEN MARGARITA

*1 cup frozen unsweetened sliced strawberries; 1½ oz. blanco tequila; 1 oz. Triple Sec; ½ oz. freshly squeezed lime juice; 4 fresh basil leaves. **Garnish:** Sugared rim; strawberry; basil leaf.*

	TEQUILA	ORANGE LIQUEUR	LIME JUICE
1 Serving	1½ oz.	1 oz.	½ oz.
2 Servings	3 oz.	2 oz.	1 oz.
4 Servings	¾ cup	½ cup	¼ cup
8 Servings	1½ cups	1 cup	½ cup
12 Servings	2¼ cups	1½ cups	¾ cup

ORANGE JUICE SPRITZER

Here's a zippy twist on regular orange juice. It's not too sweet and is refreshing with any breakfast or brunch entree.
—Michelle Krzmarzick, Torrance, CA

TAKES: 5 min. • **MAKES:** 8 servings

- 4   cups orange juice
- 1   liter ginger ale, chilled
- ¼   cup maraschino cherry juice
     Ice cubes
     Optional garnish: Orange wedges
     and maraschino cherries

In a 2-qt. pitcher, mix orange juice, ginger ale and cherry juice. Serve over ice. If desired, top servings with orange wedges and cherries.

1 CUP 103 cal., 0 fat (0 sat. fat), 0 chol., 9mg sod., 25g carb. (23g sugars, 0 fiber), 1g pro.

ROSEMARY STRAWBERRY DAIQUIRI

ROSEMARY STRAWBERRY DAIQUIRI

This strawberry daiquiri recipe is a standout with its herbal twist! I used to teach herb classes at our local technical college and everyone really enjoyed my segment on herbal cocktails like this one.
—Sue Gronholz, Beaver Dam, WI

PREP: 20 min. + cooling
MAKES: 8 servings

- 1   cup sugar
- 1   cup water
- 4   fresh rosemary sprigs

EACH SERVING
- 1   cup frozen unsweetened sliced strawberries
- 1½ oz. white rum
- 1   oz. lime juice
     Whole fresh strawberries and additional rosemary sprigs

1. In a small saucepan, bring sugar and water to a boil. Reduce heat; simmer 10 minutes. Remove from heat; add rosemary. Steep, covered, 10-15 minutes according to taste. Discard rosemary. Cool completely. Store in an airtight container in the refrigerator up to 1 month.
2. For each serving, in a blender, combine frozen strawberries, rum, lime juice and 2 Tbsp. rosemary syrup; cover and process until smooth. Pour into a chilled glass; garnish with a whole strawberry and an additional rosemary sprig.

1 SERVING 251 cal., 0 fat (0 sat. fat), 0 chol., 1mg sod., 41g carb. (32g sugars, 3g fiber), 0 pro.

STRAWBERRY
RIESLING
SPRITZERS

MINT JULEP

The subtly sweet sipper made with bourbon and fresh mint is an absolute must-have.
—Taste of Home *Test Kitchen*

- -

PREP: 30 min. + chilling
MAKES: 10 servings (2½ cups syrup)

MINT SYRUP
 2   cups sugar
 2   cups water
 2   cups loosely packed chopped
     fresh mint
EACH SERVING
 ½   to ¾ cup crushed ice
 ½   to 1 oz. bourbon
     Mint sprig

1. For syrup, combine sugar, water and chopped mint in a large saucepan. Bring to a boil over medium heat; cook until sugar is dissolved, stirring occasionally. Remove from the heat; cool to room temperature.
2. Line a mesh strainer with a double layer of cheesecloth or a coffee filter. Strain syrup; discard mint. Cover and refrigerate syrup for at least 2 hours or until chilled.
3. For each serving, place ice in a metal julep cup or rocks glass. Pour 2-4 Tbsp. mint syrup and bourbon into the glass; stir until mixture is well chilled. Garnish with mint sprig.
⅓ CUP 197 cal., 0 fat (0 sat. fat), 0 chol., 6mg sod., 42g carb. (39g sugars, 1g fiber), 1g pro.
NOTE For a bourbon-free version, add ½ cup lemon juice to syrup after straining, then chill as directed. For each serving, combine ½ cup club soda and ½ cup mint syrup in a glass filled with crushed ice. Garnish with mint.

STRAWBERRY-RIESLING SPRITZERS

Nothing says spring like strawberries and wine spritzers. The tarragon and black pepper in this refreshing cocktail complement the strawberry flavor and really make it taste special! The syrup is also delicious in lemonade, iced tea, club soda, and gin and tonics.
—*Zoe Ann McKinnon, St. Louis, MO*

- -

PREP: 10 min. • **COOK:** 30 min. + chilling
MAKES: 6 servings

 1¾ cups sliced fresh strawberries
 1   cup sugar
 1   cup water
 4   to 5 tarragon sprigs
 2   Tbsp. lime juice
 1   tsp. whole peppercorns
 3   cups sweet white wine, such as
     riesling, chilled
 3   cups club soda, chilled

1. In a small saucepan, bring the first 6 ingredients to a boil. Reduce heat; simmer for 20 minutes. Remove from heat. Cool completely. Strain through a fine-mesh strainer into a small bowl (do not press berries). Refrigerate the syrup until chilled.
2. For each serving, fill a tall glass with ice. Add ½ cup wine, ½ cup club soda and ¼ cup strawberry syrup. Garnish with additional tarragon if desired.
1 SERVING 228 cal., 0 fat (0 sat. fat), 0 chol., 31mg sod., 37g carb. (35g sugars, 0 fiber), 0 pro.

CRAZY FOR
CARAMEL
APPLES
BOARD
P. 74

BOARDS

The ultimate party centerpiece is edible! Start with a cheese plate and then branch out to fun themed boards that will have your guests amazed and delighted. And if you're wondering about which cheeses to choose, and what wine and snacks to pair them with, we've got you covered!

CAHILL
PORTER
CHEESE

MIFROMA
GRUYERE

BALLYSHANNON
CHEDDAR

*ILCHESTER
WHITE STILTON
WITH CRANBERRIES*

*PRESIDENT
BRIE*

BUILD A PERFECT CHEESE PLATTER

It's easy to build a cheese board guests won't be able to resist. Start with these tips, then turn the page for more on choosing the perfect cheeses and wines.

- Buy about 3-4 oz. of cheese per person (2 lbs. for 8 guests).

- Choose a variety of soft, firm, blue and aged cheeses. Be adventurous, but include 1 familiar type of cheese.

- Arrange soft cheeses in larger blocks so guests can slice their own. Cut or crumble harder cheeses before serving.

- Label each selection so guests know what they're sampling.

- Add visual appeal and complement cheese flavors with sweet grapes, sliced apples, cured prosciutto and toasted French bread. Add a small jar of fig jam, some almonds or other nuts—salted, spiced or plain.

- Let your cheese platter sit out about 30 minutes before guests arrive; most cheeses taste best at room temperature.

- Wines and cheeses from the same region usually go well together. Fresh, lighter cheeses go well with crisp, lighter wines; heavier, dense cheeses like bigger and bolder wines.

- Always taste the wine before the cheese for optimum effect.

ABOUT THE CHEESES
We chose these cheeses for the board shown at left. Turn the page for more cheese options and tips for wine pairings.

Cahill Porter Cheese
- Medium texture, marbling from porter beer, cow's milk
- Flavor notes: Mild, caramel, chocolaty
- Pair with Guinness or dark ale

Mifroma Gruyere
- Hard texture, aged minimum of 5 months, cow's milk
- Nutty, fruity, earthy
- Pair with chardonnay, pinot noir, cabernet sauvignon, sparkling wine.

Ballyshannon Cheddar
- Smooth yet crumbly texture, creamy, aged, cow's milk
- Rich, sweet, earthy
- Pair with riesling, sauvignon blanc, zinfandel

President Brie
- Soft texture, creamy, cow's milk, edible rind
- Mild, buttery, subtle mushroom notes
- Pair with sauvignon blanc, syrah, dry champagne

Ilchester White Stilton with Cranberries
- Soft texture, creamy, studded with cranberries, cow's milk
- Mild, fresh and milky with sweet, tangy cranberry
- Pair with riesling, zinfandel

CHEESE BOARD PAIRINGS TO TAKE YOUR SPREAD TO THE NEXT LEVEL

Learn all about the types of cheese to choose, along with serving and pairing tips for the ultimate spread.

BRIE

This soft, creamy French cheese with its hint of nuttiness and sweetness pairs well with apple and pear slices, fruit preserves, honey, nuts, prosciutto and crunchy crackers or crusty bread.
Wine: Crisp sauvignon blanc, oaked chardonnay or your favorite bubbly.

SHARP CHEDDAR

This extremely versatile hard cheese comes in a block; cut into slices or cubes. Serve with fruits such as strawberries and apples along with tangy mustards, pickles and salami.
Wine: A strong cheese needs a bold wine—malbec or cabernet sauvignon.

PECORINO ROMANO

A hard, Italian sheep's-milk cheese most often found in large wedges. Serve whole or broken into chunks. This bold, salty cheese pairs beautifully with salty salami or soppressata and sweet fruit jams or candied walnuts.
Wine: Avoid sweet wines; opt for a Chianti, dry zinfandel or chardonnay.

CHEVRE (GOAT CHEESE)

This soft, fresh cheese is perfect for serving in a whole log, sliced into discs or whipped into a spread. Serve with sliced baguette or flatbread crackers, apricots and figs, pepperoni and Marcona almonds.
Wine: A crisp, bright white such as sauvignon blanc or a bubbly rosé.

GORGONZOLA

A soft, crumbly Italian cheese with a blue marbled appearance. Its pungent flavor is best with sweet items such as fresh grapes, honey, almonds and pistachios.
Wine: A sweet riesling, moscato or a port to match its strong flavor.

PARMIGIANO REGGIANO

Its hard, dry texture and sharp flavor make this a cheese board staple. It's typically found in wedges; serve in rough chunks. Pair with tangy stone-ground mustard and salty-sweet prosciutto.
Wine: Prosecco or Champagne, or a high-acidity red such as a barbera.

BURRATA

A fresh cow's-milk cheese; the outer shell is soft mozzarella, but inside is a gooey curd. Serve whole in a small bowl, plain or drizzled with a balsamic glaze or pesto, with crackers on the side. Its light, creamy flavor goes with anything from salami and prosciutto to grapes and tomatoes.
Wine: Match its flavor with a light-bodied pinot grigio or sauvignon blanc.

HAVARTI

A creamy and versatile cheese with a sharp flavor and fine texture. Serve in slices or chunks. Pair with crisp fruits such as pear and apple slices, with salty soppressata and dill pickles for contrast.
Wine: Dry or off-dry riesling or an oaked chardonnay to match its buttery flavor.

GOUDA

A sweet and creamy cow's milk cheese; serve cut into small triangles, a wedge or chunks. It's delicious with salty and nutty options— salami, walnuts and pecans— and pickled vegetables.
Wine: Chardonnay, pinot gris or cabernet sauvignon.

FRESH MOZZARELLA

Whether served in slices, cubed or as small balls, its mild flavor pairs with practically anything. Serve with fresh basil and tomato, tapenades, fresh fruits and salty meats.
Wine: Match its light flavor with a light-bodied chardonnay or pinot grigio.

CAMEMBERT

Camembert has a stronger, earthier flavor than brie and works best with contrasting flavors, such as dried cranberries, fruit jams and honey.
Wine: Light-bodied pinot noir, chenin blanc, chardonnay or champagne.

MANCHEGO

A firm sheep's milk cheese with a buttery texture and rich salty-sweet flavor. Serve in a wedge or cut into thin triangular slices. Pair with salty meats such as salami and prosciutto, olives, sun-dried tomatoes and almonds.
Wine: Serve with a fruit-forward red (malbec or syrah) or a sparkling cava.

START WITH THE WINE

Sometimes the cheese comes first—but often you're creating your spread around a particular bottle (or bottles!) of wine. Use this guide to build a cheese shopping list when the wine is your starting point.

CHAMPAGNE OR SPARKLING WINE
Drier wines/brut Champagne: Brie, aged French and Swiss cheeses (comte and Gruyere)
Cava: Triple creme cheese like Brillat-Savarin
Prosecco: Parmigiano Reggiano

PINOT GRIGIO OR PINOT GRIS
Pinot grigio (lighter-bodied, citrus flavors): Asiago, mozzarella, burrata
Pinot gris (richer, complex, tropical fruit flavors): Aged cheddar, Gouda

CHARDONNAY
Unoaked (crisp, high acid): Chevre
Oaked: Semi-hard cheese (cheddar, Havarti)
Balanced oak: Brie, Camembert

SAUVIGNON BLANC
Chevre, Brie, feta, Asiago

RIESLING
Dry or off-dry (Kabinett): most cheeses, including Asiago, Colby, Monterey Jack, Havarti, most cheddars, raclette.
Sweet (Spatlese): salty, bolder cheeses (Gorgonzola, aged Gouda, Parmigiano Reggiano).

ROSÉ
Light rose: Fresh cheeses (burrata, chevre), Havarti
Darker, fruitier rose: Firm, bold cheeses (aged cheddar, Gouda).

PINOT NOIR
Camembert, Brie or pungent cheeses (taleggio, Reblochon, Cambozola); creamy mild blue cheese.

MALBEC
Semi-hard cheeses (cheddar, Colby, Edam)

MERLOT
Cheddar, Havarti, Swiss, taleggio

CABERNET SAUVIGNON
Aged cheddar or blue cheeses (Gorgonzola, Roquefort)

CHIANTI
Parmigiano Reggiano, provolone, pecorino Romano

ZINFANDEL
Harder cheeses (smoked Gouda, aged cheddar, Manchego), Havarti, Gruyere, Gorgonzola

SYRAH
Manchego, salty hard cheeses (cheddar, Edam, Parmigiano Reggiano)

PORT
Ruby port (sweet): Stilton, Gorgonzola
Tawny port (full bodied): Aged cheddar, Gouda, Romano
White port (drier): Gruyere

MOSCATO D'ASTI
Creamy blue cheeses (Cambozola, Gorgonzola); Camembert

FRENCH FRY FEST

Sure! You'll have fries with that, especially when served with homemade dipping sauces. You can use a variety of fries from the freezer section, or make your own.

BUILD THE BOARD:

Dipping Sauces

- **Fry Sauce**
- **Homemade Guacamole**
- Ketchup
- **Nacho Cheese Dip**
- **Ranch Dressing**
- Sour cream

Fries

- Crinkle-cut fries
- Curly fries
- Shoestring potatoes
- **Air-Fryer Sweet Potato Fries**
- Tater Tots
- Waffle fries

Toppings

- Bacon, cooked and crumbled
- Chives, chopped
- Shredded cheddar cheese
- **Garlic-Parmesan Fry Seasoning**

GARLIC-PARMESAN FRY SEASONING P. 69

FRY SAUCE P. 69

PAIRS WITH

UNCLE MERLE'S BLOODY MARY, P. 45

RANCH DRESSING P. 69

NACHO CHEESE DIP P. 68

MAKE AIR-FRYER SWEET POTATO FRIES, P. 97

HOMEMADE GUACAMOLE P. 69

RANCH DRESSING

Why buy bottled ranch dressing when the from-scratch version is so easy to make (and tastes so much better)? Fresh chives are a colorful addition if you have them on hand.
—Taste of Home *Test Kitchen*

TAKES: 10 min. • **MAKES:** 1 cup

- ⅔ cup buttermilk
- ½ cup mayonnaise
- ½ cup sour cream
- 2 Tbsp. minced fresh parsley
- 2 garlic cloves, minced
- ½ tsp. sugar
- 1 tsp. dill weed
- ½ tsp. salt
- ½ tsp. onion powder
- ½ tsp. ground mustard
- ¼ tsp. pepper

In a bowl, combine all the ingredients. Whisk until smooth. Refrigerate, covered, until serving.
2 TBSP. 66 cal., 7g fat (2g sat. fat), 3mg chol., 131mg sod., 1g carb. (1g sugars, 0 fiber), 1g pro.

NACHO CHEESE DIP

NACHO CHEESE DIP

With jobs, school and sport activities, evening is our time for family fun. We munch on this zippy dip while visiting or watching a movie.
—Dawn Taylor, Milton, KY

TAKES: 10 min. • **MAKES:** 3 cups

- ¼ lb. bulk spicy pork or Mexican-style sausage
- 2 Tbsp. chopped green pepper
- 2 Tbsp. chopped onion
- 1 lb. American cheese, cubed
- ¾ cup salsa

In a 1½-qt. microwave-safe container, microwave sausage, green pepper and onion on high for 1-2 minutes or until the sausage is fully cooked; drain. Add the cheese and salsa. Microwave, covered, on high for 1-2 minutes, stirring frequently until the cheese is melted and the mixture is smooth.
2 TBSP. 75 cal., 6g fat (3g sat. fat), 14mg chol., 279mg sod., 2g carb. (2g sugars, 0 fiber), 4g pro.

GARLIC-PARMENSAN FRY SEASONING

Bake a 32-oz. bag of fries as directed. In small saucepan, melt 2 Tbsp. butter over medium-low heat; add 4 garlic cloves, minced. Cook, stirring constantly, 2-3 minutes. Reduce heat. Add an additional 4 Tbsp. butter; cook until melted. Pour butter over hot fries; toss to coat. Sprinkle with ½ cup grated Parmesan and 2 Tbsp. minced fresh parsley.

FRY SAUCE

HOMEMADE GUACAMOLE

Nothing is better than freshly made guacamole when you're eating something spicy! It is easy to whip together in a matter of minutes and quickly tames anything that's too hot.
—Joan Hallford, Fort Worth, TX

TAKES: 10 min. • **MAKES:** 2 cups

- 3 medium ripe avocados, peeled and cubed
- 1 garlic clove, minced
- ¼ to ½ tsp. salt
- 1 small onion, finely chopped
- 1 to 2 Tbsp. lime juice
- 1 Tbsp. minced fresh cilantro
- 2 medium tomatoes, seeded and chopped, optional
- ¼ cup mayonnaise, optional

Mash avocados with garlic and salt. Stir in remaining ingredients, adding tomatoes and mayonnaise if desired.
¼ CUP 90 cal., 8g fat (1g sat. fat), 0 chol., 78mg sod., 6g carb. (1g sugars, 4g fiber), 1g pro. **DIABETIC EXCHANGES** 1½ fat.

FRY SAUCE

Want a change of pace from dipping your french fries into ketchup? Try a favorite condiment from Utah: fry sauce. It's a spiced-up blend of ketchup and mayo.
—Taste of Home *Test Kitchen*

TAKES: 5 min. • **MAKES:** 1½ cups

- 1 cup mayonnaise
- ½ cup ketchup
- 4 tsp. sweet pickle juice
- ½ tsp. hot pepper sauce
- ½ tsp. onion powder
- ¼ tsp. pepper
- ⅛ tsp. salt
- 1 Tbsp. sweet pickle relish, optional

In a small bowl, whisk the first 7 ingredients; if desired, add pickle relish. Refrigerate leftovers in airtight container.
2 TBSP. 133 cal., 13g fat (2g sat. fat), 1mg chol., 261mg sod., 3g carb. (3g sugars, 0 fiber), 0 pro.

TEST KITCHEN TIP

Bake your fries on several 15x10x1-in. baking pans. While the fries are baking, place your sauces and toppings on the board. That way, everything will be ready as soon as the fries are done and you can eat them while they're hot!

JUST WING IT!

People's love of wings never wanes, so why not dedicate a board to them?

BUILD THE BOARD:

Dipping Sauces

- **Buffalo Wing Sauce**
- Cilantro lime salad dressing
- **Garlic Blue Cheese Dip**
- **Spicy Barbecue Sauce**

Snacks

- **Best Ever Fried Chicken Wings**
- Onion rings
- Snack mix

Vegetables

- Carrots
- Celery
- Cucumbers
- Radishes
- Sugar snap peas

BEST EVER FRIED CHICKEN WINGS P. 72

MAKE CRISPY FRIED ONION RINGS, P. 96

PAIRS WITH

RIESLING OR GEWURZTRAMINER

BUFFALO WING SAUCE P. 72

GARLIC BLUE CHEESE DIP P. 72

SPICY BARBECUE SAUCE P. 72

GARLIC BLUE CHEESE DIP

This thick, creamy dip is my mom's recipe and a family favorite. It also makes a tasty substitute for mayonnaise on chicken and turkey sandwiches.
—*Lillian Nardi, Richmond, CA*

- -

TAKES: 10 min. • **MAKES:** About 1½ cups

½   cup milk
1   pkg. (8 oz.) cream cheese, cubed
1   cup (4 oz.) crumbled blue cheese
2   garlic cloves, peeled
    Assorted vegetables or crackers

In a blender, combine the milk, cream cheese, blue cheese and garlic; cover and process until blended. If desired, top with additional crumbled blue cheese just before serving. Serve with vegetables or crackers.
2 TBSP. 113 cal., 10g fat (6g sat. fat), 31mg chol., 218mg sod., 1g carb. (1g sugars, 0 fiber), 4g pro.

BEST EVER FRIED CHICKEN WINGS

For game days, I shake up these saucy wings. When I run out, friends hover by the snack table until I bring out more. When they ask me how I fry chicken wings, they never believe it's so easy!
—*Nick Iverson, Denver, CO*

- -

PREP: 10 min. + chilling • **COOK:** 20 min.
MAKES: about 4 dozen

4   lbs. chicken wings
2   tsp. kosher salt
    Oil for deep-fat frying
BUFFALO WING SAUCE
¾   cup Louisiana-style hot sauce
¼   cup unsalted butter, cubed
2   Tbsp. molasses
¼   tsp. cayenne pepper
SPICY THAI SAUCE
1   Tbsp. canola oil
1   tsp. grated fresh gingerroot
1   garlic clove, minced
1   minced Thai chile pepper or ¼ tsp. crushed red pepper flakes
¼   cup packed dark brown sugar
2   Tbsp. lime juice
2   Tbsp. minced fresh cilantro
1   Tbsp. fish sauce
SPICY BARBECUE SAUCE
¾   cup barbecue sauce
2   chipotle peppers in adobo sauce, finely chopped
2   Tbsp. honey
1   Tbsp. cider vinegar

1. Using a sharp knife, cut through the 2 wing joints; discard wing tips. Pat chicken dry with paper towels. Toss wings with kosher salt. Place on a wire rack in a 15x10x1-in. baking pan. Refrigerate at least 1 hour or overnight.
2. In an electric skillet or deep-fat fryer, heat oil to 375°. Fry wings in batches until skin is crisp and meat is tender, 8-10 minutes. Remove from pan with a slotted spoon; drain on paper towels.

3. For **Buffalo Wing sauce**, bring hot sauce just to a boil in a small saucepan. Remove from heat; whisk in butter 1 piece at a time. Stir in molasses and cayenne pepper.
4. For **Spicy Thai sauce**, heat oil in a small saucepan over medium heat. Add ginger, garlic and chile pepper; cook and stir until fragrant, about 2 minutes. Stir in brown sugar and lime juice. Bring to a boil; cook until slightly thickened, about 5 minutes. Stir in cilantro and fish sauce.
5. For **Spicy Barbecue sauce**, heat prepared barbecue sauce in a small saucepan over medium heat. Stir in chipotle peppers, honey and vinegar. Bring to a boil; cook and stir until slightly thickened, about 5 minutes.
6. Toss wings with desired sauce.
NOTE Wear disposable gloves when cutting hot peppers; the oils can burn skin. Avoid touching your face.
1 PIECE 87 cal., 8g fat (2g sat. fat), 15mg chol., 218mg sod., 1g carb. (1g sugars, 0 fiber), 4g pro.

TEST KITCHEN TIPS

- Toss these sauces with chicken nuggets, grilled shrimp, even steamed veggies. Mix leftover sauce into ground beef for burgers to spice things up..

- Tossing the wings with salt helps dry the skin; dryness is the key to perfect crispness when the wings are fried.

- Use enough oil to cover the wings by at least 1 inch with no danger of bubbling over the top.

- Fry in batches to ensure you don't crowd the pan. If there isn't enough room between the wings, the oil will cool down and the wings won't cook evenly.

- Between batches, let the oil heat back up to 375° before frying more wings.

BEST EVER FRIED CHICKEN WINGS

PREPPING CHICKEN WINGS

Step 1: Using a sharp, thin knife, cut through the joint between the wing tip and the wingette. Discard the wing tip.

Step 2: Move the joint between the wingette and drumette to see where to slice, then separate them with a sharp knife.

CRAZY FOR CARAMEL APPLES

You'll be the apple of everyone's eye with this seasonal spread—it's just the thing for fall get-togethers, when the weather starts to turn colder!

BUILD THE BOARD:

Dippers

- Apples
- Graham crackers
- Pretzel rods

Dips

- Caramel dip
- **Fluffy Caramel Apple Dip**
- Peanut butter

Toppings

- Chopped nuts
- Craisins
- Mini chocolate chips
- Mini M&M's
- Mini marshmallows
- Shredded coconut
- Sprinkles

Treats

- **Caramel Apple Rice Krispies Treats**
- **Creamy Caramels**

CREAMY CARAMELS P. 77

PAIRS
WITH

TAWNY PORT

FLUFFY
CARAMEL
APPLE DIP
P. 77

CARAMEL APPLE
RICE KRISPIES
TREATS
P. 78

FLUFFY
CARAMEL
APPLE DIP

FLUFFY CARAMEL APPLE DIP

This sweet, smooth and fluffy dip is really a crowd-pleaser. Be careful—it's so good that you won't want to stop eating it!
—Taste of Home *Test Kitchen*

TAKES: 30 min. • **MAKES:** 2 cups

- 1   pkg. (8 oz.) cream cheese, softened
- ½   cup packed brown sugar
- ¼   cup caramel ice cream topping
- 1   tsp. vanilla extract
- 1   cup marshmallow creme
    Apple slices

In a small bowl, beat cream cheese, brown sugar, caramel topping and vanilla until smooth; fold in marshmallow creme. Serve with apple slices.

2 TBSP. 110 cal., 5g fat (3g sat. fat), 14mg chol., 69mg sod., 15g carb. (14g sugars, 0 fiber), 1g pro.

TEST KITCHEN TIPS

When slicing apples, it's a race against time before unappetizing brown spots appear. Keep apple slices looking white and wonderful for a couple of hours with one of these easy hacks.

- Place in a bowl of cold salted water (about ½ tsp. salt per cup of water). Soak for 5 minutes. Drain and rinse.

- Soak in cold lemon water (about 1 Tbsp. juice per cup of water) for 5 minutes. Drain and rinse.

- Mix ½ tsp. honey with 1 cup water. Add apple slices; soak for 5 minutes. Drain and rinse.

- Soak in lemon-lime soda for 5 minutes. Drain (there's no need to rinse).

- Store in an airtight container and refrigerate until ready to serve.

CREAMY CARAMELS

CREAMY CARAMELS

I discovered this recipe in a local newspaper years ago and have made these soft, buttery caramels ever since. I make them for Christmas, picnics and charity auctions—they're so much better than the store-bought version.
—*Marcie Wolfe, Williamsburg, VA*

PREP: 10 min. • **COOK:** 30 min. + cooling
MAKES: 64 pieces (2½ lbs.)

- 1   tsp. plus 1 cup butter, divided
- 1   cup sugar
- 1   cup dark corn syrup
- 1   can (14 oz.) sweetened condensed milk
- 1   tsp. vanilla extract

1. Line an 8-in. square pan with foil; grease foil with 1 tsp. butter.
2. In a large heavy saucepan, combine sugar, corn syrup and remaining 1 cup butter; bring to a boil over medium heat, stirring constantly. Boil slowly for 4 minutes without stirring.
3. Remove from heat; stir in milk. Reduce heat to medium-low and cook until a candy thermometer reads 238° (soft-ball stage), stirring constantly. Remove from heat; stir in vanilla.
4. Pour into prepared pan (do not scrape saucepan). Cool. Using foil, lift candy out of pan. Discard foil; cut candy into 1-in. squares. Wrap individually in waxed paper; twist ends.
NOTE We recommend you test your candy thermometer before each use by bringing water to a boil; the thermometer should read 212°. Adjust your recipe temperature up or down based on your test.
1 PIECE 72 cal., 3g fat (2g sat. fat), 10mg chol., 45mg sod., 10g carb. (8g sugars, 0 fiber), 1g pro.

HOW TO MAKE CARAMEL APPLES

Farm-fresh apples wrapped in sweet caramel are impossible to resist. Follow these steps to make your own batch to accompany your board. The caramel can be kept warm and used for dipping individual apple slices, too!

INGREDIENTS
- 6 small Gala apples
- 6 wooden pop sticks
- 1 package (14 oz.) caramels, unwrapped
- 2 Tbsp. milk

DIRECTIONS

Step 1: Remove the stems and thoroughly wash the apples. Store-bought apples can have a waxy coating, so scrub them with a dishcloth until they look natural and dull. Dry the apples; insert a wooden pop stick into the top of each. Line a baking sheet with a piece of greased parchment or waxed paper. (Greasing the paper is so the caramel won't stick later.) Set the baking sheet on a counter close to the stovetop.

Step 2: Place the caramels in a saucepan with the milk. Heat over medium-low heat, stirring frequently, until mixture is smooth, 3-5 minutes. Remove from heat.

Step 3: Tip the saucepan and lower an apple into the caramel. Rotate the apple until the surface is completely covered. Allow excess caramel to drip off. If the caramel runs off the apples, don't worry—it might just be a touch too warm. Wait a minute and dip the apple again.

Step 4: Place each apple on the lined baking sheet. Let stand until the caramel is set, about 10 minutes, before eating. These caramel apples can be kept refrigerated for a week or so. Take them out of the fridge 10-15 minutes before eating to allow the caramel to soften.

TEST KITCHEN TIPS

- We like Gala apples for their sweet flavor, but feel free to use whatever apple you prefer. Granny Smiths are a traditional option for tartness and a good crunch.

- Don't limit yourself to plain caramel! After dipping, while the caramel is still sticky, roll the apples in nuts, sprinkles or candies or drizzle them with melted chocolate. If you like salty with your sweet, sprinkle a little sea salt on top when the caramel is just about set.

CARAMEL APPLE
RICE KRISPIES
TREATS

CARAMEL APPLE RICE KRISPIES TREATS

Ooey, gooey caramel meets your favorite crisped rice treat in impossible-to-resist recipe.

—Taste of Home *Test Kitchen*

- -

PREP: 20 + cooling • **MAKES:** 1 dozen

1 pkg. (10 oz.) miniature marshmallows
3 Tbsp. canola oil
5 cups Rice Krispies
1 cup dried apples, chopped
1 pkg. (11 oz.) caramels

In a microwave or a large saucepan over low heat, melt marshmallows and oil; stir until smooth. Remove from heat; stir in cereal and dried apples. Shape ⅓ cup mixture into an apple shape. Insert a paper straw or pop stick into center; repeat with remaining mixture. Let cool to room temperature. Melt caramels according to package directions. Spread caramel onto apples and set on waxed paper to cool.

1 TREAT 278 cal., 6g fat (1g sat. fat), 2mg chol., 165mg sod., 56g carb. (36g sugars, 1g fiber), 3g pro.

STRAWBERRY
SHORTCAKE
SALAD
P. 86

SIDES & SALADS

The right side dish can elevate a good meal to great. Whether you're planning a dinner party for a few close friends or a blow-out bash for a crowd, these stunning salads and tasty supporting acts might just end up stealing the show!

LAYERED FRESH FRUIT SALAD

ORZO WITH CARAMELIZED BUTTERNUT SQUASH & BACON

The year my garden produced a bumper crop of butternut squash, I made so many new dishes trying to use up my bounty! This is a tasty, easy side with pretty colors, and it makes plenty. To make it into a main dish, add some shrimp or shredded chicken.

—*Kallee Krong-McCreery, Escondido, CA*

- -

PREP: 20 min. • **COOK:** 20 min.
MAKES: 6 servings

- 1½ cups uncooked orzo pasta
- 4 bacon strips, chopped
- 2 cups cubed peeled butternut squash (½-in. cubes)
- ½ cup chopped onion
- 1 cup cut fresh or frozen green beans, thawed
- 1 garlic clove, minced
- 1 Tbsp. butter
- 1 tsp. garlic salt
- ¼ tsp. pepper
- ¼ cup grated Parmesan cheese
  Minced fresh parsley

1. In a large saucepan, cook orzo according to the package directions.
2. Meanwhile, in a large skillet, cook bacon over medium heat until crisp, stirring occasionally. Remove with a slotted spoon; drain on paper towels. Cook and stir squash and onion in the bacon drippings until tender, 8-10 minutes. Add beans and garlic; cook 1 minute longer.
3. Drain orzo; stir into the squash mixture. Add butter, garlic salt, pepper and bacon; heat through. Sprinkle with Parmesan cheese and parsley.

¾ CUP 329 cal., 11g fat (4g sat. fat), 20mg chol., 533mg sod., 47g carb. (4g sugars, 3g fiber), 11g pro.

LAYERED FRESH FRUIT SALAD

Fresh fruit flavor shines through in this medley, which is always welcome at potlucks. It's got a little zing from citrus zest and cinnamon—and is just sweet enough to feel like dessert.

—*Page Alexander, Baldwin City, KS*

- -

PREP: 20 min. + chilling
COOK: 10 min. + cooling
MAKES: 12 servings

- ½ tsp. grated orange zest
- ⅔ cup orange juice
- ½ tsp. grated lemon zest
- ⅓ cup lemon juice
- ⅓ cup packed light brown sugar
- 1 cinnamon stick

FRUIT SALAD

- 2 cups cubed fresh pineapple
- 2 cups sliced fresh strawberries
- 2 medium kiwifruit, peeled and sliced
- 3 medium bananas, sliced
- 2 medium oranges, peeled and sectioned
- 1 medium red grapefruit, peeled and sectioned
- 1 cup seedless red grapes

1. Place the first 6 ingredients in a saucepan; bring to a boil. Reduce heat; simmer, uncovered, 5 minutes. Cool completely. Remove cinnamon stick.
2. Layer fruit in a large glass bowl. Pour the juice mixture over top. Refrigerate, covered, several hours.

1 SERVING 110 cal., 0 fat (0 sat. fat), 0 chol., 5mg sod., 28g carb. (21g sugars, 2g fiber), 1g pro. **DIABETIC EXCHANGES** 1 starch, 1 fruit.

ORZO WITH CARAMELIZED BUTTERNUT SQUASH & BACON

ZUCCHINI FRIES

These aren't anything like potato fries—in a good way! They are air-fried to crispy perfection and oh, so flavorful. Enjoy them as an appetizer or a low-carb alternative to french fries. If you don't have an air fryer, you can bake them in a convection oven for the same length of time.

—*Jen Pahl, West Allis, WI*

PREP: 20 min. • **COOK:** 10 min./batch
MAKES: 4 servings

- 2 medium zucchini
- 1 cup panko bread crumbs
- 2 tsp. dried basil, divided
- 1½ tsp. seasoned salt
- 1 tsp. garlic powder
- 1 tsp. dried oregano
- ½ cup plus 2 Tbsp. grated Parmesan cheese, divided
- 2 large eggs, lightly beaten
  Cooking spray
  Marinara sauce, warmed

1. Preheat air fryer to 375°. Cut each zucchini in half lengthwise and then in half crosswise. Cut each piece lengthwise into ¼-in. slices.
2. In a shallow bowl, mix bread crumbs, 1 tsp. basil, salt, garlic powder, oregano and ½ cup Parmesan. In a separate shallow bowl, combine eggs and the remaining 1 tsp. basil. Dip zucchini in the egg mixture and then in the crumb mixture, patting to help coating adhere.
3. In batches, place zucchini pieces in a single layer on greased tray in air-fryer basket; spritz with cooking spray. Cook until lightly browned, 6-8 minutes. Flip each piece; cook until golden brown, 3-5 minutes longer.
4. Sprinkle hot fries with the remaining 2 Tbsp. Parmesan cheese; serve with marinara sauce.
1 CUP 91 cal., 4g fat (2g sat. fat), 52mg chol., 389mg sod., 9g carb. (2g sugars, 1g fiber), 6g pro. **DIABETIC EXCHANGES** 1 vegetable, 1 fat.

ZUCCHINI FRIES

BERRY NECTARINE SALAD

I've been making this recipe for years. Whenever my family has a summer get-together, everyone requests it. The nectarines and berries look beautiful together, and the cream cheese topping is the perfect accent.

—*Mindee Myers, Lincoln, NE*

- -

PREP: 15 min. + chilling
MAKES: 8 servings

- 4 medium nectarines, sliced
- ¼ cup sugar
- 1 tsp. lemon juice
- ½ tsp. ground ginger
- 3 oz. reduced-fat cream cheese
- 2 cups fresh raspberries
- 1 cup fresh blueberries

1. In a large bowl, toss nectarines with sugar, lemon juice and ginger. Refrigerate, covered, for 1 hour, stirring once.

2. Drain nectarines, reserving juices. Gradually beat the reserved juices into cream cheese. Gently combine nectarines and berries; serve with cream cheese mixture.

1 SERVING 109 cal., 3g fat (2g sat. fat), 8mg chol., 46mg sod., 21g carb. (15g sugars, 4g fiber), 2g pro. **DIABETIC EXCHANGES** 1 fruit, ½ starch, ½ fat.

HOW TO SET A TABLE

BASIC SETTING

Set the plate in the center, with the fork to the left and the knife and spoon to the right. The water glass goes above the knife, and a napkin is placed under the fork or on the plate.

INFORMAL

Start with a basic setting. Depending on your menu, add:

- If you'll serve salad, the salad fork goes to the left of the dinner fork. Place the dessert fork to the right of the dinner fork, or wait to bring dessert forks to the table when you serve dessert.

- If soup is on the menu, place the bowl on the plate and a soup spoon to the right of the knife.

- Salad or bread plates go to the left of the dinner plate, above the fork(s). If needed, set the butter spreader across the plate.

- Place cup and saucer above the spoon(s), with the handle angled to the right. Wine or water glasses are positioned to the left of the coffee cup.

FORMAL DINNER

Begin with the setting for an informal dinner or luncheon and add to it using the following ideas:

- If you'll be serving different wines with each course, add wine glasses by the water glass to the left of the coffee cup.

- To dress it up more, place a charger under the dinner plate.

MORE WAYS TO MAKE A SIT-DOWN DINNER SPECIAL
Consider these ways to add flair to your table.

- Bring out your china, crystal, silver and best linen cloths.

- Use place cards so guests don't have to guess where to sit.

- Buy or arrange a floral centerpiece for the table. Make sure it's on the shorter side (10 to 12 inches), so people can see each other across the table.

- Before calling guests to the table, fill water glasses.

STRAWBERRY
SHORTCAKE
SALAD

TRIPLE-CHEESE MACARONI

No truly southern meal is complete without macaroni and cheese. Three types of cheese and a squirt of mustard make this comforting dish sing!
—Katie Sloan, Charlotte, NC

- -

PREP: 20 min. • **BAKE:** 25 min.
MAKES: 6 servings

- 1 pkg. (16 oz.) elbow macaroni
- 2 large eggs, room temperature
- 1 can (12 oz.) evaporated milk
- ¼ cup butter, melted
- 2 Tbsp. prepared mustard
- 1 tsp. seasoned salt
- 1 tsp. pepper
- 8 oz. Velveeta, melted
- 2 cups shredded mild cheddar cheese, divided
- 2 cups shredded sharp cheddar cheese, divided

1. Cook macaroni according to package directions. Preheat oven to 350°.
2. Meanwhile, in a large bowl, whisk eggs, milk, butter, mustard, seasoned salt and pepper until combined. Stir in Velveeta and 1½ cups of each cheddar cheese.
3. Drain macaroni; stir into the cheese mixture. Pour into a greased 3-qt. baking dish. Top with the remaining cheeses. Bake, uncovered, until cheese is melted and edges are bubbly, 25-30 minutes.
1½ CUPS 830 cal., 45g fat (30g sat. fat), 213mg chol., 1368mg sod., 67g carb. (11g sugars, 3g fiber), 39g pro.

#GIRLDINNER

This mac & cheese will keep in the fridge for up to 5 days, making it a perfect base for one-off dinners throughout the week. Good protein add-ins include seasoned chicken strips, pulled pork and sausage—like Polish sausage or spicy chorizo!

STRAWBERRY SHORTCAKE SALAD

This fabulous recipe transforms a classic dessert into a bright, refreshing twist on traditional salad. Creamy Gorgonzola, crispy pancetta and a strawberry-yogurt dressing make this a celebration of spring in a salad bowl.
—Adrienne Vradenburg, Bakersfield, CA

- -

TAKES: 25 min. • **MAKES:** 4 servings

- 4 oz. chopped pancetta
- 1 Tbsp. extra virgin olive oil
- 2 individual round shortcakes, cubed
- 3 Tbsp. minced fresh parsley, divided
- ½ tsp. kosher salt, divided
- ½ cup strawberry custard-style yogurt
- 1 Tbsp. fresh lemon juice
- ¼ tsp. coarsely ground pepper
- 4 cups fresh arugula
- 1 cup fresh strawberries, sliced
- ½ cup crumbled Gorgonzola cheese
- ¼ cup pine nuts, toasted

1. In a large skillet, cook pancetta over medium-high heat until crispy, about 5 minutes. Remove to paper towels to drain. Add olive oil to the drippings. Add shortcake cubes; cook, stirring frequently, until golden brown, 3-4 minutes. Transfer to bowl; stir in 2 Tbsp. parsley and ¼ tsp. salt.
2. For dressing, in a small bowl, stir together the yogurt, lemon juice, the remaining 1 Tbsp. parsley and ¼ tsp. salt, and pepper.
3. In a salad bowl, toss the arugula, strawberries, Gorgonzola, pine nuts, pancetta and shortcake croutons. Drizzle with the dressing. Serve immediately.
1 SERVING 330 cal., 24g fat (8g sat. fat), 51mg chol., 1074mg sod., 18g carb. (11g sugars, 2g fiber), 12g pro.

SUMMER
GARDEN
COUSCOUS
SALAD

SUMMER GARDEN COUSCOUS SALAD

This refreshing salad makes the most of summer's bounty with a light and tasty lemon vinaigrette replacing heavy mayo.
—*Priscilla Yee, Concord, CA*

TAKES: 30 min. • **MAKES:** 9 servings

- 3 medium ears sweet corn, husks removed
- 1 cup reduced-sodium chicken broth or vegetable broth
- 1 cup uncooked couscous
- 1 medium cucumber, halved and sliced
- 1½ cups cherry tomatoes, halved
- ½ cup crumbled feta cheese
- ¼ cup chopped red onion
- 3 Tbsp. minced fresh parsley
- 3 Tbsp. olive oil
- 3 Tbsp. lemon juice
- 1 tsp. dried oregano
- ¾ tsp. ground cumin
- ½ tsp. salt
- ½ tsp. pepper

1. Place corn in a Dutch oven; cover with water. Bring to a boil; cover and cook for 6-9 minutes or until tender. Meanwhile, in a small saucepan, bring broth to a boil. Stir in couscous. Remove from the heat; cover and let stand for 5-10 minutes or until water is absorbed. Fluff with a fork and set aside to cool slightly.
2. In a large bowl, combine cucumber, tomatoes, cheese, onion and parsley. Drain the corn and immediately place in ice water. Drain and pat dry; cut the kernels from the cobs. Add to the cucumber mixture. Stir in couscous.
3. In a small bowl, whisk oil, lemon juice and seasonings. Pour over the couscous mixture; toss to coat. Serve immediately or cover and refrigerate until chilled.
¾ CUP 173 cal., 6g fat (1g sat. fat), 3mg chol., 264mg sod., 25g carb. (4g sugars, 2g fiber), 6g pro. **DIABETIC EXCHANGES** 1½ starch, 1 fat.

OVEN FRIES

I jazz up my fries with paprika and garlic powder. Something about the combination of spices packs a punch. The leftovers are even good cold!
—*Heather Byers, Pittsburgh, PA*

PREP: 10 min. • **BAKE:** 40 min.
MAKES: 4 servings

- 4 medium potatoes
- 1 Tbsp. olive oil
- 2½ tsp. paprika
- ¾ tsp. salt
- ¾ tsp. garlic powder

1. Preheat oven to 400°. Cut each potato into 12 wedges. In a large bowl, combine oil, paprika, salt and garlic powder. Add potatoes; toss to coat.
2. Transfer to a greased 15x10x1-in. baking pan. Bake until tender, 40-45 minutes, turning once.
12 FRIES 200 cal., 4g fat (1g sat. fat), 0 chol., 457mg sod., 38g carb. (2g sugars, 5g fiber), 5g pro.

GREEK TORTELLINI SALAD

A bold homemade dressing gives this pasta salad a burst of flavor. Watch it disappear from your buffet table.
—*Sue Braunschweig, Delafield, WI*

- -

PREP: 20 min. + chilling
MAKES: 10 servings

16 to 18 oz. refrigerated or frozen cheese tortellini
1 medium sweet red pepper, julienned
1 medium green pepper, julienned
¾ cup sliced red onion
¼ cup sliced ripe olives
½ cup olive oil
½ cup white wine vinegar
3 Tbsp. minced fresh mint or 1 Tbsp. dried mint flakes
3 Tbsp. lemon juice
1½ tsp. seasoned salt
1 tsp. garlic powder
½ tsp. pepper
⅛ to ¼ tsp. crushed red pepper flakes
½ cup crumbled feta cheese

1. Cook tortellini according to package directions; drain and rinse in cold water. In a large bowl, combine the tortellini, peppers, onion and olives.
2. In a jar with a tight-fitting lid, combine oil, vinegar, mint, lemon juice, seasoned salt, garlic powder, pepper and pepper flakes; shake well. Pour over the salad; toss to coat. Refrigerate, covered, for at least 4 hours. Just before serving, sprinkle with feta cheese.
¾ CUP 267 cal., 16g fat (4g sat. fat), 23mg chol., 477mg sod., 24g carb. (3g sugars, 2g fiber), 8g pro.

GARDEN PESTO PASTA SALAD

GARDEN PESTO PASTA SALAD

My family and I live on a homestead in the Missouri Ozarks and grow much of our own food. In the summer, when the garden is bursting with fresh produce and it's too hot to cook, I like to use the seasonal vegetables for pasta salads and other cool meals.
—*Sarah Mathews, Ava, MO*

- -

PREP: 15 min. + chilling
MAKES: 10 servings

3 cups uncooked spiral pasta (about 9 oz.)
1 cup prepared pesto
3 Tbsp. white wine vinegar
1 Tbsp. lemon juice
½ tsp. salt
¼ tsp. pepper
¼ cup olive oil
1 medium zucchini, halved and sliced
1 medium sweet red pepper, chopped
1 medium tomato, seeded and chopped
1 small red onion, halved and thinly sliced
½ cup grated Parmesan cheese

1. Cook pasta according to the package directions; drain. Rinse with cold water and drain well.
2. Meanwhile, whisk together pesto, vinegar, lemon juice, salt and pepper. Gradually whisk in oil until blended.
3. Combine vegetables and pasta. Drizzle with the pesto dressing; toss to coat. Refrigerate, covered, until cold, about 1 hour. Serve with Parmesan cheese.
¾ CUP 267 cal., 17g fat (3g sat. fat), 5mg chol., 431mg sod., 24g carb. (2g sugars, 2g fiber), 6g pro. **DIABETIC EXCHANGES** 3 fat, 1½ starch.

CLASSIC MACARONI SALAD

This never-fail recipe is a refreshingly light take on an all-time favorite. It's perfect for a fast weeknight dinner or a weekend barbecue.
—*Dorothy Bayes, Sardis, OH*

- -

TAKES: 30 min. • **MAKES:** 8 servings

2 cups uncooked elbow macaroni
1 cup fat-free mayonnaise
2 Tbsp. sweet pickle relish
2 tsp. sugar
¾ tsp. ground mustard
¼ tsp. salt
⅛ tsp. pepper
½ cup chopped celery
⅓ cup chopped carrot
¼ cup chopped onion
1 hard-boiled large egg, chopped
Dash paprika

1. Cook macaroni according to the package directions; drain and rinse with cold water. Cool completely.
2. For dressing, in a small bowl, combine mayonnaise, pickle relish, sugar, mustard, salt and pepper. In a large bowl, combine the macaroni, celery, carrot and onion. Add the dressing and toss gently to coat.
3. Refrigerate until serving. Garnish with egg and paprika.

¾ CUP 115 cal., 2g fat (0 sat. fat), 27mg chol., 362mg sod., 21g carb. (6g sugars, 2g fiber), 4g pro. **DIABETIC EXCHANGES** 1½ starch.

TEST KITCHEN TIP

Don't be tempted to skip the rinsing step! Rinsing under cold water speeds cooling and prevents the pasta from overcooking. It also removes the starches that coat cooked pasta, ensuring the dressing coats it evenly. Making sure your pasta is rinsed and cold creates the creamiest salad.

MAC ATTACK

Try a twist on classic mac salad and watch as guests elbow their way through to scoop it up!

Basic Macaroni Salad

In a small bowl, combine 1 cup mayonnaise, 2 tsp. sugar, ¾ tsp. ground mustard, ¼ tsp. salt and ⅛ tsp. pepper. Place 4 cups cooked elbow macaroni in a large bowl. Stir in the dressing and additional ingredients; toss gently to coat. Refrigerate until serving.

CHICKEN CAESAR MACARONI SALAD

Add 2 Tbsp. Italian salad dressing mix; 1 cup chopped cooked chicken; one 14-oz. can water-packed artichoke hearts, drained and chopped; ¼ cup grated Parmesan cheese; and 2 Tbsp. capers, drained. Top with croutons if desired.
—SHAWN BARTO, PALMETTO, FL

CAPRESE MACARONI SALAD

Add 1 Tbsp. Italian salad dressing mix; 1 pint cherry tomatoes, halved; and 1 cup fresh mozzarella cheese pearls. Top with minced fresh basil and grated Parmesan cheese.
—DEBBIE GLASSCOCK, CONWAY, AR

MIDDLE EASTERN MACARONI SALAD

Add ½ lb. cooked ground lamb; one 16-oz. can chickpeas, rinsed and drained; ¼ cup chopped onion; and 1 tsp. za'atar seasoning. Top with plain yogurt and grated lemon zest if desired.
—RUTH HARTUNIAN-ALUMBAUGH, WILLIMANTIC, CT

GRECIAN MACARONI SALAD

Add 2 tsp. dried oregano; 2 tsp. grated lemon zest; ½ cup crumbled feta cheese; ½ cup chopped peeled cucumber; ½ cup sliced red onion; ½ cup cherry tomatoes, halved; and ¼ cup Greek olives, chopped.
—BRIGETTE SCHROEDER, YORKVILLE, IL

SCANDINAVIAN MACARONI SALAD

Add 2 tsp. snipped fresh dill; 1 cup peeled and deveined cooked shrimp; 1 small cucumber, chopped; and 1 small red onion, thinly sliced. Top with additional dill if desired.
—KALLEE KRONG-MCCREERY, ESCONDIDO, CA

CHICKEN TACO MACARONI SALAD

Add 2 Tbsp. reduced-sodium taco seasoning; 2 cups cubed cooked chicken; 1 small sweet yellow or orange pepper, chopped; and 1 jalapeno pepper, seeded and chopped. Top with fresh cilantro leaves if desired.
—LISA ALLEN, JOPPA, AL

BARBECUE MACARONI SALAD

Add 1 to 3 Tbsp. barbecue sauce; 1 Tbsp. ranch salad dressing mix; 2 hard-boiled eggs, chopped; and 2 Tbsp. sweet pickle relish. Drizzle with additional barbecue sauce if desired.
—ANDREA BOLDEN, UNIONVILLE, TN

POLYNESIAN MACARONI SALAD

Add one 12-oz. can Spam, cubed and cooked; one 8-oz. can water chestnuts, drained; 1 chopped red pepper; and one 8-oz. can unsweetened pineapple tidbits, drained. Top with chopped green onions if desired.
—SUSAN BICKTA, KUTZTOWN, PA

SHRIMP & CRAB MACARONI SALAD

Add 2 tsp. Old Bay Seasoning; 1 tsp. garlic powder; 6 oz. imitation crabmeat; 1 small cucumber, chopped; and 1 cup peeled and deveined cooked shrimp. Top with chopped green onions if desired.
—DARLA ANDREWS, BOERNE, TX

CUBANO MACARONI SALAD

Add 1 cup shredded Swiss cheese, 1 cup cubed cooked pork, 1 cup cubed fully cooked ham, ½ cup chopped sweet pickles and ½ cup chopped onion.
—MARINA CASTLE KELLEY, CANYON COUNTRY, CA

SZECHUAN
SUGAR
SNAP PEAS

SZECHUAN SUGAR SNAP PEAS

Simple seasonings transform crisp and sweet sugar snap peas into an unbeatable side dish. You can use chopped walnuts instead of cashews if you prefer.

—*Jeanne Holt, Mendota Heights, MN*

TAKES: 25 min. • **MAKES:** 8 servings

    6   cups fresh sugar snap peas
    2   tsp. peanut oil
    1   tsp. sesame oil
    3   Tbsp. thinly sliced green onions
    1   tsp. grated orange zest
    ½   tsp. minced garlic
    ½   tsp. minced fresh gingerroot
    ⅛   tsp. crushed red pepper flakes
    1   Tbsp. minced fresh cilantro
    ¼   tsp. salt
    ⅛   tsp. pepper
    ⅓   cup salted cashew halves

1. In a Dutch oven, saute peas in peanut oil and sesame oil until crisp-tender. Add onions, orange zest, garlic, ginger and pepper flakes; saute 1 minute longer.
2. Remove from heat; stir in cilantro, salt and pepper. Sprinkle with cashews just before serving.

¾ CUP 107 cal., 5g fat (1g sat. fat), 0 chol., 121mg sod., 10g carb. (5g sugars, 4g fiber), 5g pro. **DIABETIC EXCHANGES** 2 vegetable, 1 fat.

TEST KITCHEN TIP
Once cooked and chilled, these zesty snap peas make a great addition to salads!

STRAWBERRY PINEAPPLE COLESLAW

STRAWBERRY-PINEAPPLE COLESLAW

Sweet fruit, tangy coleslaw dressing and colorful, crisp cabbage make a wonderful combination. I like to include the nuts for an added healthy crunch.

—*Victoria Pederson, Ham Lake, MN*

PREP: 15 min. + chilling
MAKES: about 14 servings

    2   pkg. (14 oz. each) coleslaw mix
    1   jar (13 oz.) coleslaw salad dressing
    1   cup salted cashews or macadamia
        nuts
    1   cup dried cranberries
    1   cup chopped fresh or canned
        pineapple
    1   cup chopped fresh sugar snap peas
    1   cup chopped fresh strawberries
    ½   cup sweetened shredded coconut
    ½   cup chopped green onions

Combine all ingredients in a large bowl; toss to coat. Refrigerate, covered, until serving.

¾ CUP 244 cal., 15g fat (3g sat. fat), 3mg chol., 272mg sod., 26g carb. (19g sugars, 3g fiber), 3g pro.

FRESH CUCUMBER SALAD

Crisp garden-fresh cukes are always in season when we hold our family reunion, and they really shine in this simple cucumber salad. The recipe can easily be expanded to make even larger quantities too.

—*Betsy Carlson, Rockford, IL*

PREP: 10 min. + chilling
MAKES: 10 servings

    3   medium cucumbers, sliced
    1   cup sugar
    ¾   cup water
    ½   cup white vinegar
    3   Tbsp. minced fresh dill or parsley

Place cucumbers in a 1½- or 2-qt. glass container. In a jar with a tight-fitting lid, shake the remaining ingredients until combined. Pour over the cucumbers. Refrigerate, covered, overnight. Serve with a slotted spoon.

½ CUP 87 cal., 0 fat (0 sat. fat), 0 chol., 0 sod., 22g carb. (21g sugars, 1g fiber), 1g pro.

SPICY
THAI-INSPIRED
NOODLE
WATERMELON
SALAD

FRENCH POTATO SALAD

French potato salad is vinegar-based instead of creamy, made with Dijon mustard, olive oil, scallions or shallots, and fresh herbs.

—*Denise Cassady, Phoenix, MD*

- -

PREP/COOK TIME: 25 min.
MAKES: 6 cups

- 1 lb. baby red potatoes
- 1 lb. baby yellow potatoes
- 1 garlic clove
- ¼ cup olive oil
- 2 Tbsp. champagne vinegar or white wine vinegar
- 2 tsp. Dijon mustard
- ½ tsp. salt
- ½ tsp. pepper
- 1 shallot, finely chopped
- 1 Tbsp. each minced fresh chervil, parsley and chives
- 1 tsp. minced fresh tarragon

1. Place potatoes in a large saucepan; add water to cover. Bring to a boil. Reduce heat; cook, uncovered, until tender, 10-15 minutes. With a slotted spoon, remove potatoes to a colander; cool slightly. Return water to a boil. Add garlic; cook, uncovered, for 1 minute. Remove garlic and immediately drop into ice water. Drain and pat dry; mince. Reserve ¼ cup cooking liquid.
2. Cut cooled potatoes into ¼-in. slices; transfer to a large bowl. In a small bowl, whisk the reserved cooking liquid, oil, vinegar, mustard, minced garlic, salt and pepper until blended. Pour over the potato mixture; toss gently to coat. Gently stir in the remaining ingredients. Serve warm or at room temperature.
1 CUP 201 cal., 9g fat (1g sat. fat), 0 chol., 239mg sod., 29g carb. (1g sugars, 2g fiber), 3g pro. **DIABETIC EXCHANGES** 2 starch, 2 fat.

SPICY THAI-INSPIRED NOODLE WATERMELON SALAD

Our county is famous for its fabulous Green River melons. This unusual and refreshing salad is definitely our favorite way to eat watermelon all summer long!
—*Carmell Childs, Orangeville, UT*

- -

PREP: 25 min. • **COOK:** 25 min.
MAKES: 10 servings

- 4½ cups cubed watermelon, divided
- ½ cup sweet chili sauce
- 3 Tbsp. fish sauce or soy sauce
- 2 Tbsp. lime juice
- ½ tsp. minced fresh gingerroot
- 7 oz. uncooked stir-fry rice noodles
- 1½ cups julienned carrots
- 1 small red onion, halved and thinly sliced
- ½ cup fresh cilantro leaves, chopped
- 3 Tbsp. minced fresh mint
- 1¼ cups salted peanuts, chopped
  Lime wedges

1. Place 2 cups watermelon in a blender; cover and puree until smooth. Press through a fine-mesh strainer into a bowl; discard pulp.
2. Pour 1 cup of the watermelon juice into a small saucepan (save any remaining juice for another use). Add chili sauce, fish sauce, lime juice and ginger to the saucepan. Bring to a boil; cook until the liquid is slightly thickened, 20-25 minutes. Remove from heat. Refrigerate until cooled.
3. Meanwhile, prepare noodles according to package directions; rinse with cold water and drain well. Place noodles in a large bowl. Add carrots, red onion, cilantro, mint and the remaining 2½ cups watermelon. Drizzle with dressing; toss to coat. Serve with peanuts and lime wedges.
¾ CUP 240 cal., 10g fat (2g sat. fat), 0 chol., 721mg sod., 34g carb. (14g sugars, 3g fiber), 7g pro.

HARISSA SWEET POTATO FRITTERS

I had extra sweet potatoes and had to think up a new way to use them. I flavored these fun fritters with a little harissa— just enough for flavor but not too spicy. If you want more heat, you can adjust the spice to please your taste buds.
—*Teri Schloessmann, Tulsa, OK*

PREP: 20 min. + standing
COOK: 5 min./batch • **MAKES:** 6 servings

- 6 cups boiling water
- 3 cups shredded and peeled sweet potatoes, slightly packed (about 2 medium)
- 2 large eggs
- ¼ cup all-purpose flour
- 1 tsp. baking powder
- 1 tsp. cornstarch
- 1 tsp. seasoned salt
- 2 to 3 tsp. harissa
- 1 small onion, grated
- ¼ cup coconut oil
- ½ cup crumbled queso fresco
  Optional: Sliced avocado, sliced tomato and minced fresh cilantro

1. Pour boiling water over shredded sweet potatoes in a large bowl; let stand 20 minutes. Drain, squeezing to remove excess liquid. Pat dry.
2. In a large bowl, whisk the eggs, flour, baking powder, cornstarch, seasoned salt and harissa. Add the sweet potatoes and onion; toss to coat.
3. In a large nonstick skillet, heat 2 Tbsp. coconut oil over medium heat. Working in batches, drop sweet potato mixture by ¼ cupfuls into oil; press slightly to flatten. Fry for 1-2 minutes on each side until golden brown, using remaining oil as needed. Drain on paper towels. Serve with queso fresco and desired optional ingredients.

2 FRITTERS 217 cal., 13g fat (10g sat. fat), 69mg chol., 421mg sod., 20g carb. (3g sugars, 2g fiber), 6g pro.

HARISSA SWEET POTATO FRITTERS

BEER-CHEESE GREEN BEAN CASSEROLE

Being from Wisconsin, where beer, cheese and snap beans abound, I thought I'd try a local spin on a beloved casserole. My mom deemed this even better than the traditional recipe. One point to America's dairyland!
—*Sue Gronholz, Beaver Dam, WI*

PREP: 25 min. • **BAKE:** 30 min.
MAKES: 8 servings

- 5   Tbsp. butter, divided
- ¼   cup all-purpose flour
- 1   cup 2% milk
- ½   cup lager beer or chicken broth
- 1½ cups shredded cheddar cheese
- ½   tsp. salt
- ½   tsp. Worcestershire sauce
- ⅛   tsp. cayenne pepper
- ⅛   tsp. smoked paprika
- 6   cups frozen cut green beans (about 24 oz.), thawed
- 1   Tbsp. finely chopped onion
- ½   cup dry bread crumbs

1. Preheat oven to 350°. In a large saucepan, melt 4 Tbsp. butter over medium heat. Stir in flour until smooth; gradually whisk in milk and beer. Bring to a boil, stirring constantly; cook and stir until thickened, 1-2 minutes. Stir in cheese, salt, Worcestershire sauce, cayenne and paprika until blended. Add green beans and onion; stir to combine.
2. Transfer to a greased 2-qt. baking dish. Melt remaining 1 Tbsp. butter; stir into bread crumbs. Sprinkle over casserole. Bake, uncovered, until casserole is bubbly and top is golden brown, 30-35 minutes.

¾ CUP 235 cal., 15g fat (9g sat. fat), 43mg chol., 410mg sod., 16g carb. (4g sugars, 2g fiber), 9g pro.

CRISPY FRIED ONION RINGS

CRISPY FRIED ONION RINGS

These crispy onion rings are tasty on their own, as an add-in to give salads a little crunch, or as an extra element to already fantastic burgers.
—*Taste of Home Test Kitchen*

TAKES: 25 min. • **MAKES:** 12 servings

- ½   cup all-purpose flour
- ½   cup water
- 1   large egg, lightly beaten
- 1   tsp. seasoned salt
- ½   tsp. baking powder
- 1   large onion, very thinly sliced
      Oil for deep-fat frying

In a shallow bowl, whisk the first 5 ingredients. Separate onion slices into rings. Dip rings into batter. In a deep-fat fryer, heat 1 in. oil to 375°. In batches, fry onion rings until golden brown, 1-1½ minutes on each side. Drain on paper towels. Serve immediately.

½ CUP 71 cal., 5g fat (0 sat. fat), 16mg chol., 153mg sod., 5g carb. (1g sugars, 0 fiber), 1g pro.

RED ONION RINGS Substitute a red onion for the onion. With the flour mixture, whisk in ¼ tsp. cayenne.

BAKED ONION RINGS Beat egg in a shallow bowl. In another shallow bowl, mix ⅔ cup dry bread crumbs, ½ tsp. seasoned salt and ¼ tsp. pepper. Dip onion rings into egg, then roll in crumbs. Place on a baking sheet coated with cooking spray. Bake at 425° until golden brown, 15-18 minutes, turning once.

*HONEY PECAN &
GOAT CHEESE SALAD*

AIR-FRYER SWEET POTATO FRIES

I can never get enough of these sweet potato fries! Even though my grocery store sells them in the frozen foods section, I still love to pull sweet potatoes out of my garden and slice them up fresh!
—Amber Massey, Argyle, TX

TAKES: 20 min. • **MAKES:** 4 servings

- 2 large sweet potatoes, cut into thin strips
- 2 Tbsp. canola oil
- 1 tsp. garlic powder
- 1 tsp. paprika
- 1 tsp. kosher salt
- ¼ tsp. cayenne pepper

Preheat air fryer to 400°. Combine all ingredients; toss to coat. Place on greased tray in air-fryer basket. Cook until lightly browned, 10-12 minutes, stirring once. Serve immediately.
1 SERVING 243 cal., 7g fat (1g sat. fat), 0 chol., 498mg sod., 43g carb. (17g sugars, 5g fiber), 3g pro.

HONEY PECAN & GOAT CHEESE SALAD

I make this salad for my wife and son while our pizza is in the oven—the creamy cheese makes a perfect companion to spicy, saucy pizza. My son loves goat cheese—one of my dreams is to own a herd of goats and make our own cheese!
—Greg Fontenot, The Woodlands, TX

TAKES: 25 min. • **MAKES:** 4 servings

- ½ cup chopped pecans
- 2 tsp. plus 1 Tbsp. honey, divided
- ⅓ cup plus 3 Tbsp. olive oil, divided
- 2 Tbsp. balsamic vinegar
- ½ tsp. salt
- ⅛ tsp. pepper
- ¼ cup all-purpose flour
- 1 large egg, beaten
- ¾ cup seasoned bread crumbs
- 8 oz. fresh goat cheese
- 4 cups spring mix salad greens

1. In a shallow microwave-safe dish, combine pecans and 2 tsp. honey; microwave, uncovered, on high until toasted, 1½-2 minutes, stirring twice. Immediately transfer to a waxed paper-lined baking sheet to cool.
2. For dressing, in a small bowl, whisk ⅓ cup oil, vinegar, remaining 1 Tbsp. honey, salt and pepper; set aside.
3. Place flour, egg and bread crumbs in 3 separate shallow bowls. Shape cheese into 8 balls; flatten slightly. Coat cheese with flour, then dip in the egg and coat with the bread crumbs.
4. Heat the remaining 3 Tbsp. oil in a large skillet over medium-hight heat. Fry cheese until golden brown, 1-2 minutes on each side. Drain on paper towels.
5. Divide salad greens among 4 plates; top with cheese. Drizzle with dressing and sprinkle with honey pecans.
1 SERVING 570 cal., 47g fat (10g sat. fat), 64mg chol., 763mg sod., 29g carb. (11g sugars, 3g fiber), 11g pro.

CARAMELIZED
HAM & SWISS BUNS
P. 113

SLIDERS, SANDWICHES & PARTY SUBS

Sandwiches might just be the perfect party food—they're easy to assemble and easy to make in large numbers, and always popular with guests, no matter what the occasion.

REUBEN PUFF PASTRY STROMBOLI

I love this quick-to-fix, layered Reuben Stromboli. I used a different sandwich recipe as a guide but made it with Reuben fixings. To switch things up, make it a "Rachel" by using sliced turkey and coleslaw instead of corned beef and sauerkraut.
—*Joan Hallford, Fort Worth, TX*

PREP: 25 min. • **BAKE:** 40 min. + standing
MAKES: 6 servings

- 1 sheet frozen puff pastry, thawed
- 2/3 cup Thousand Island salad dressing, divided
- 3 Tbsp. dill pickle relish
- 1/2 lb. thinly sliced deli corned beef
- 1/2 lb. thinly sliced deli pastrami
- 4 Tbsp. spicy brown mustard
- 8 slices Swiss or fontina cheese
- 1½ cups sauerkraut, rinsed and well drained
- 1 large egg white, lightly beaten
- 2 tsp. caraway seeds or sesame seeds

1. Preheat oven to 400°. On a lightly floured surface, unfold puff pastry. Roll into a 14x11-in. rectangle. Spread 1/3 cup dressing to within 1/2 in. of edges. Sprinkle with relish. Layer with corned beef, pastrami, mustard, cheese and sauerkraut. Roll up jelly-roll style, starting with a long side. Place on a parchment-lined baking sheet, seam side down; tuck ends under and press to seal.

2. Brush with egg white and sprinkle with caraway seeds; cut small slits in top. Bake until top is golden brown and pastry is cooked through, 40-45 minutes. Let stand 10 minutes before slicing. Serve with remaining 1/3 cup dressing.
1 PIECE 491 cal., 32g fat (10g sat. fat), 50mg chol., 1566mg sod., 32g carb. (4g sugars, 4g fiber), 18g pro.

BBQ BACON PULLED CHICKEN SANDWICHES

BBQ BACON PULLED CHICKEN SANDWICHES

This simple recipe tastes amazing. It makes a great spread for a party; prepare the chicken and let your guests design their own sandwiches using a variety of toppings!
—*Jennifer Darling, Ventura, CA*

PREP: 20 min. • **COOK:** 3 hours
MAKES: 12 servings

- 1 bottle (18 oz.) barbecue sauce
- 1/2 cup amber beer or root beer
- 1/4 cup cider vinegar
- 2 green onions, chopped
- 2 Tbsp. dried minced onion
- 2 Tbsp. Dijon mustard
- 2 Tbsp. Worcestershire sauce
- 4 garlic cloves, minced
- 1 Tbsp. dried parsley flakes
- 2 lbs. boneless skinless chicken breasts
- 12 hamburger buns, split and toasted
- 24 cooked bacon strips
- 12 lettuce leaves

In a large bowl, combine the first 9 ingredients. Place chicken in a greased 4- or 5-qt. slow cooker; pour sauce over top. Cook, covered, on low, 3-4 hours or until tender. Shred chicken with 2 forks. Serve on buns with bacon and lettuce.
FREEZE OPTION Freeze cooled, cooked chicken mixture in freezer containers. To use, partially thaw in refrigerator overnight. Heat through in a saucepan, stirring occasionally; add water or broth if necessary.
1 SANDWICH 401 cal., 12g fat (4g sat. fat), 65mg chol., 1175mg sod., 43g carb. (19g sugars, 2g fiber), 28g pro.

TEST KITCHEN TIP
Offer your guests a selection of toppings, starting with something creamy—mayonnaise, ranch dressing or blue cheese dressing. Lettuce and bacon are a great starting point; try cheddar or Muenster cheese, tomato and onion as well.

PHILLY CHEESESTEAK SLIDERS

PHILLY CHEESESTEAK SLIDERS

This is a wonderful way to use leftover roast beef, but using sliced roast beef from the deli also works.

—*Debra Waggoner, Grand Island, NE*

PREP: 20 min. + chilling • **BAKE:** 25 min.
MAKES: 2 dozen

- 2 large green peppers, sliced
- 1 large sweet onion, sliced
- 1 Tbsp. olive oil
- 2 pkg. (12 oz. each) Hawaiian sweet rolls
- 1½ lbs. sliced deli roast beef
- 12 slices provolone cheese
- ¾ cup butter
- 1½ tsp. dried minced onion
- 1½ tsp. Worcestershire sauce
- 1 tsp. garlic powder

1. In a large skillet, cook green peppers and onion in oil over medium-high heat until tender, 8-10 minutes. Without separating rolls, cut each package in half horizontally; arrange bottom halves in a greased 13x9-in. baking pan. Layer with roast beef, pepper mixture and cheese; replace top halves of rolls.
2. In a small saucepan, melt butter; add dried onion, Worcestershire sauce and garlic powder. Drizzle over rolls. Refrigerate, covered, 8 hours or overnight.
3. Preheat oven to 350°. Remove rolls from refrigerator 30 minutes before baking. Bake, uncovered, 15 minutes. Cover with foil; bake until cheese is melted, 10 minutes longer.

1 SLIDER 247 cal., 14g fat (8g sat. fat), 56mg chol., 413mg sod., 18g carb. (7g sugars, 1g fiber), 14g pro.

PAIRS WITH

CABERNET FRANC

SOURDOUGH BREAD BOWL SANDWICH

I created this recipe for when my husband and I go to the lake. I don't like to spend a lot of time hovering over a stove or grill, especially in the hot Oklahoma summer months, and this filling sandwich is ready in minutes. For extra flavor, brush melted garlic and herb butter over the top prior to cooking.
—Shawna Welsh-Garrison, Owasso, OK

PREP: 15 min. • **COOK:** 25 min. + standing
MAKES: 8 servings

    1   round loaf sourdough bread (1½ lbs.)
    ½   cup honey mustard salad dressing
    4   slices sharp cheddar cheese
    ⅓   lb. thinly sliced deli ham
    4   slices smoked provolone cheese
    ⅓   lb. thinly sliced deli smoked turkey
    1   Tbsp. butter, melted

1. Prepare a grill or campfire for low heat. Cut a thin slice off top of bread loaf. Hollow out bottom of loaf, leaving a ½-in.-thick shell (save removed bread for another use). Spread dressing on the inside of the hollowed loaf and under the bread top. Layer cheddar, ham, provolone and turkey inside the loaf. Replace top. Place on a piece of heavy-duty foil (about 24x18 in.). Brush loaf with butter. Fold foil edges over the top, crimping to seal.
2. Cook over grill or campfire until heated through, 25-30 minutes. Let stand for 15 minutes before removing foil. Cut into wedges.
1 WEDGE 346 cal., 17g fat (6g sat. fat), 46mg chol., 865mg sod., 30g carb. (5g sugars, 1g fiber), 19g pro.

ITALIAN HERO BRAID

ITALIAN HERO BRAID

My mother-in-law used to make these pastry pockets for my husband when he was growing up. After we got married, I changed her recipe a little to fit our family's tastes.
—Amanda Kohler, Redmond, WA

PREP: 20 min. • **BAKE:** 25 min.
MAKES: 8 servings

    ½   lb. bulk Italian sausage
    1   pkg. (¼ oz.) active dry yeast
    1   cup warm water (110° to 115°)
    2¾ to 3¼ cups all-purpose flour
    1   Tbsp. butter, melted
    ⅓   lb. sliced provolone cheese
    ⅓   lb. thinly sliced Genoa salami
    1   cup shredded cheddar cheese
    1   large egg white

1. Preheat oven to 400°. In a large skillet over medium heat, cook and crumble Italian sausage until no longer pink, 4-6 minutes; drain.
2. Meanwhile, dissolve yeast in warm water. In another bowl, combine 1½ cups flour and butter; add yeast mixture. Beat on medium speed until smooth. Stir in enough of the remaining flour to form a soft dough.
3. Turn dough onto a lightly floured surface; roll into a 13x10-in. rectangle. Transfer to a parchment-lined baking sheet. Layer cheese and salami slices down the center of the rectangle; top with crumbled sausage and shredded cheddar. On each long side, cut 1-in.-wide strips about 2 in. into the center. Starting at 1 end, fold alternating strips at an angle across the filling. Pinch both ends to seal.
4. Whisk egg white; brush over pastry. Bake until golden brown, 25-30 minutes.
1 PIECE 436 cal., 23g fat (11g sat. fat), 64mg chol., 823mg sod., 35g carb. (0 sugars, 1g fiber), 21g pro.

CHEESY PEPPERONI BUNS

NUTTY CHICKEN SANDWICHES

Crushed pineapple gives these chicken salad sandwiches a bit of sweetness, while pecans add a bit of crunch.
—*Nancy Johnson, Laverne, OK*

PREP: 20 min. + chilling
MAKES: 16 tea sandwiches

- 1 cup shredded cooked chicken breast
- 1 hard-boiled large egg, chopped
- ½ cup unsweetened crushed pineapple, drained
- ⅓ cup mayonnaise
- ½ tsp. salt
- ⅛ tsp. pepper
- ¼ cup chopped pecans, toasted
- ½ cup fresh baby spinach
- 8 slices white bread, crusts removed

1. In a small bowl, combine chicken, egg, pineapple, mayonnaise, salt and pepper. Refrigerate, covered, for at least 1 hour.
2. Just before serving, stir in pecans. Place spinach on 4 slices of bread; top with chicken salad and the remaining bread. Cut each sandwich into quarters.
1 SANDWICH 103 cal., 6g fat (1g sat. fat), 19mg chol., 178mg sod., 9g carb. (2g sugars, 1g fiber), 4g pro.

CHEESY PEPPERONI BUNS

A pizza version of the sloppy joe, this hot and melty open-faced sandwich is a surefire crowd pleaser.
—*Tanya Belt, Newcomerstown, OH*

TAKES: 25 min. • **MAKES:** 12 servings

- 1 lb. lean ground beef (90% lean)
- 2 cups pizza sauce or pasta sauce
- 1 pkg. (3½ oz.) sliced pepperoni, chopped
- 4 slices American cheese, chopped
- 12 mini buns, split
- 2 cups shredded part-skim mozzarella cheese

1. In a large skillet, cook beef over medium heat until no longer pink, 5-7 minutes, breaking into crumbles; drain. Stir in pizza sauce, pepperoni and American cheese. Cook and stir until cheese is melted, 4-5 minutes.
2. Place buns on a baking sheet, cut sides up. Spoon meat mixture onto buns; top with mozzarella cheese. Bake at 350° until cheese is melted, about 5 minutes. If desired, serve with additional warmed pizza sauce.
2 OPEN-FACED SANDWICHES 280 cal., 14g fat (6g sat. fat), 46mg chol., 612mg sod., 18g carb. (4g sugars, 1g fiber), 18g pro.

#GIRLDINNER

These sandwiches make a great quick weeknight dinner, especially if you make the sauce ahead of time. Then just assemble and bake; use a toaster oven or air fryer to make it even faster. You can use full-size buns for a dinner-sized portion.

MIDNIGHT CARIBBEAN PORK SANDWICHES

These sandwiches are so tasty! They have depth of flavor—savory, sweet, piquant, subtle and sublime. They're super easy to make and worth the (slow-cooker) wait.
—*Elizabeth Bennett, Mill Creek, WA*

PREP: 25 min. • **COOK:** 6 hours
MAKES: 12 servings

- 1 Tbsp. canola oil
- 3 medium onions, cut into ½-in. slices
- 1 bottle (12 oz.) amber beer or 1½ cups chicken broth
- ¼ cup packed brown sugar
- 10 garlic cloves, minced and divided
- 2 Tbsp. ground cumin
- 7 tsp. minced chipotle peppers in adobo sauce, divided
- ½ tsp. salt
- ½ tsp. pepper
- 1 boneless pork shoulder butt roast (2 to 3 lbs.)
- 1 cup mayonnaise
- ½ cup minced fresh cilantro
- 12 Hawaiian sweet hamburger buns
- 2 medium ripe avocados, peeled and sliced

1. In a large skillet, heat oil over medium-high heat. Add onions; cook and stir until tender, 6-8 minutes. Add beer, brown sugar, 8 garlic cloves, cumin, 5 tsp. chipotle peppers, salt and pepper; cook and stir until combined.
2. Place roast in a 5- or 6-qt. slow cooker. Pour onion mixture over meat. Cook, covered, on low 6-8 hours, until pork is tender.
3. Meanwhile, combine mayonnaise, cilantro, remaining 2 garlic cloves and 2 tsp. chipotle peppers. Refrigerate, covered, until serving.
4. Remove roast; shred with 2 forks. Strain cooking juices. Reserve vegetables and 1 cup juices; discard remaining juices. Skim fat from reserved juices. Return pork and reserved vegetables and cooking juices to slow cooker; heat through. Serve on buns with avocado slices and mayonnaise mixture.
FREEZE OPTION Place shredded pork and vegetables in freezer containers; top with cooking juices. Cool and freeze. To use, partially thaw in refrigerator overnight. Heat through in a covered saucepan, stirring gently. Add broth or water if necessary.
1 SANDWICH 484 cal., 29g fat (7g sat. fat), 71mg chol., 400mg sod., 36g carb. (15g sugars, 3g fiber), 18g pro.

MANGO JALAPENO SLOPPY JOE SLIDERS

I've loved sloppy joes since I can remember. In an attempt to give them a makeover, I thought of this idea, which was a big hit with my family, friends and co-workers! If you can't find a mango, chopped pineapple would work just as well.
—*Shea Goldstein, Royal Palm Beach, FL*

PREP: 10 min. • **COOK:** 25 min.
MAKES: 12 servings

- 1 lb. ground beef
- ½ cup water
- 1 envelope taco seasoning
- 2 Tbsp. hot pepper sauce
- 2 Tbsp. steak sauce
- 2 Tbsp. olive oil
- 1 small onion, halved and sliced
- 1 small green pepper, sliced
- 1 medium mango, peeled and chopped
- 1 tsp. sugar
- 1 jalapeno pepper, sliced
- ¼ tsp. salt
- 12 dinner or slider rolls, split
- ¼ cup butter, melted
- 1 cup mayonnaise
- ½ cup salsa verde
- 1½ cups shredded sharp white cheddar cheese

1. In a large cast-iron or other heavy skillet, cook beef over medium heat until no longer pink, 8-10 minutes; crumble beef; drain. Add water, taco seasoning, pepper sauce and steak sauce; cook and stir until sauce thickens, 2-4 minutes. Remove and keep warm.
2. In another skillet, heat oil over medium-high heat. Add onion, green pepper, mango, sugar, jalapeno and salt; cook and stir until lightly browned, 8-10 minutes.
3. Meanwhile, place rolls, cut side up, on an ungreased baking sheet. Broil 3-4 in. from heat until golden brown, 2-3 minutes. Spread with melted butter. Combine mayonnaise and salsa verde; spread over roll bottoms. Top with beef mixture, pepper mixture and cheese; replace tops. Serve with extra sauce.
NOTE Wear disposable gloves when cutting hot peppers; the oils can burn skin. Avoid touching your face.
1 SLIDER 443 cal., 31g fat (10g sat. fat), 66mg chol., 870mg sod., 28g carb. (7g sugars, 2g fiber), 14g pro.

MANGO
JALAPEÑO
SLOPPY JOE
SLIDERS

SLAW-TOPPED BEEF SLIDERS

When I was working full time, I would rely on these delicious, fast-to-fix beef sliders for simple meals. To ease on prep time and avoid extra cleanup, I used bagged coleslaw mix and bottled slaw dressing.
—*Jane Whittaker, Pensacola, FL*

PREP: 20 min. • **COOK:** 6 hours
MAKES: 1 dozen

- 3 cups coleslaw mix
- ½ medium red onion, chopped (about ⅔ cup)
- ⅛ tsp. celery seed
- ¼ tsp. pepper
- ⅓ cup coleslaw salad dressing

SANDWICHES
- 1 boneless beef chuck roast (2 lbs.)
- 1 tsp. salt
- ½ tsp. pepper
- 1 can (6 oz.) tomato paste
- ¼ cup water
- 1 tsp. Worcestershire sauce
- 1 small onion, diced
- 1 cup barbecue sauce
- 12 slider buns or dinner rolls, split

1. Combine coleslaw, onion, celery seed and pepper. Add salad dressing; toss to coat. Refrigerate until serving.
2. Sprinkle roast with salt and pepper; transfer roast to a 5-qt. slow cooker. Mix tomato paste, water and Worcestershire sauce; pour over roast. Top with onion. Cook, covered, on low 6-8 hours or until meat is tender.
3. Shred meat with 2 forks; return to slow cooker. Stir in barbecue sauce; heat through. Place beef on buns; top with coleslaw. Replace bun tops.

1 SLIDER 322 cal., 12g fat (4g sat. fat), 67mg chol., 726mg sod., 34g carb. (13g sugars, 3g fiber), 20g pro.

SLAW-TOPPED BEEF SLIDERS

*PESTO-TURKEY
LAYERED LOAF*

PAIRS
WITH

PINOT GRIGIO

CHICKEN PARMESAN STROMBOLI

I love chicken Parmesan and my family loves stromboli, so one day I combined the two using a few convenience products. It turned out better than I could have hoped. It's now a staple in our house.
—*Cyndy Gerken, Naples, FL*

PREP: 20 min. • **BAKE:** 20 min.
MAKES: 6 servings

- 4 frozen breaded chicken tenders (about 1½ oz. each)
- 1 tube (13.8 oz.) refrigerated pizza crust
- 8 slices part-skim mozzarella cheese
- ⅓ cup shredded Parmesan cheese
- 1 Tbsp. olive oil
- ½ tsp. garlic powder
- ¼ tsp. dried oregano
- ¼ tsp. pepper
  Marinara sauce, warmed

1. Prepare chicken tenders according to package directions. Preheat oven to 400°. Unroll pizza crust onto a parchment-lined baking sheet. Layer with mozzarella, chicken tenders and Parmesan to within ½ in. of edges. Roll up jelly-roll style, starting with a short side; pinch seam to seal and tuck ends under. Combine olive oil, garlic powder, oregano and pepper; brush over top.
2. Bake until crust is dark golden brown, 18-22 minutes. Let stand 5 minutes before slicing. Serve with marinara sauce for dipping.
1 PIECE 408 cal., 18g fat (7g sat. fat), 34mg chol., 859mg sod., 42g carb. (5g sugars, 2g fiber), 21g pro.

PESTO-TURKEY LAYERED LOAF

This yummy sandwich is easy to make and travels well to picnics and potlucks. Use any meat, veggies and cheese you like.
—*Marion Sundberg, Yorba Linda, CA*

PREP: 20 min. • **BAKE:** 25 min. + standing
MAKES: 6 servings

- 1 loaf (1 lb.) French bread
- 1 cup prepared pesto
- 1 lb. thinly sliced deli turkey
- ½ lb. provolone cheese, thinly sliced
- 2 small zucchini, thinly sliced
- 2 medium tomatoes, thinly sliced
- 1 medium red onion, thinly sliced

1. Preheat oven to 350°. Cut the top fourth off loaf of bread. Carefully hollow out the bottom, leaving a ½-in. shell. (Discard removed bread or save for another use.) Spread pesto on the inside of top and bottom of bread. Set top aside.
2. In the bottom of the bread, layer turkey, cheese, zucchini, tomatoes and onion. Gently press layers together. Replace bread top and wrap tightly in foil.
3. Place on a baking sheet. Bake until heated through, 25-30 minutes. Let stand 10 minutes before cutting.
1 PIECE 544 cal., 30g fat (11g sat. fat), 67mg chol., 1828mg sod., 41g carb. (7g sugars, 3g fiber), 29g pro.

FIVE-SPICE CHICKEN LETTUCE WRAPS

FIVE-SPICE CHICKEN LETTUCE WRAPS

With this lettuce wrap, I get all the satisfaction without all the carbs. The pickled carrots really make it feel special. Use them on other sandwiches and wraps for an extra pop of flavor, crunch and color.

—*Stacy Schneidmiller, Beaumont, AB*

PREP: 25 min. + marinating
GRILL: 20 min. • **MAKES:** 6 servings

- 3 Tbsp. soy sauce
- 4 garlic cloves, crushed
- 1 Tbsp. packed brown sugar
- 2 tsp. Chinese five-spice powder
- 1 tsp. salt, divided
- 2 lbs. boneless skinless chicken thighs
- ½ cup white vinegar
- ¼ cup water
- 1 Tbsp. sugar
- 2 medium carrots, shredded
- 12 Bibb lettuce leaves
- ¼ cup thinly sliced green onions
- 2 Tbsp. fresh cilantro leaves
   Sweetened shredded coconut, optional

1. In a bowl or shallow dish, combine the first 4 ingredients and ½ tsp. salt. Add chicken and turn to coat. Cover and refrigerate 8 hours or overnight.
2. In a small saucepan, combine vinegar, water, sugar and remaining ½ tsp. salt. Bring to a boil; whisk until sugar is dissolved. Remove from heat. Place carrots in a small bowl; pour vinegar mixture over top. Refrigerate 8 hours or overnight.
3. Drain chicken, discarding marinade. On a lightly oiled rack, grill chicken, covered, over medium heat or broil 4 in. from heat until a thermometer reads 170°, 6-8 minutes on each side. Cool slightly; slice into strips.
4. Divide chicken among lettuce leaves; top with pickled carrots, green onions and cilantro. Sprinkle with coconut if desired.
2 WRAPS 236 cal., 11g fat (3g sat. fat), 101mg chol., 625mg sod., 4g carb. (2g sugars, 1g fiber), 29g pro. **DIABETIC EXCHANGES** 4 lean meat.

BACON-CHICKEN CRESCENT RING

This ring makes a really impressive display as part of a party spread, but it's really very easy to put together. It's so good that people always ask me for the recipe.

—*Michele McWhorter, Jacksonville, NC*

PREP: 25 min. • **BAKE:** 20 min.
MAKES: 8 servings

- 2 tubes (8 oz. each) refrigerated crescent rolls
- 1 can (10 oz.) chunk white chicken, drained and flaked
- 1½ cups shredded Swiss cheese
- ¾ cup mayonnaise
- ½ cup finely chopped sweet red pepper
- ¼ cup finely chopped onion
- 6 bacon strips, cooked and crumbled
- 2 Tbsp. Dijon mustard
- 1 Tbsp. Italian salad dressing mix

1. Preheat oven to 375°. Grease a 14-in. pizza pan. Unroll crescent roll dough; separate into 16 triangles. Place the wide end of 1 triangle 3 in. from edge of prepared pan with point overhanging the edge of the pan. Repeat with the remaining triangles along outer edge of pan, overlapping the wide ends (dough will look like a sun when complete). Lightly press the wide ends together.
2. Combine remaining ingredients. Spoon over the wide ends of dough. Fold points of triangles over filling and tuck under the wide ends (filling will be visible). Bake until golden brown, 20-25 minutes.
2 PIECES 502 cal., 34g fat (7g sat. fat), 42mg chol., 1002mg sod., 26g carb. (7g sugars, 0 fiber), 21g pro.

TACO SANDWICH

This is like a taco on French bread—a great option when you don't have taco shells! The cream cheese-salsa spread adds a delicious flavor boost.
—*Melody Stoltzfus, Parkesburg, PA*

TAKES: 20 min. • **MAKES:** 6 servings

   1   loaf (1 lb.) unsliced Italian bread
   1   lb. ground beef
   2   Tbsp. taco seasoning
   4   oz. cream cheese, softened
   ½   cup salsa
   1   cup shredded lettuce
   1   large tomato, sliced
   6   slices American cheese

1. Cut bread in half lengthwise; hollow out top and bottom of loaf, leaving a ½-in. shell (save removed bread for another use).
2. In a large skillet, cook beef over medium heat until no longer pink, breaking into crumbles, 5-7 minutes; drain. Stir in taco seasoning.
3. Beat cream cheese and salsa until blended. Spread inside top and bottom of bread shell. Add lettuce, tomato, beef mixture and cheese to bottom shell. Replace bread top. Cut into slices.
1 PIECE 477 cal., 21g fat (11g sat. fat), 71mg chol., 1173mg sod., 45g carb. (4g sugars, 3g fiber), 25g pro.

MOROCCAN-SPICED CHICKEN SLIDERS

MOROCCAN-SPICED CHICKEN SLIDERS

This recipe is great for both fast and easy weeknight dinners and for entertaining! Ras el hanout is a mixture of ground spices that typically includes various peppers, cardamom, ginger, cinnamon, nutmeg, turmeric and mace. It can be found in the spice section of well-stocked supermarkets. For a more peppery slider, substitute baby arugula for the leaf lettuce.
—*Kathi Jones-DelMonte, Rochester, NY*

PREP: 25 min. • **COOK:** 10 min.
MAKES: 8 servings

   1   container (6 oz.) plain yogurt, divided
   2   Tbsp. Dijon mustard
   2   tsp. grated lemon zest
   1   tsp. grated orange zest

CHICKEN SLIDERS
   3   Tbsp. chopped fresh mint
   4   tsp. minced garlic
   2   tsp. ras el hanout (Moroccan seasoning)
   1½ tsp. coarsely ground pepper
   1   tsp. ground cumin
   1   tsp. kosher salt
   1   lb. ground chicken
   2   Tbsp. canola oil
   4   miniature pita pockets, halved and warmed
   8   red leaf lettuce leaves
   8   slices tomato

1. Stir together ⅔ cup yogurt, mustard and zests. Refrigerate until serving.
2. In a large bowl, combine the remaining 2 Tbsp. yogurt, mint, garlic, ras el hanout, pepper, cumin and salt. Crumble chicken into bowl; mix lightly but thoroughly. Shape into 8 ½-in.-thick patties; press a small indention in middle of each patty.
3. In a large nonstick skillet, heat oil over medium heat. Add patties; cook until golden brown and no longer pink, 4-5 minutes on each side. Serve patties inside pita pocket with sauce, lettuce and tomato.
1 SLIDER 173 cal., 9g fat (2g sat. fat), 40mg chol., 456mg sod., 11g carb. (2g sugars, 1g fiber), 12g pro.

KENTUCKY HOT BROWN SLIDERS

KENTUCKY HOT BROWN SLIDERS

I transformed the classic Hot Brown sandwich, traditionally open-faced, into a party-ready slider. This easy-to-eat finger food was originally meant for a Kentucky Derby get-together, but it's so tasty, I now serve it anytime. Just cover and refrigerate the assembled sandwiches so you can pop them in the oven when company arrives.
—*Blair Lonergan, Rochelle, VA*

PREP: 20 min. • **BAKE:** 30 min.
MAKES: 12 servings

- 1 pkg. (12 oz.) Hawaiian sweet rolls
- 3 Tbsp. mayonnaise
- 12 slices deli turkey, folded into quarters
- 12 slices cooked bacon strips, halved widthwise
- 1 jar (4 oz.) diced pimientos, drained, or 2 plum tomatoes, cut into 12 slices
- 6 slices Gruyere cheese, halved
- ¼ cup grated Parmesan cheese
- ½ cup butter, cubed
- 2 Tbsp. finely chopped onion
- 2 Tbsp. brown sugar
- 1½ tsp. Worcestershire sauce
- ¼ tsp. garlic powder

1. Preheat oven to 350°. Without separating rolls, cut the package of rolls in half horizontally; arrange bottom halves in a greased 11x7-in. baking pan. Spread mayonnaise evenly across the bottom halves. Top each with turkey, bacon, pimientos, Gruyere and Parmesan cheese. Replace top halves of rolls.

2. In a small skillet, melt butter over medium heat. Add onion; cook and stir until tender, 1-2 minutes. Whisk in brown sugar, Worcestershire sauce and garlic powder. Cook and stir until sugar is dissolved; drizzle over sandwiches.

3. Cover and bake 25 minutes. Uncover; bake until golden brown, 5-10 minutes longer.

1 SLIDER 327 cal., 21g fat (10g sat. fat), 67mg chol., 652mg sod., 20g carb. (9g sugars, 1g fiber), 16g pro.

CHICKEN CORDON BLEU STROMBOLI

If chicken cordon bleu and stromboli had a baby, this would be it. Serve with jarred Alfredo sauce, homemade Alfredo sauce or classic Mornay sauce on the side if desired.
—*Cyndy Gerken, Naples, FL*

TAKES: 30 min. • **MAKES:** 6 servings

- 1 tube (13.8 oz.) refrigerated pizza crust
- 4 thin slices deli ham
- 1½ cups shredded cooked chicken
- 6 slices Swiss cheese
- 1 Tbsp. butter, melted
   Roasted garlic Alfredo sauce, optional

1. Preheat oven to 400°. Unroll pizza dough onto a baking sheet. Layer with ham, chicken and cheese to within ½ in. of edges. Roll up jelly-roll style, starting with a long side; pinch seam to seal and tuck ends under. Brush with melted butter.

2. Bake until crust is dark golden brown, 18-22 minutes. Let stand for 5 minutes before slicing. If desired, serve with Alfredo sauce for dipping.

1 PIECE 298 cal., 10g fat (4g sat. fat), 53mg chol., 580mg sod., 32g carb. (4g sugars, 1g fiber), 21g pro.

HOT ITALIAN PARTY SANDWICHES

It doesn't get much easier or more delicious than these warm little Italian sandwiches. They are wonderful as an appetizer for gatherings or a hungry family, and are a fantastic party food that is quick to prepare.

—*Joan Hallford, Fort Worth, TX*

PREP: 20 min. • **BAKE:** 15 min.
MAKES: 12 sandwiches

- 1 pkg. (12 oz.) Hawaiian sweet rolls
- ½ cup mayonnaise
- 2 Tbsp. prepared pesto
- 6 slices part-skim mozzarella or provolone cheese
- 6 thin slices deli ham
- 9 thin slices hard salami
- 6 thin slices deli pastrami
- 1¼ cups giardiniera
- ½ cup shredded Parmesan cheese
- 1 cup fresh basil leaves
- ½ cup sliced red onion
- ¼ cup prepared zesty Italian salad dressing
  Pepperoncini

1. Preheat oven to 350°. Cut rolls horizontally in half; place roll bottoms in a greased 11x7-in. baking dish. Mix mayonnaise and pesto until combined. Spread over cut sides of rolls. Layer bottoms with mozzarella cheese, ham, salami, pastrami, giardiniera, shredded Parmesan cheese, basil leaves and red onion. Place bun tops over filling; gently press to flatten.
2. Bake for 10 minutes. Remove from oven; brush with salad dressing. Bake until golden brown and cheese is melted, about 5 minutes longer. Cool slightly before cutting. Serve with pepperoncini and additional giardiniera if desired.
1 SANDWICH 290 cal., 17g fat (6g sat. fat), 44mg chol., 1026mg sod., 20g carb. (7g sugars, 1g fiber), 15g pro.

CAPRESE EGGPLANT HERO

CAPRESE EGGPLANT HERO

During the summer when tomatoes are at the most delicious, I love to create new recipes to eat as many tomatoes as possible! This recipe is so tasty that my family enjoys eating it in every season. Change it up and add sliced mushrooms in addition to or instead of the spinach.

—*Stacy Corday, Waxhaw, NC*

PREP: 20 min+ standing • **GRILL:** 10 min.
MAKES: 6 servings

- 1 large eggplant
- 1 tsp. kosher salt, divided
- ¼ cup olive oil, divided
- 3 Tbsp. honey
- 1 tsp. coarsely ground pepper
- ¼ cup balsamic glaze, divided
- 1 loaf (1 lb.) unsliced Italian bread
- 2 large tomatoes, cut into ¼-in. slices
- 1 lb. fresh mozzarella cheese, thinly sliced
- 2 cups fresh arugula
- ½ cup fresh basil leaves, julienned

1. Peel and slice eggplant lengthwise into ¼-in.-thick slices. Place in a colander over a plate; sprinkle with ½ tsp. salt and toss. Let stand 30 minutes.
2. Brush eggplant slices with 2 Tbsp. oil. Drizzle with honey; sprinkle with remaining ½ tsp. salt and pepper. Grill eggplant, covered, over medium heat until tender, 3-4 minutes per side. Drizzle with 2 Tbsp. balsamic glaze.
3. Cut bread in half horizontally. Drizzle cut sides with remaining 2 Tbsp. olive oil and 2 Tbsp. balsamic glaze. Layer eggplant, tomato and mozzarella slices on bread bottom; top with arugula and basil. Replace top. Cut crosswise into 6 slices.
1 PIECE 600 cal., 28g fat (12g sat. fat), 59mg chol., 856mg sod., 64g carb. (22g sugars, 6g fiber), 22g pro.

TEST KITCHEN TIP

If you prefer, you don't have to peel the eggplant; it's a taste preference. The peel adds some texture and nutrients, and it helps hold the form a little better.

CARAMELIZED
HAM & SWISS BUNS

CARAMELIZED HAM & SWISS BUNS

My next-door neighbor shared this recipe with me and I simply cannot improve it! You can assemble it ahead and cook it quickly when company arrives. The combo of poppy seeds, ham, cheese, horseradish and brown sugar makes it so delicious.
—*Iris Weihemuller, Baxter, MN*

PREP: 25 min. + chilling • **BAKE:** 30 min.
MAKES: 1 dozen

- 1 pkg. (12 oz.) Hawaiian sweet rolls
- ½ cup horseradish sauce
- ¾ lb. sliced deli ham
- 6 slices Swiss cheese, halved
- ½ cup butter, cubed
- 2 Tbsp. finely chopped onion
- 2 Tbsp. brown sugar
- 1 Tbsp. spicy brown mustard
- 2 tsp. poppy seeds
- 1½ tsp. Worcestershire sauce
- ¼ tsp. garlic powder

1. Without separating the rolls, cut rolls in half horizontally. Place bottom halves of rolls in a greased 9x9-in. baking pan. Spread cut side of roll bottoms with horseradish sauce. Layer with ham and cheese; replace top half of the rolls.
2. In a small skillet, heat butter over medium-high heat. Add onion; cook and stir until tender, 1-2 minutes. Stir in remaining ingredients. Pour over rolls. Refrigerate, covered, for several hours or overnight.
3. Preheat oven to 350°. Remove rolls from refrigerator 30 minutes before baking. Bake, covered, 25 minutes. Uncover and bake until golden brown, 5-10 minutes longer.
1 SANDWICH 315 cal., 17g fat (9g sat. fat), 61mg chol., 555mg sod., 29g carb. (13g sugars, 2g fiber), 13g pro.

HOW TO SPLIT BUNS

Place 1 hand over the top of the buns to hold them steady. Using a serrated knife, gently cut horizontally through the buns. Carefully remove top to separate. Place bottom half in baking dish.

CLASSIC ALMOND
RICOTTA CAKE
P. 140

SWEET THINGS

Girls night just got a lot sweeter! After all, nothing caps off a fun time like a sugary nosh. Turn here for everything from cute cookies and cakes to coffee-shop staples, frosty bites and fruity favorites.

DARK
CHOCOLATE
ESPRESSO
TAPIOCA
PUDDING

DARK CHOCOLATE ESPRESSO TAPIOCA PUDDING

I've been experimenting with espresso powder in different dishes. I really enjoy this recipe, and I hope you do, too!
—*Shelly Bevington, Hermiston, OR*

PREP: 15 min. + standing
COOK: 20 min. + cooling
MAKES: 12 servings

- 2   cups water
- ⅔   cup pearl tapioca
- 1   carton (32 oz.) unsweetened almond milk
- 4   large eggs, separated
- 1¼ cups sugar, divided
- 1   to 2 Tbsp. instant espresso powder
- ½   tsp. salt
- ¼   cup dark baking cocoa
- 1   tsp. vanilla extract
     Chopped chocolate-covered espresso beans, optional

1. In a large saucepan, combine water and tapioca; let stand 30 minutes. Whisk in almond milk, egg yolks, ½ cup sugar, espresso powder and salt. Bring to a boil; reduce heat. Simmer, uncovered, until slightly thickened, 10-15 minutes, stirring frequently. Combine ¼ cup sugar and baking cocoa; stir into pan. Cook and stir 2 minutes longer.
2. In a large bowl, beat egg whites on medium speed until foamy. Gradually add remaining ½ cup sugar, 1 Tbsp. at a time, beating on high after each addition until sugar is dissolved. Continue beating until soft glossy peaks form.
3. Gently fold a small amount of the tapioca mixture into the egg whites; return all to pan, whisking constantly. Cook and stir 2 minutes. Remove from heat. Cool 15 minutes; stir in vanilla. Transfer to dessert dishes. Press plastic wrap onto surface of pudding. Refrigerate until cold (pudding will thicken upon cooling). If desired, garnish with chopped espresso beans.
¾ CUP 156 cal., 3g fat (1g sat. fat), 62mg chol., 182mg sod., 31g carb. (21g sugars, 1g fiber), 3g pro.

VANILLA CREAM FRUIT TART

It's well worth the effort to whip up this creamy tart bursting with juicy summer berries. A friend gave me the recipe, and it always receives rave reviews at gatherings.
—*Susan Terzakis, Andover, MA*

PREP: 25 min. + chilling • **BAKE:** 25 min.
MAKES: 12 servings

- ¾   cup butter, softened
- ½   cup confectioners' sugar
- 1½ cups all-purpose flour
- 1   pkg. (10 to 12 oz.) white baking chips, melted and cooled
- ¼   cup heavy whipping cream
- 1   pkg. (8 oz.) cream cheese, softened
- ½   cup pineapple juice
- ¼   cup sugar
- 1   Tbsp. cornstarch
- ½   tsp. lemon juice
- 4   cups assorted fresh fruit

1. Preheat oven to 300°. Cream butter and confectioners' sugar until light and fluffy. Beat in flour (mixture will be crumbly). Pat onto a greased 12-in. pizza pan. Bake until lightly browned, 25-28 minutes. Cool.
2. Beat melted chips and cream until smooth. Beat in cream cheese until smooth. Spread over crust. Refrigerate 30 minutes. Meanwhile, in a small saucepan, combine pineapple juice, sugar, cornstarch and lemon juice. Bring to a boil over medium heat; cook and stir until thickened, about 2 minutes. Cool.
3. Arrange fruit over cream cheese layer; brush with pineapple mixture. Refrigerate 1 hour before serving.
1 PIECE 433 cal., 28g fat (17g sat. fat), 60mg chol., 174mg sod., 43g carb. (28g sugars, 2g fiber), 5g pro.

VANILLA
CREAM
FRUIT TART

MINI BLUEBERRY BUNDT CAKES

MINI BLUEBERRY BUNDT CAKES

These pretty little blueberry cakes are topped with a yummy lemon-flavored glaze. The recipe makes 12 mini cakes so you might want to bake up a couple of batches if you plan to serve more people.
—*Cathy Isaak, Rivers, MB*

- -

PREP: 20 min. • **BAKE:** 30 min. + cooling
MAKES: 1 dozen

- 1   cup butter, softened
- 2   cups sugar
- 4   large eggs, room temperature
- 2   tsp. vanilla extract
- 4   cups all-purpose flour
- 1   tsp. baking powder
- 1   tsp. salt
- 1   cup 2% milk
- 4   cups fresh blueberries

LEMON ICING
- 2   cups confectioners' sugar
- 2   Tbsp. 2% milk
- 4   tsp. lemon juice

1. Preheat oven to 350°. In a large bowl, cream butter and sugar until light and fluffy, 5-7 minutes. Beat in the eggs and vanilla. In another bowl, combine flour, baking powder and salt; add to creamed mixture alternately with milk, beating well after each addition. Fold in the blueberries.

2. Scoop into 12 greased 4-in. fluted tube pans. Place pans on a large baking sheet. Bake until a toothpick inserted in the center comes out clean, 30-35 minutes. Cool for 10 minutes before removing from tube pans to wire racks to cool completely.

3. For icing, in a small bowl, combine the confectioners' sugar, milk and lemon juice; drizzle over cakes. If desired, garnish with additional blueberries.

1 MINI CAKE 560 cal., 18g fat (11g sat. fat), 105mg chol., 395mg sod., 94g carb. (59g sugars, 2g fiber), 8g pro.

BOUQ-YAY!

A smart tape trick takes the fuss out of floral arranging. A stunning display is just moments away.

- With ¼-in. clear tape, create 3-4 rows (depending on the width of your vase) horizontally and vertically to make a grid.

- Place a few trimmed stems in each hole of the grid, then conceal the tape by adding a shorter layer of flowers or foliage around the edge of the vase.

LAVENDER SHORTBREAD

LAVENDER SHORTBREAD

Lavender flowers can be used fresh or dried in cooking. The flowers have an intense flavor, so they are best used sparingly.
—Taste of Home *Test Kitchen*

- -

PREP: 45 min. + standing
BAKE: 20 min. + cooling
MAKES: 4 dozen

- 2 cups confectioners' sugar
- 2 Tbsp. plus 2 tsp. finely snipped dried lavender flowers, divided
- 1 cup butter, softened
- ⅔ cup sugar
- 2 cups all-purpose flour
- ½ cup cornstarch
- ⅛ tsp. salt

1. In a bowl, combine confectioners' sugar and 2 tsp. lavender; cover and set aside at room temperature for 24 hours.
2. In a bowl, cream butter, sugar and remaining lavender. Combine flour, cornstarch and salt; add to the creamed mixture. Divide dough in half. Cover and refrigerate until easy to handle, 2 hours.
3. Preheat oven to 325°. On a lightly floured surface, roll out 1 portion of dough to ¼-in. thickness. Cut into 1½-in. squares. Repeat with remaining dough.
4. Place 1 in. apart on ungreased baking sheets. Prick with a fork several times. Bake until edges are lightly browned, 18-22 minutes. Cool for 1 minute before removing to wire racks to cool completely. Sift reserved lavender sugar; discard lavender. Sprinkle cookies with the sugar. Store in airtight containers.

NOTE Look for dried lavender flowers in spice shops. If using lavender from the garden, make sure it hasn't been treated with chemicals.

1 COOKIE 88 cal., 4g fat (2g sat. fat), 10mg chol., 37mg sod., 13g carb. (8g sugars, 0 fiber), 1g pro.

NUTELLA HAND PIES

These pint-sized Nutella hand pies made with puff pastry are too good to keep to yourself!
—Taste of Home *Test Kitchen*

TAKES: 30 min. • **MAKES:** 9 servings

- 1 large egg
- 1 Tbsp. water
- 1 sheet frozen puff pastry, thawed
- 3 Tbsp. Nutella
- 1 to 2 tsp. grated orange zest

ICING
- ⅓ cup confectioners' sugar
- ½ tsp. orange juice
- ⅛ tsp. grated orange zest
  Additional Nutella, optional

1. Preheat oven to 400°. In a small bowl, whisk egg with water.
2. Unfold puff pastry; cut into 9 squares. Place 1 tsp. Nutella in center of each; sprinkle with orange zest. Brush edges of pastry with egg mixture. Fold 1 corner over filling to form a triangle; press edges to seal. Transfer to an ungreased baking sheet.
3. Bake until pastry is golden brown and cooked through, 17-20 minutes. Cool slightly.
4. In a small bowl, mix confectioners' sugar, orange juice and orange zest; drizzle over pies. If desired, warm additional Nutella in a microwave and drizzle over tops.

1 HAND PIE 190 cal., 10g fat (2g sat. fat), 21mg chol., 100mg sod., 24g carb. (8g sugars, 2g fiber), 3g pro.

NUTELLA HAND PIES

BANANA PUDDING PARFAIT

BROWNIE KISS CUPCAKES

It's fun to make these individual brownie cupcakes with a chocolaty surprise inside. My goddaughter asked me to make them for her birthday to share with classmates at school. She requested 32 treats. I later found out she needed only 27. I wonder where the others went!
—Pamela Lute, Mercersburg, PA

- -

TAKES: 30 min. • **MAKES:** 9 servings

⅓ cup butter, softened
1   cup sugar
2   large eggs, room temperature
1   tsp. vanilla extract
¾   cup all-purpose flour
½   cup baking cocoa
¼   tsp. baking powder
¼   tsp. salt
9   milk chocolate kisses

1. Preheat oven to 350°. In a large bowl, cream butter and sugar until light and fluffy, 5-7 minutes. Beat in eggs and vanilla. Combine the flour, cocoa, baking powder and salt; gradually add to the creamed mixture and mix well.
2. Fill 9 paper- or foil-lined muffin cups two-thirds full. Place 1 chocolate kiss tip end down in the center of each.
3. Bake until top of brownie springs back when lightly touched, 20-25 minutes.
1 CUPCAKE 239 cal., 10g fat (5g sat. fat), 66mg chol., 163mg sod., 36g carb. (24g sugars, 1g fiber), 4g pro.

TEST KITCHEN TIP

For a tasty change of pace, swap out the chocolate kisses with mini peanut butter cups. Or, bake half a pan of each for 2 treats in 1.

BANANA PUDDING PARFAIT

A tasty blend of cream cheese, sweetened condensed milk and whipped topping are mixed into instant pudding, then layered in this creamy concoction with vanilla wafers and sliced bananas. Serve it in a pretty glass bowl for a visually fancy yet surprisingly fuss-free dessert.
—Edna Perry, Rice, TX

- -

PREP: 15 min. + chilling
MAKES: 12 servings

1   pkg. (8 oz.) cream cheese, softened
1   can (14 oz.) sweetened condensed milk
1   cup cold 2% milk
1   pkg. (3.4 oz.) instant vanilla pudding mix
1   carton (8 oz.) frozen whipped topping, thawed
52 vanilla wafers
4   medium firm bananas, sliced

1. In a large bowl, beat cream cheese until smooth. Beat in condensed milk. In another bowl, whisk milk and pudding mix; add to cream cheese mixture. Fold in whipped topping.
2. Place a third of the vanilla wafers in a 2½-qt. glass bowl. Top with a third of the bananas and pudding mixture. Repeat layers twice.
3. Cover and refrigerate at least 4 hours or overnight. If desired, garnish with additional whipped topping, sliced bananas and wafers.
¾ CUP 376 cal., 16g fat (10g sat. fat), 35mg chol., 225mg sod., 52g carb. (41g sugars, 1g fiber), 5g pro.

NO-BAKE
OREO PIE

NO-BAKE OREO PIE

You need only 5 ingredients and just 15 minutes of prep to make this cool and creamy dessert. It's the perfect make-ahead treat in the heat of summer.
—Taste of Home *Test Kitchen*

- -

PREP: 15 min. + chilling
MAKES: 8 servings

- 30 Oreo cookies, finely crushed
- ½ cup butter, melted

FILLING
- 1 pkg. (8 oz.) cream cheese, softened
- ¼ cup sugar
- 2 cups whipped topping
- 18 Oreo cookies, divided

1. In a small bowl, mix crushed cookies and butter. Press onto bottom and up side of an ungreased 9-in. pie plate. Refrigerate for 30 minutes.
2. In a large bowl, beat cream cheese and sugar until smooth. Fold in whipped topping. Coarsely chop 10 cookies; fold into cream cheese mixture. Spoon over the crust.
3. Refrigerate, covered, at least 2 hours before serving. If desired, garnish with additional whipped topping and crushed cookies. Arrange remaining 8 whole cookies over pie.
1 PIECE 595 cal., 38g fat (20g sat. fat), 59mg chol., 450mg sod., 62g carb. (39g sugars, 2g fiber), 4g pro.

TEST KITCHEN TIP
Add a drop or 2 of food coloring to the filling to jazz things up a bit. Make it pink for a baby shower or green for St Paddy's Day.

BOURBON BRIOCHE BREAD PUDDING

BOURBON BRIOCHE BREAD PUDDING

My husband wasn't a fan of bread pudding until I had him try a bite of mine from a local restaurant. I replicated it with some added bourbon, walnuts and a different type of bread. It's a keeper!
—*Cindy Worth, Lapwai, ID*

- -

PREP: 15 min. + standing • **BAKE:** 35 min.
MAKES: 6 servings

- ½ cup bourbon, divided
- ½ cup raisins
- 2½ cups cubed brioche bread, toasted
- ⅓ cup finely chopped walnuts
- 4 large eggs
- 1¾ cups heavy whipping cream
- ⅓ cup sugar
- 1 tsp. ground cinnamon
- 1 tsp. vanilla extract
- ½ tsp. ground nutmeg
- ¼ tsp. salt
  Optional: Confectioners' sugar and whipped cream

1. Preheat oven to 375°. Pour ¼ cup bourbon over raisins in a small bowl; let stand 5 minutes. Place bread in a greased 8-in. square baking dish. Top with walnuts, raisins and soaking liquid.
2. In a large bowl, whisk eggs, cream, sugar, cinnamon, vanilla, nutmeg, salt and remaining ¼ cup bourbon until blended. Pour over bread; let stand until bread is softened, about 15 minutes.
3. Bake, uncovered, until puffed, golden and a knife inserted in the center comes out clean, 35-40 minutes. Serve warm. If desired, sprinkle with confectioners' sugar and serve with whipped cream.
1 SERVING 469 cal., 34g fat (19g sat. fat), 213mg chol., 218mg sod., 30g carb. (22g sugars, 1g fiber), 9g pro.

COOKIES & CREAM

Pair up two sweet treats—plus some tempting toppings—to make these easy, freeze-y twists on an ice cream sandwich

MINT COOKIE

COOKIE OVERLOAD

FROZEN S'MORE

COOKIE-BUTTER LOVER

TOTALLY TROPICAL

COOKIE-BUTTER LOVER
Place 1 scoop coffee ice cream between 2 Biscoff biscuits. Drizzle with ¼ cup melted Biscoff creamy cookie butter. Freeze until serving.

COOKIE OVERLOAD
Place 1 scoop cookie dough ice cream between 2 chocolate chip cookies. Roll in ¼ cup mixture of frozen cookie dough bites and mini chocolate chips. Freeze until serving.

MINT COOKIE
Place 1 scoop mint chip ice cream between 2 mint Milano cookies. Freeze until serving.

MINI BAKED ALASKA
Place 1 scoop strawberry ice cream onto 1 shortbread cookie. Spread ¼ cup marshmallow creme over the top, covering all ice cream. Blow-torch marshmallow until browned. Serve immediately.

FROZEN S'MORE
Place 1 scoop s'mores ice cream onto 1 graham cracker half. Spread ⅛ cup marshmallow fluff over ice cream; top with remaining graham cracker half. Freeze until solid. Dip half the sandwich into ½ cup milk chocolate coating. Freeze until serving.

MINI
BAKED
ALASKA

POP
TART

LEMON
BLUEBERRY

CHOCOLATE
CHERRY

SNICKERDOODLE

TOTALLY TROPICAL
Place 1 scoop mango sorbet between 2 Keebler Coconut Dreams Fudge, Coconut & Caramel Cookies. Roll in ⅛ cup toasted sweetened shredded coconut. Thread 2 maraschino cherries on a toothpick and place in the center. Freeze until serving.

CHOCOLATE CHERRY
Place 1 scoop black cherry ice cream between 2 classic chocolate wafer cookies. Freeze until serving.

SNICKERDOODLE
Place 1 scoop cinnamon ice cream between 2 snickerdoodle cookies. Roll in ½ cup coarse sugar. Freeze until serving.

POP TART
Place 1 scoop blue moon ice cream between 2 Wild Berry Pop-Tarts. Roll in sprinkles. Freeze until serving.

LEMON BLUEBERRY
Place 1 scoop lemon bar ice cream onto 1 windmill cookie. Drizzle with ⅛ cup warmed blueberry preserves. Top with second windmill cookie. Freeze until serving.

CHOCOLATE-DIPPED STRAWBERRIES

Plump berries from our strawberry patch turned into a real treat when I dipped them in chocolate! I like to make these before dinner and put them in the fridge so they're ready when we're finished eating.

—*Valerie Gee, Depew, NY*

TAKES: 20 min.
MAKES: about 9 strawberries

- 1 pint large strawberries
- 4 oz. semisweet chocolate, chopped
- 1 Tbsp. plus ½ tsp. shortening, divided
- 1 oz. white baking chocolate
- 4 drops food coloring, optional

1. Wash strawberries and gently pat with paper towels until completely dry. In a microwave-safe bowl, melt semisweet chocolate and 1 Tbsp. shortening at 50% power; stir until smooth. Dip each strawberry and place on a waxed paper-lined baking sheet. Freeze strawberries for 5 minutes.
2. Meanwhile, microwave white chocolate and remaining shortening at 30% power until melted; stir until smooth. Stir in food coloring if desired. Drizzle over strawberries. Refrigerate until serving.

1 STRAWBERRY 57 cal., 4g fat (2g sat. fat), 1mg chol., 4mg sod., 6g carb. (5g sugars, 1g fiber), 1g pro.

TEST KITCHEN TIP
For a twist on this classic recipe, dunk your strawberries in melted caramel and enjoy!

CHOCOLATE-DIPPED STRAWBERRIES

PAIRS WITH

BRACHETTO D'ACQUI

PECAN TARTS

FRESH PLUM KUCHEN

In summer when plums are in season, this tender fruit-topped cake is simply delectable! For variety, you can use fresh pears or apples instead.
—*Anna Daley, Montague, PE*

- -

PREP: 20 min. • **BAKE:** 40 min. + cooling
MAKES: 12 servings

- ¼ cup butter, softened
- ¾ cup sugar
- 2 large eggs, room temperature
- 1 cup all-purpose flour
- 1 tsp. baking powder
- ¼ cup 2% milk
- 1 tsp. grated lemon zest
- 2 cups sliced fresh plums (about 4 medium)
- ½ cup packed brown sugar
- 1 tsp. ground cinnamon
  Confectioners' sugar, optional

1. Preheat oven to 350°. In a small bowl, cream butter and sugar until light and fluffy, 5-7 minutes. Beat in eggs. Combine flour and baking powder; add to the creamed mixture alternately with milk, beating well after each addition. Add lemon zest. Pour into a greased 10-in. springform pan. Arrange plums on top; gently press into batter. Sprinkle the top with brown sugar and cinnamon.
2. Place pan on a baking sheet. Bake until top is golden and a toothpick inserted in the center comes out clean, 40-50 minutes. Cool 10 minutes. Run a knife around edge of pan; remove rim. Cool on a wire rack. If desired, dust with confectioners' sugar just before serving.
1 PIECE 185 cal., 5g fat (3g sat. fat), 46mg chol., 89mg sod., 33g carb. (24g sugars, 1g fiber), 3g pro.

PECAN TARTS

The flaky crust combined with a rich center makes these little tarts a satisfying snack. They look so appealing on a pretty platter and make a great finger-food dessert when you're entertaining. They also freeze well.
—*Jean Rhodes, Tignall, GA*

- -

PREP: 20 min. + chilling
BAKE: 25 min. + cooling
MAKES: about 20

- 3 oz. cream cheese, softened
- ½ cup butter, softened
- 1 cup all-purpose flour
- ¼ tsp. salt
FILLING
- 1 large egg
- ¾ cup packed dark brown sugar
- 1 Tbsp. butter, melted
- 1 tsp. vanilla extract
  Pecan halves, optional
- ⅔ cup chopped pecans

1. In a small bowl, beat cream cheese and butter until fluffy; blend in flour and salt. Refrigerate for 1 hour.
2. Preheat oven to 325°. Shape into 1-in. balls; press onto the bottom and up the sides of greased mini-muffin cups.
3. For filling, in a small bowl, beat the egg. Add brown sugar, butter and vanilla; mix well. Stir in pecans. Spoon into tart shells. If desired, top each tart with a pecan half.
4. Bake until lightly browned and set, 25-30 minutes. Cool for 15 minutes before carefully removing from pans.
1 TART 145 cal., 10g fat (4g sat. fat), 29mg chol., 101mg sod., 14g carb. (8g sugars, 1g fiber), 2g pro.

LEMON ICE

Pucker up for this sweet-tart treat. The delicious lemon dessert is a perfectly refreshing way to end a summer meal... or any meal, for that matter.
—*Concetta Maranto Skenfield, Bakersfield, CA*

- -

PREP: 15 min. + freezing
MAKES: 6 servings

  2 cups sugar
  1 cup water
  2 cups lemon juice
      Optional: Lemon slices and fresh
      mint leaves

1. In a large saucepan over low heat, cook and stir sugar and water until sugar is dissolved. Remove from heat; stir in lemon juice.
2. Pour into a freezer container. Freeze until mixture becomes slushy, about 8 hours or overnight. If desired, top servings with lemon slices and mint.
½ CUP 278 cal., 0 fat (0 sat. fat), 0 chol., 1mg sod., 73g carb. (69g sugars, 0 fiber), 0 pro.

AIR-FRYER APPLE PIE EGG ROLLS

AIR-FRYER APPLE PIE EGG ROLLS

These easy apple pie egg rolls can be prepared as needed, using egg roll wrappers as vessels for the fruit rather than traditional pie crust. The air-fryer method of cooking results in a crispy, crunchy crust with a tender, juicy filling. Flavored cream cheese spread may be used instead of plain, depending on availability.
—*Sheila Joan Suhan, Scottdale, PA*

- -

PREP: 25 min. • **COOK:** 10 min./batch
MAKES: 8 servings

  3 cups chopped peeled tart apples
  ½ cup packed light brown sugar
2½ tsp. ground cinnamon, divided
  1 tsp. cornstarch
  8 egg roll wrappers
  ½ cup spreadable cream cheese
      Butter-flavored cooking spray
  1 Tbsp. sugar
  ⅔ cup hot caramel ice cream topping

1. Preheat air fryer to 400°. In a small bowl, combine apples, brown sugar, 2 tsp. cinnamon and cornstarch. With a corner of an egg roll wrapper facing you, spread 1 scant Tbsp. cream cheese to within 1 in. of edges. Place ⅓ cup apple mixture just below center of wrapper. (Cover remaining wrappers with a damp paper towel until ready to use.)
2. Fold bottom corner over filling; moisten remaining wrapper edges with water. Fold side corners toward center over filling. Roll egg roll up tightly, pressing at tip to seal. Repeat.
3. In batches, arrange egg rolls in a single layer on greased tray in air-fryer basket; spritz with cooking spray. Cook until golden brown, 5-6 minutes. Turn; spritz with cooking spray. Cook until golden brown and crisp, 5-6 minutes longer. Combine sugar and remaining ½ tsp. cinnamon; roll hot egg rolls in mixture. Serve with caramel sauce.
1 ROLL 273 cal., 4g fat (2g sat. fat), 13mg chol., 343mg sod., 56g carb. (35g sugars, 2g fiber), 5g pro.

AIR-FRYER
FRIED
COOKIES

4-INGREDIENT CHOCOLATE DUMP CAKE

This is a very moist cake with chocolate chips on top instead of frosting. It tastes wonderful served warm with ice cream.
—*Kim Rodney, Archbald, PA*

- -

PREP: 5 min. • **COOK:** 40 min.
MAKES: 12 servings

1   chocolate cake mix (regular size)
1   pkg. (3.9 oz.) instant chocolate pudding mix
2   cups (12 oz. each) semisweet chocolate chips, divided
2   cups 2% milk
    Vanilla ice cream, optional

1. Preheat oven to 350°. Evenly sprinkle dry cake mix into a greased 13x9-in. baking dish. Sprinkle dry pudding mix over cake mix and top with 1¾ cups chocolate chips. Drizzle milk over the top. Gently stir to combine (mixture will appear thick and lumpy). Sprinkle with remaining ¼ cup chocolate chips.
2. Bake until top appears set and edges pull away from sides of dish, 35-40 minutes. Cool slightly on a wire rack. Serve warm, with ice cream if desired.
½ CUP 460 cal., 19g fat (12g sat. fat), 3mg chol., 338mg sod., 76g carb. (53g sugars, 4g fiber), 6g pro.

AIR-FRYER FRIED COOKIES

Deep-fried Oreos are quickly becoming a county fair favorite. Thanks to this recipe, you can make them at home quickly, easily and mess free.
—*Margarita Torres, Bayamon, Puerto Rico*

- -

PREP: 10 min. + freezing
COOK: 5 min./batch • **MAKES:** 1½ dozen

18   Oreo cookies
1   large egg, room temperature
¼   cup 2% milk
¼   tsp. almond extract
1   cup biscuit/baking mix
    Confectioners' sugar

1. On each of eighteen 4-in. wooden skewers, thread 1 cookie, inserting pointed end of skewer into filling. Freeze until firm, about 1 hour.
2. Preheat air fryer to 350°. Cut pieces of parchment to fit the bottom of the air fryer. In a shallow bowl, whisk together egg, milk and extract; add biscuit mix and stir just until moistened. Dip cookie into biscuit mixture to coat both sides; shake off excess. Place a sheet of parchment in air fryer; spray parchment with cooking spray. In batches, arrange cookies in a single layer ½ in. apart, placing 1 cookie in each corner of the paper so it doesn't fly around during cooking.
3. Cook until golden brown, 5-7 minutes. Dust with confectioners' sugar before serving.
NOTE In our testing, we find cook times vary dramatically between brands of air fryers. As a result, we give wider than normal ranges on suggested cook times. Begin checking at the first time listed and adjust as needed.
1 COOKIE 84 cal., 3g fat (1g sat. fat), 11mg chol., 115mg sod., 13g carb. (5g sugars, 0 fiber), 1g pro.

DOUBLE PEANUT BUTTER CAKE

My family loves peanut butter cake, so I came up with a recipe that packs in as much peanut butter as possible. Easy to say, they can't get enough of it.
—Marie Hoyer, Hodgenville, KY

PREP: 20 min. • **BAKE:** 30 min.
MAKES: 9 servings

- ½ cup creamy peanut butter
- ¼ cup butter, softened
- ¾ cup sugar
- 2 large eggs, room temperature
- 1½ cups all-purpose flour
- 2 tsp. baking powder
- ¼ tsp. salt
- ¾ cup 2% milk

FROSTING
- ⅓ cup chunky peanut butter
- 3 Tbsp. butter, softened
- 3 cups confectioners' sugar
- ¼ cup 2% milk
- 1½ tsp. vanilla extract
  Chopped salted peanuts, optional

1. Preheat oven to 350°. In a large bowl, cream peanut butter, butter and sugar until light and fluffy, 3-5 minutes. Add eggs, 1 at a time, beating well after each addition. Combine flour, baking powder and salt; add to creamed mixture alternately with milk, beating well after each addition.
2. Pour into a greased 9 in. square baking pan. Bake until a toothpick inserted in center comes out clean, 30-35 minutes. Cool in pan on a wire rack. For frosting, cream peanut butter and butter. Add sugar, milk and vanilla; beat until smooth. Spread over top of cake. If desired, sprinkle with chopped peanuts.
1 PIECE 548 cal., 23g fat (9g sat. fat), 67mg chol., 380mg sod., 79g carb. (60g sugars, 2g fiber), 10g pro.

SALTED CARAMEL CUPCAKES

SALTED CARAMEL CUPCAKES

To help balance the sweetness of the brown sugar cupcake, our Test Kitchen experts created a unique salty frosting. It's the best of both worlds!
—Taste of Home Test Kitchen

PREP: 25 min. + chilling
BAKE: 20 min. + cooling
MAKES: 10 cupcakes

- ½ cup butter, softened
- ½ cup packed brown sugar
- ¼ cup sugar
- 2 large eggs, room temperature
- 1 tsp. vanilla extract
- 1¼ cups all-purpose flour
- ¾ tsp. baking powder
- ¼ tsp. salt
- ½ cup 2% milk

FROSTING
- ⅓ cup sugar
- 4 tsp. water
- ⅛ tsp. salt
- 1⅓ cups heavy whipping cream
  Optional: Caramel ice cream topping and flaky sea salt

1. Preheat oven to 350°. In a large bowl, cream butter and sugars until light and fluffy, 5-7 minutes. Add eggs, 1 at a time, beating well after each addition. Beat in vanilla. Combine flour, baking powder and salt; add to creamed mixture alternately with milk, beating well after each addition.
2. Fill 10 paper-lined muffin cups three-fourths full. Bake 18-22 minutes or until a toothpick inserted in center comes out clean. Cool 10 minutes before removing from pan to a wire rack to cool completely.
3. For frosting, in a large, heavy saucepan, combine sugar, water and salt. Cook over medium-low heat until sugar begins to melt. Gently pull melted sugar to center of pan until sugar melts evenly. Cook, without stirring, until mixture turns an amber color.
4. Remove from heat; gradually stir in cream until smooth. Transfer to a small bowl; cover and refrigerate for 4 hours. Beat until stiff peaks form. Frost cupcakes. If desired, top with caramel topping and sea salt.
1 CUPCAKE 416 cal., 22g fat (14g sat. fat), 111mg chol., 224mg sod., 52g carb. (39g sugars, 0 fiber), 4g pro.

MAPLE &
BACON BARS

MAPLE & BACON BARS

This bacon maple bar recipe is the perfect treat when you're craving both salty and sweet. The aroma will tantalize you while the bars are baking.
—Taste of Home *Test Kitchen*

PREP: 15 min. • **BAKE:** 20 min. + cooling
MAKES: 9 servings

- ½ cup butter, softened
- ¾ cup packed brown sugar
- 2 large eggs, room temperature
- 1 Tbsp. 2% milk
- 1 tsp. vanilla extract
- ¾ cup all-purpose flour
- ¾ cup quick-cooking oats
- ½ tsp. baking powder
- ¼ tsp. salt
- 4 bacon strips, cooked and crumbled
- ⅓ cup chopped pecans, toasted

MAPLE GLAZE
- 1 cup confectioners' sugar
- 2 Tbsp. maple syrup
- ½ to 1 tsp. maple flavoring, optional

1. Preheat oven to 350°. In a large bowl, cream butter and brown sugar until light and fluffy, 5-7 minutes. Beat in eggs, milk and vanilla. Combine flour, oats, baking powder and salt; gradually add to creamed mixture. Fold in the bacon and pecans.

2. Spread into a greased 9-in. square baking pan. Bake until a toothpick inserted in center comes out clean, 20-25 minutes. Cool on a wire rack. For glaze, in a small bowl, mix confectioners' sugar, syrup and, if desired, maple flavoring. Drizzle over bars; let stand until set.

1 BAR 351 cal., 16g fat (8g sat. fat), 72mg chol., 261mg sod., 48g carb. (34g sugars, 1g fiber), 5g pro.

BEST EVER CHEESECAKE

PEACHY BUTTERMILK SHAKES

My husband and grandkids sure enjoy the tang of buttermilk blended with sweet peaches in these delightful change-of-pace shakes.
—Anna Mayer, Fort Branch, IN

TAKES: 10 min. • **MAKES:** 3 servings

- 1 cup buttermilk
- 3 cups fresh or frozen unsweetened sliced peaches, thawed
- 1 cup vanilla ice cream, softened
- ¼ cup sugar
- ¾ tsp. ground cinnamon
  Optional: Whipped cream and additional sliced peaches

Place the first 5 ingredients in a blender; cover and process until smooth. Pour into chilled glasses; serve immediately. If desired, top with whipped cream and additional sliced peaches.
1 CUP 250 cal., 6g fat (3g sat. fat), 23mg chol., 191mg sod., 46g carb. (42g sugars, 3g fiber), 6g pro.

BEST EVER CHEESECAKE

I've passed this recipe on to dozens of folks. My daughter was so fond of it that she served it for her wedding instead of traditional cake.
—Howard Koch, Lima, OH

PREP: 20 min. • **BAKE:** 45 min. + chilling
MAKES: 8 servings

- 1¼ cups graham cracker crumbs
- ⅓ cup butter, melted
- ¼ cup sugar
  FILLING/TOPPING
- 2 pkg. (8 oz. each) cream cheese, softened
- 2 large eggs, room temperature, lightly beaten
- ⅔ cup sugar, divided
- 2 tsp. vanilla extract, divided
  Dash salt
- 1 cup sour cream
  Whipped cream, optional

1. Preheat oven to 350°. In a bowl, combine the graham cracker crumbs, butter and sugar. Pat into the bottom and 1 in. up the side of an 8-in. springform pan. Chill.
2. For filling, beat cream cheese and eggs in a bowl on medium speed for 1 minute. Add ⅓ cup sugar, 1 tsp. vanilla and salt. Continue beating until well blended, about 1 minute. Pour into crust.
3. Place pan on a baking sheet. Bake for 35 minutes. Cool for 10 minutes. For topping, combine the sour cream and remaining sugar and vanilla in a small bowl; spread over cheesecake. Bake 10 minutes longer. Cool completely on a wire rack. Refrigerate 3 hours or overnight. If desired, serve with whipped cream.
1 PIECE 504 cal., 36g fat (20g sat. fat), 131mg chol., 357mg sod., 40g carb. (30g sugars, 1g fiber), 7g pro.

BEER & PRETZEL CARAMELS

BEER & PRETZEL CARAMELS

Beer and pretzels are a natural combination—mix them with smooth caramel and you have an awesome candy. The guys will go wild over these crunchy, chunky chews.
—*Jenni Sharp, Milwaukee, WI*

PREP: 1 hour + cooling
COOK: 50 min. + standing
MAKES: about 3 lbs. (81 servings)

PRETZELS
- ⅓ cup sugar
- ½ tsp. salt
- 2 cups miniature pretzels
- 1 Tbsp. canola oil
- 1 Tbsp. vanilla extract

CARAMELS
- 4 cups dark beer
- 1 tsp. plus 1 cup butter, divided
- 3 cups sugar
- ⅔ cup corn syrup
- 2 cups heavy whipping cream, divided
- ⅓ cup water
- 1 tsp. salt
- ½ tsp. kosher salt

1. Preheat oven to 350°. For pretzels, in a small bowl, combine sugar and salt. In a large bowl, combine the pretzels, oil and vanilla. Add sugar mixture; toss to coat. Transfer to a 15x10x1-in. foil-lined baking pan coated with cooking spray.
2. Bake until sugars have melted and caramelized, 10-13 minutes, stirring occasionally. Do not overcook or sugar may burn. Cool completely. Coarsely chop pretzels.
3. In a large saucepan, bring beer to a boil; cook until reduced to ⅔ cup. Set aside to cool.
4. Meanwhile, line a 9-in. square pan with foil; grease the foil with 1 tsp. butter.
5. In a Dutch oven, combine the sugar, corn syrup, ⅔ cup cream, water, salt and remaining 1 cup butter. Cook and stir over medium heat until a candy thermometer reads 238°, about 20 minutes. In a small bowl, combine reduced beer and remaining 1⅓ cups cream; slowly stir into sugar mixture.
6. Using a pastry brush dipped in cold water, wash down the sides of the pan to eliminate sugar crystals. Cook, stirring constantly, until a candy thermometer reads 245° (firm-ball stage), about 30 minutes.
7. Remove from the heat. Pour into prepared pan (do not scrape saucepan); sprinkle with candied pretzels and kosher salt. Let stand until firm, about 5 hours or overnight. Using foil, lift candy out of pan. Discard foil; cut candy into 1-in. squares using a buttered knife. Wrap individually in waxed paper; twist ends.

NOTE We recommend that you test your candy thermometer before each use by bringing water to a boil; the thermometer should read 212°. Adjust your recipe temperature up or down based on your test.

1 PIECE 90 cal., 5g fat (3g sat. fat), 14mg chol., 91mg sod., 12g carb. (9g sugars, 0 fiber), 0 pro.

SNAP, CRACKLE, SWAP!

Give the crispy-chewy cereal treat a little extra pop with fun and flavorful stir-ins.

Basic Rice Krispies Treats
In a large saucepan over low heat or in a microwave, melt a 10-oz. pkg. of miniature marshmallows in 3 Tbsp. canola oil; stir until smooth. Remove from the heat; stir in 5 cups Rice Krispies cereal plus any mix-ins. Press mixture into a lightly greased 13x9-in. baking pan using waxed paper or a lightly greased spatula. Cool to room temperature. Cut into bars.

WATERMELON

SPARKLY PRINCESS

CHOCOLATE RASPBERRY

SALTED CARAMEL PRETZEL

ROCKY ROAD

MAPLE BACON

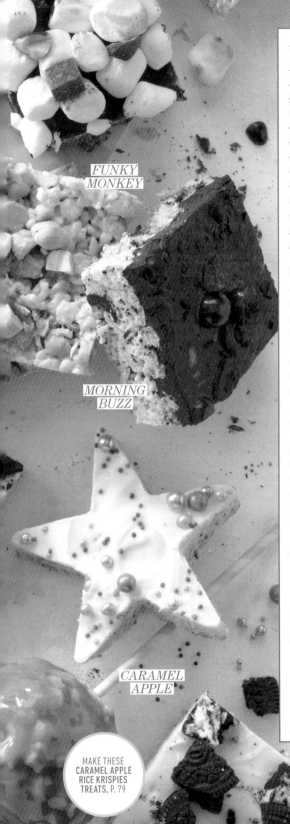

MAKE THESE
CARAMEL APPLE
RICE KRISPIES
TREATS, P. 79

*FUNKY
MONKEY*

*MORNING
BUZZ*

*CARAMEL
APPLE*

OREO

WATERMELON

Stir 1 tsp. watermelon extract into melted marshmallows. Stir ¼ tsp. green food coloring paste into half the marshmallow mixture. Add 3 cups cereal. Press mixture around inside edge of 2 lightly greased 9-in. round cake pans. Stir ¼ tsp. pink food coloring paste and ⅛ tsp. red food coloring paste into the remaining marshmallow mixture; add 3 cups cereal. Press into center of the cake pans. Press mini chocolate chips into pink portion for seeds.

SPARKLY PRINCESS

Stir 2 tsp. strawberry extract into melted marshmallows. Stir in ⅔ cup rainbow sprinkles when adding cereal. Melt an 11½-oz. pkg. white baking chips; spread over cooled bars. Sprinkle with ⅓ cup rainbow sprinkles. Use cookie cutters to cut out shapes if desired.

ROCKY ROAD

When adding the cereal, stir in 5 whole graham crackers, crumbled; 1 cup chopped salted almonds; and 1 cup chocolate chunks. Melt an 11½-oz. pkg. chocolate chunks; spread over cooled bars. Top with a 10-oz. pkg. mini marshmallows. Using a kitchen torch, toast the marshmallows until golden brown. Sprinkle the bars with ¼ cup almonds and ¾ cup chocolate chunks.

SALTED CARAMEL PRETZEL

Add ⅔ cup each chopped caramels and pretzels when adding the cereal. Melt an 11½-oz. pkg. milk chocolate chips; spread over the cooled bars. Top with ⅓ cup each coarsely chopped caramels and pretzels. Sprinkle bars with sea salt.

MAPLE BACON

Stir 2 tsp. maple flavoring into melted marshmallows. Add 9 cooked, crumbled bacon strips when adding the cereal.

CHOCOLATE RASPBERRY

Stir 1 tsp. raspberry extract into the melted marshmallows. Add 1 cup mini chocolate chips and 1 cup freeze-dried raspberries when adding the cereal.

FUNKY MONKEY

Stir 1½ tsp. banana extract into the melted marshmallows. Add a 10-oz. pkg. peanut butter chips, 1 cup chopped dried banana chips and ½ cup chopped dry roasted peanuts when adding cereal. Press ½ cup chopped dry roasted peanuts on top of the warm bars.

MORNING BUZZ

Stir 2 tsp. coffee extract into the melted marshmallows. Add ½ cup coarsely chopped chocolate-covered espresso beans when adding cereal. Melt an 11-oz. pkg. dark chocolate chips; spread on top of the cooled bars. Sprinkle with ½ cup coarsely chopped chocolate-covered espresso beans.

OREO

Add 1 cup coarsely chopped Oreo cookies when adding the cereal. Melt a 10-oz. pkg. white baking chips and spread over cooled bars. Sprinkle with 1 cup coarsely chopped Oreo cookies.

STICKY TOFFEE PUDDING WITH BUTTERSCOTCH SAUCE

STICKY TOFFEE PUDDING WITH BUTTERSCOTCH SAUCE

Sticky toffee pudding is a classic dessert in Britain. I love that I can easily enjoy the traditional treat with its rich butterscotch sauce at home.
—Agnes Ward, Stratford, ON

- -

PREP: 30 min. + cooling • **BAKE:** 50 min.
MAKES: 15 servings (2½ cups sauce)

- 2   cups coarsely chopped dates (about 12 oz.)
- 2½ cups water
- 2   tsp. baking soda
- 1⅔ cups sugar
- ½   cup butter, softened
- 4   large eggs, room temperature
- 2   tsp. vanilla extract
- 3¼ cups all-purpose flour
- 2   tsp. baking powder

BUTTERSCOTCH SAUCE
- 7   Tbsp. butter, cubed
- 2¼ cups packed brown sugar
- 1   cup half-and-half cream
- 1   Tbsp. brandy
- ¼   tsp. vanilla extract
     Whipped cream, optional

1. Preheat oven to 350°. In a small saucepan, combine dates and water; bring to a boil. Remove from heat; stir in baking soda. Cool to lukewarm.
2. In a large bowl, cream sugar and butter until light and fluffy, 5-7 minutes. Add eggs, 1 at a time, beating well after each addition. Beat in vanilla. In another bowl, mix flour and baking powder; gradually add to creamed mixture. Stir in date mixture.
3. Transfer to a greased 13x9-in. baking pan. Bake until a toothpick inserted in center comes out clean, 50-60 minutes. Cool slightly in pan on a wire rack.
4. Meanwhile, in a small saucepan, melt butter; add brown sugar and cream. Bring to a boil over medium heat, stirring constantly. Remove from heat. Stir in brandy and vanilla. Serve sauce warm with warm cake. If desired, top cake with whipped cream.

1 PIECE WITH ABOUT 2 TBSP. SAUCE
521 cal., 15g fat (9g sat. fat), 88mg chol., 361mg sod., 93g carb. (70g sugars, 3g fiber), 6g pro.

CHOCOLATE-STUFFED PEANUT BUTTER SKILLET COOKIE

A surprise chocolate filling makes this dessert extra delicious! Serve warm from the oven with a scoop of your favorite ice cream.
—Andrea Price, Grafton, WI

- -

PREP: 20 min. • **BAKE:** 35 min. + cooling
MAKES: 12 servings

- 1   cup creamy peanut butter
- ¾   cup butter, softened
- 1¼   cups plus 1 Tbsp. sugar, divided
- 1   large egg, room temperature
- 1   tsp. vanilla extract
- 1½   cups all-purpose flour
- ½   tsp. baking soda
- ½   tsp. salt
- 1   cup milk chocolate chips
      Vanilla ice cream, optional

1. Preheat oven to 350°. In a large bowl, cream peanut butter, butter and 1¼ cups sugar until blended. Beat in egg and vanilla. In another bowl, whisk flour, baking soda and salt; gradually beat into creamed mixture. Press half the dough into a well greased 10-in. cast-iron or other ovenproof skillet. Sprinkle chocolate chips over dough in skillet to within ½ in. of edge. Drop remaining dough over chocolate chips; spread until even. Sprinkle remaining 1 Tbsp. sugar over the top.
2. Bake until a toothpick inserted in center comes out with moist crumbs, 35-40 minutes. Cool completely on a wire rack. If desired, serve with vanilla ice cream.

1 PIECE 453 cal., 27g fat (12g sat. fat), 49mg chol., 351mg sod., 47g carb. (32g sugars, 2g fiber), 8g pro.

CHOCOLATE-STUFFED
PEANUT BUTTER
SKILLET COOKIE

LITTLE LEMON
POUND CAKES

LITTLE LEMON POUND CAKES

My mother-in-law follows a gluten-free diet, so when she comes to visit I like to make her a delicious dessert. I decided to convert my grandma's whipped pound cake to be gluten- and dairy-free. My husband, who is not a fan of gluten-free baked goods, thought my version was truly amazing.
—Sue Gronholz, Beaver Dam, WI

PREP: 20 min. • **BAKE:** 25 min. + cooling
MAKES: 6 servings

- ½ cup vegan butter-style sticks
- 1½ cups sugar
- 3 large eggs, room temperature
- 2 tsp. grated lemon zest
- 1½ tsp. lemon extract
- 1½ cups gluten-free baking flour (with xanthan gum)
- ½ cup dairy-free heavy whipping cream
    Confectioners' sugar, optional

1. Preheat oven to 325°. Grease six 4-in. fluted tube pans.
2. In a large bowl, cream butter-style sticks and sugar until light and fluffy, 5-7 minutes. Add eggs, 1 at a time, beating well after each addition. Beat in extract and zest. Add flour to creamed mixture alternately with cream, beating well after each addition.
3. Transfer to prepared pans. Bake until a toothpick inserted in center comes out clean, 25-30 minutes. Cool in pans 10 minutes before removing to wire racks to cool completely. If desired, dust with confectioners' sugar.

1 CAKE 497 cal., 17g fat (7g sat. fat), 93mg chol., 206mg sod., 81g carb. (50g sugars, 0 fiber), 5g pro.

PINEAPPLE RUMCHATA SHORTCAKES

PINEAPPLE RUMCHATA SHORTCAKES

This deliciously different dessert, with a soft inside and a crumbly crust, is made in the slow cooker in jars instead of in the oven. When done, add final touches to the cooled shortcake jars and serve.
—Joan Hallford, Fort Worth, TX

PREP: 20 min. • **COOK:** 1½ hours + chilling
MAKES: 6 servings

- 1½ cups all-purpose flour
- ¼ cup sugar
- 1 tsp. baking powder
- ½ tsp. salt
- ¼ tsp. baking soda
- ⅓ cup cold butter
- 1 large egg, room temperature
- ¾ cup sour cream
- 3 Tbsp. RumChata liqueur

TOPPING

- 1½ cups fresh pineapple, cut into ½-in. pieces
- 3 Tbsp. sugar, divided
- 1 to 2 Tbsp. RumChata liqueur
- 1 tsp. grated lime zest
- ½ cup heavy whipping cream
- 1 medium lime, thinly sliced, optional

1. In a large bowl, whisk flour, sugar, baking powder, salt and baking soda. Cut in butter until mixture resembles coarse crumbs. In another bowl, whisk egg, sour cream and RumChata. Add to flour mixture; stir just until moistened.
2. Spoon mixture into 6 greased half-pint jars. Center lids on jars and screw on bands until fingertip tight. Place jars in a 6- or 7-qt. oval slow cooker; add enough hot water to reach halfway up the jars, about 5 cups. Cook, covered, on high 1½ to 2 hours or until a toothpick inserted in center of shortcake comes out clean.
3. Meanwhile, for the topping, combine pineapple, 2 Tbsp. sugar, RumChata and lime zest. Refrigerate, covered, at least 1 hour. Remove jars from slow cooker to wire racks to cool completely. In a large bowl, beat cream until it begins to thicken. Add remaining 1 Tbsp. sugar; beat until soft peaks form.
4. Top shortcakes with pineapple mixture, whipped cream and, if desired, lime slices.

1 SHORTCAKE 463 cal., 28g fat (17g sat. fat), 101mg chol., 442mg sod., 47g carb. (20g sugars, 1g fiber), 6g pro.

ICE CREAM BOWLS

Once you sample these homemade waffle ice cream bowls, you'll want to serve them time and again! You can either prepare them with pretty designs in a special pizzelle cookie maker or without designs in the oven.
—Taste of Home *Test Kitchen*

PREP: 15 min. • **BAKE:** 35 min.
MAKES: 16 servings

    3   large eggs, room temperature
    ¾   cup sugar
    ½   cup butter, melted
    2   tsp. vanilla extract
    1½ cups all-purpose flour
    2   tsp. baking powder

1. In a small bowl, beat eggs on medium speed until blended. Gradually beat in sugar until thick and lemon colored. Add butter and vanilla. Combine flour and baking powder; gradually add to egg mixture. Invert two 6-oz. custard cups on paper towels; coat with cooking spray.
2. Prepare cookies in a preheated pizzelle cookie maker according to manufacturer's directions, using 2 Tbsp. batter for each cookie. Immediately remove pizzelles and drape over inverted custard cups. To shape cookies into bowls, place another custard cup coated with cooking spray over each pizzelle. Let stand until set. Remove from custard cups and set aside. Repeat with remaining batter.
NOTE To make ice cream bowls in the oven, line a baking sheet with parchment. Draw two 7-in. circles on the paper. Spread 2 Tbsp. batter over each circle. Bake at 400° for 4-5 minutes or until edges are golden brown. Immediately remove cookies and drape over inverted custard cups. Shape into bowls as directed above. Store in an airtight container.
1 BOWL 145 cal., 7g fat (4g sat. fat), 50mg chol., 119mg sod., 19g carb. (10g sugars, 0 fiber), 2g pro.

CLASSIC ALMOND RICOTTA CAKE

CLASSIC ALMOND RICOTTA CAKE

After I started making homemade ricotta cheese, I was inspired to use it in dessert recipes, not just savory dishes. This is a simple, yet delicious dessert full of almond flavor and melt-in-your-mouth texture. It is elegant enough to serve to guests, while simple enough for a sweet snack during the week. You can use a hand mixer if you do not have a stand mixer. You can even add ingredients like lemon zest or fresh blueberries for a change of pace.
—Carrie Dault, Baxter, TN

PREP: 20 min. • **BAKE:** 45 min. + cooling
MAKES: 12 servings

    ½   cup unsalted butter, softened
    1   cup sugar
    2   large eggs, room temperature
    1¼   tsp. almond extract
    1   tsp. vanilla extract
    1½   cups all-purpose flour
    1¼   tsp. baking powder
    ¼   tsp. salt
    1   carton (15 oz.) whole-milk ricotta cheese
    ¾   cup sliced almonds
         Confectioners' sugar, optional

1. Preheat oven to 350°. In a large bowl, cream butter and sugar until light and fluffy, 5-7 minutes. Add eggs, 1 at a time, beating well after each addition. Beat in extracts. Sift flour, baking powder and salt together; gradually add to creamed mixture alternately with ricotta. Spread into a greased 9-in. springform pan. Sprinkle with almonds.
2. Bake until a toothpick inserted near the center comes out with moist crumbs, 45-50 minutes. Cool on a wire rack for 15 minutes. Loosen sides from pan with a knife; remove rim from pan. Allow cake to cool completely. If desired, dust with confectioners' sugar before serving.
1 PIECE 289 cal., 15g fat (8g sat. fat), 66mg chol., 155mg sod., 32g carb. (19g sugars, 1g fiber), 8g pro.

BOURBON ICE CREAM

BOURBON ICE CREAM

The brown sugar in this decadent ice cream gives a hint of caramel flavor, which complements the bourbon. When the custard is still liquid, before it goes into the ice cream maker, you can add more or less bourbon to suit your taste.
—*Peggy Woodward, Shullsburg, WI*

PREP: 15 min. + chilling
PROCESS: 25 min./batch + freezing
MAKES: 5 cups

- 2 cups heavy whipping cream
- 2 cups 2% milk
- ¾ cup packed brown sugar
- ⅛ tsp. salt
- 6 large egg yolks
- 3 to 4 Tbsp. bourbon
- 2 tsp. vanilla extract

1. In a large heavy saucepan, combine cream, milk, sugar and salt. Heat over medium heat until bubbles form around side of pan, stirring to dissolve sugar.
2. In a small bowl, whisk a small amount of the hot mixture into the egg yolks; return all to the pan, whisking constantly. Cook over low heat until mixture is just thick enough to coat a metal spoon and temperature reaches 180°, stirring constantly. Do not allow to boil. Immediately transfer to a bowl.
3. Place bowl in a pan of ice water. Stir gently and occasionally for 2 minutes. Stir in bourbon and vanilla. Press waxed paper onto surface of mixture. Refrigerate several hours or overnight.
4. Fill cylinder of ice cream maker two-thirds full; freeze according to manufacturer's directions. (Refrigerate remaining mixture until ready to freeze.) Transfer ice cream to a freezer container; freeze until firm, 4-6 hours. Repeat with remaining mixture.

½ CUP 295 cal., 21g fat (13g sat. fat), 169mg chol., 75mg sod., 20g carb. (20g sugars, 0 fiber), 5g pro.

GRANDMA'S
STRAWBERRY
SHORTCAKE

GRANDMA'S STRAWBERRY SHORTCAKE

I can still taste the juicy berries piled over warm biscuits and topped with a dollop of fresh whipped cream. My father added even more indulgence to the dessert by first buttering his biscuits.

—Shirley Joan Helfenbein, Lapeer, MI

PREP: 30 min. • **BAKE:** 20 min. + cooling
MAKES: 8 servings

- 2 cups all-purpose flour
- 2 Tbsp. sugar
- 3 tsp. baking powder
- ½ tsp. salt
- ½ cup cold butter, cubed
- 1 large egg, room temperature, beaten
- ⅔ cup half-and-half cream
- 1 cup heavy whipping cream
- 2 Tbsp. confectioners' sugar
- ⅛ tsp. vanilla extract
  Additional butter
- 1½ cups fresh strawberries, sliced

1. Preheat oven to 450°. In a large bowl, combine flour, sugar, baking powder and salt. Cut in butter until mixture resembles coarse crumbs. In another bowl, whisk egg and half-and-half. Add all at once to crumb mixture; stir just until moistened.
2. Spread batter into a greased 8-in. round baking pan, slightly building up the edge. Bake until golden brown, 16-18 minutes. Remove from pan; cool on a wire rack.
3. Beat heavy cream until it begins to thicken. Add confectioners' sugar and vanilla; beat until stiff peaks form. Split cake in half crosswise; butter bottom layer. Spoon half the strawberries over bottom layer. Spread with some whipped cream. Cover with top cake layer. Top with remaining berries and whipped cream. Cut into wedges.
1 PIECE 381 cal., 25g fat (16g sat. fat), 98mg chol., 447mg sod., 32g carb. (8g sugars, 1g fiber), 6g pro.

JUMBO BROWNIE COOKIES

JUMBO BROWNIE COOKIES

Bring these deeply fudgy cookies to a party, and you're sure to make a friend. A little espresso powder in the dough makes them over-the-top good.

—Rebecca Cababa, Las Vegas, NV

PREP: 20 min. • **BAKE:** 15 min./batch
MAKES: about 1½ dozen

- 2⅔ cups 60% cacao bittersweet chocolate baking chips
- ½ cup unsalted butter, cubed
- 4 large eggs, room temperature
- 1½ cups sugar
- 4 tsp. vanilla extract
- 2 tsp. instant espresso powder, optional
- ⅔ cup all-purpose flour
- ½ tsp. baking powder
- ¼ tsp. salt
- 1 pkg. (11½ oz.) semisweet chocolate chunks

1. Preheat oven to 350°. In a large saucepan, melt chocolate chips and butter over low heat, stirring until smooth. Remove from heat; cool until mixture is warm.
2. In a small bowl, whisk the eggs, sugar, vanilla and, if desired, espresso powder until blended. Whisk into chocolate mixture. In another bowl, mix the flour, baking powder and salt; add to chocolate mixture, mixing well. Fold in chocolate chunks; let stand until mixture thickens slightly, about 10 minutes.
3. Drop by ¼ cupfuls 3 in. apart onto parchment-lined baking sheets. Bake until set, 12-14 minutes. Cool on pans 1-2 minutes. Remove to wire racks to cool.
1 COOKIE 350 cal., 19g fat (11g sat. fat), 60mg chol., 65mg sod., 48g carb. (40g sugars, 3g fiber), 4g pro.

COLORFUL DEVILED EGGS P. 159

WHAT CAN I BRING?

Sometimes the party isn't at your place and you're asked to bring a dish. Or your guests need a little guidance on what they can contribute. Read on for a treasure trove of recipes that are travel-worthy and always welcome at any potluck.

SMOKY
MACARONI
& CHEESE

MISSISSIPPI MUD PIE

My grandmother, mother and aunts always made this dish for family gatherings. Now I make it for just about every event because it's so easy to prepare and everyone loves it—there are never any leftovers!
—*Elizabeth Williston, Thibodaux, LA*

PREP: 30 min. • **BAKE:** 15 min. + cooling
MAKES: 12 servings

- 1 cup all-purpose flour
- 1 cup chopped pecans
- ½ cup butter, softened
- 1 pkg. (5.9 oz.) instant chocolate pudding mix
- 1 pkg. (8 oz.) cream cheese, softened
- 1 cup confectioners' sugar
- 1 container (16 oz.) frozen whipped topping, thawed, divided
  Optional: Toasted chopped pecans and chocolate curls

1. Preheat oven to 350°. In a large bowl, beat flour, pecans and butter until blended. Press into bottom of a 13x9-in. baking dish. Bake until golden brown, about 15 minutes. Remove to a wire rack; cool completely.
2. Make chocolate pudding according to package directions; let stand 5 minutes.
3. Beat cream cheese and confectioners' sugar until smooth; fold in 1 cup whipped topping. Spread cream cheese mixture over cooled crust. Spread pudding over cream cheese layer; top with remaining whipped topping. If desired, top with additional pecans and chocolate curls.
1 PIECE 466 cal., 29g fat (17g sat. fat), 46mg chol., 214mg sod., 44g carb. (28g sugars, 2g fiber), 5g pro.

SMOKY MACARONI & CHEESE

I found this recipe years ago and kept experimenting until I found the perfect combination. You can make it in the oven, but grilling or smoking it is the best way to go. Assemble it at home and cook it on the grill at a cookout, or cook it at home and reheat for a potluck.
—*Stacey Dull, Gettysburg, OH*

PREP: 40 min. • **GRILL:** 20 min. + standing
MAKES: 2 casseroles (8 servings each)

- 6 cups small pasta shells
- 12 oz. Velveeta, cut into small cubes
- 2 cups shredded smoked cheddar cheese, divided
- 1 cup shredded cheddar cheese
- 1 cup 2% milk
- 4 large eggs, lightly beaten
- ¾ cup heavy whipping cream
- ⅔ cup half-and-half cream
- ½ cup shredded provolone cheese
- ½ cup shredded Colby-Monterey Jack cheese
- ½ cup shredded pepper jack cheese
- 1 tsp. salt
- ½ tsp. pepper
- ½ tsp. smoked paprika
- ½ tsp. liquid smoke, optional
  Dash cayenne pepper, optional
- 8 bacon strips, cooked and crumbled, optional

1. Preheat grill or smoker to 350°. Cook pasta according to package directions for al dente. Drain and transfer to a large bowl. Stir in Velveeta, 1 cup smoked cheddar, cheddar cheese, milk, eggs, heavy cream, half-and-half, provolone, Colby-Monterey Jack, pepper jack, salt, pepper, paprika and, if desired, liquid smoke and cayenne pepper.
2. Transfer to 2 greased 13x9-in. baking pans; sprinkle with the remaining 1 cup smoked cheddar cheese. Place on grill or smoker rack. Grill or smoke, covered, until a thermometer reads at least 160°, 20-25 minutes, rotating pans partway through cooking. Do not overcook. Let stand 10 minutes before serving; if desired, sprinkle with bacon.
1 CUP 403 cal., 23g fat (13g sat. fat), 117mg chol., 670mg sod., 30g carb. (4g sugars, 1g fiber), 18g pro.

MISSISSIPPI MUD PIE

MACARONI COLESLAW

My friend Peggy brought this coleslaw to one of our picnics, and everyone liked it so much, we all had to have the recipe.
—*Sandra Matteson, Westhope, ND*

PREP: 25 min. + chilling
MAKES: 16 servings

- 1 pkg. (7 oz.) ring macaroni or ditalini
- 1 pkg. (14 oz.) coleslaw mix
- 2 medium onions, finely chopped
- 2 celery ribs, finely chopped
- 1 medium cucumber, finely chopped
- 1 medium green pepper, finely chopped
- 1 can (8 oz.) whole water chestnuts, drained and chopped

DRESSING
- 1½ cups Miracle Whip Light
- ⅓ cup sugar
- ¼ cup cider vinegar
- ½ tsp. salt
- ¼ tsp. pepper

1. Cook macaroni according to package directions; drain and rinse in cold water. Transfer to a large bowl; add coleslaw mix, onions, celery, cucumber, green pepper and water chestnuts.
2. In a small bowl, whisk the dressing ingredients. Pour over salad; toss to coat. Cover and refrigerate for at least 1 hour.
¾ CUP 150 cal., 5g fat (1g sat. fat), 6mg chol., 286mg sod., 24g carb. (12g sugars, 2g fiber), 3g pro. **DIABETIC EXCHANGES** 1 starch, 1 vegetable, 1 fat.

"KOOL" FACT

The term coleslaw is derived from the Dutch word *koolsla*, literally translated as "cabbage salad." The term has evolved to refer to many types of crunchy, shredded-vegetable salads that hold up well after being dressed.

PEACH CRUMB BARS

PEACH CRUMB BARS

I had the most beautiful peaches and really wanted to bake with them. I started with my blueberry crumb bar recipe, and after a couple of tries, I was so happy with the results. My co-worker taste testers were too!
—*Amy Burns, Newman, IL*

PREP: 30 min. • **BAKE:** 40 min. + cooling
MAKES: 2 dozen

- 3 cups all-purpose flour
- 1½ cups sugar, divided
- 1 tsp. baking powder
- ½ tsp. salt
   Dash ground cinnamon
- 1 cup shortening
- 1 large egg
- 1 tsp. vanilla extract
- 3 lbs. peaches, peeled and chopped
- 1 tsp. almond extract
- 4 tsp. cornstarch

1. Preheat oven to 375°. Whisk flour, 1 cup sugar, baking powder, salt and cinnamon; cut in shortening until crumbly. In another bowl, whisk egg and vanilla until blended; add to the flour mixture, stirring with a fork until crumbly.
2. Reserve 2½ cups of the crumb mixture for topping. Press the remaining mixture onto the bottom of a greased 13x9-in. baking pan.
3. Toss peaches with almond extract. In another bowl, mix cornstarch and remaining sugar; add to the peaches and toss to coat. Spread over crust; sprinkle with the reserved topping.
4. Bake until topping is lightly browned and filling is bubbly, 40-45 minutes. Cool completely in pan on a wire rack. Cut into bars.
1 BAR 207 cal., 9g fat (2g sat. fat), 8mg chol., 73mg sod., 30g carb. (17g sugars, 1g fiber), 2g pro.

TAKE A DIP!

Spontaneous potlucks call for simple, scrumptious snacks. These five-ingredient (or less!) dips will make a splash at any bash.

GARLIC BLUE CHEESE DIP

SMOKED SALMON DIP

MUSTARD DIP

BACON CHEDDAR DIP

YUMMY CHOCOLATE DIP

BACON CHEDDAR DIP

Combine 2 cups sour cream, 1 cup finely shredded cheddar cheese, 1 envelope ranch salad dressing mix and 2-4 cooked and crumbled strips of bacon. Refrigerate, covered, for at least 1 hour. Serve with crackers and/or vegetables.

CUCUMBER ONION DIP

Beat one 8-oz. pkg. softened cream cheese, ½ cup finely chopped seeded peeled cucumber, ¼ cup finely chopped onion, 2 Tbsp. mayonnaise, ⅛ tsp. salt and ⅛ tsp. pepper until blended. Refrigerate until serving. Serve with rye chips or crackers.

GARLIC BLUE CHEESE DIP

In a blender, combine ½ cup milk, one 8-oz. pkg. cubed cream cheese, 1 cup crumbled blue cheese and 2 cloves peeled garlic; cover and process until blended. Serve with crackers.

HONEY PEANUT APPLE DIP

Beat one 8-oz. pkg. cream cheese until smooth. Beat in 1 cup finely chopped peanuts, ⅔ cup honey and 1 tsp. vanilla extract until combined. Serve with apples. Refrigerate leftovers.

HORSERADISH CRAB DIP

Beat one 8-oz. pkg. cream cheese, 2-3 Tbsp. picante sauce and 1-2 Tbsp. prepared horseradish until blended. Stir in one 6-oz. can crabmeat. Serve with celery.

With a variety of dips, offer a choice of dunkers and dippers: sliced fresh fruit, crackers, pretzels, breadsticks, warm pita bread or thick potato chips.

MUSTARD DIP

Combine one 14-oz. can sweetened condensed milk, ¼ cup ground or prepared mustard, 3 Tbsp. prepared horseradish and 1 Tbsp. Worcestershire sauce until smooth (dip will thicken as it stands). Serve with pretzels. Store in the refrigerator.

PEANUT BUTTER FRUIT DIP

Combine 1 cup vanilla yogurt, ½ cup peanut butter and ⅛ tsp. ground cinnamon; mix well. Fold in ½ cup whipped topping. Refrigerate until serving. Serve with fruit.

RANCH JALAPENO DIP

In a blender or food processor, prepare 1 envelope ranch salad dressing mix according to package directions. Add 2 pickled seeded jalapeno peppers, 1 seeded jalapeno pepper and 2 Tbsp. minced fresh cilantro; cover and process 2-3 minutes or until combined. Refrigerate, covered, at least 1 hour. Serve with tortilla chips.

SMOKED SALMON DIP

Place one 16-oz. can drained pitted ripe olives and 8 green onions cut into 2-in. pieces in a blender or food processor; cover and process for about 15 seconds. Add one 14¾-oz. can pink salmon, ⅔ cup mayonnaise and, if desired, 8 drops liquid smoke; process until dip reaches desired consistency. Chill. Serve with crackers.

YUMMY CHOCOLATE DIP

In a microwave, melt ¾ cup semisweet chocolate chips; stir until smooth. Stir in ½ cup of one 8-oz. carton whipped topping, ½ tsp. ground cinnamon and ½ tsp. rum or vanilla extract; cool for 5 minutes. Fold in remaining whipped topping. Serve with fruit. Refrigerate leftovers.

SHRIMP COCKTAIL WITH HOMEMADE DIPPING SAUCE

During the '60s, shrimp cocktail was one of the most popular party foods around, and it's still a crowd favorite. I serve it for every special occasion as well as small plate-style meals.
—*Peggy Allen, Pasadena, CA*

PREP: 30 min. + chilling
MAKES: about 6 dozen (1¼ cups sauce)

- 3 qt. water
- 1 small onion, sliced
- ½ medium lemon, sliced
- 2 sprigs fresh parsley
- 1 Tbsp. salt
- 5 whole peppercorns
- 1 bay leaf
- ¼ tsp. dried thyme
- 3 lbs. uncooked large shrimp, peeled and deveined (tails on)

SAUCE
- 1 cup chili sauce
- 2 Tbsp. lemon juice
- 2 Tbsp. prepared horseradish
- 4 tsp. Worcestershire sauce
- ½ tsp. salt
  Dash cayenne pepper
  Lemon wedges, optional

1. In a Dutch oven, combine the first 8 ingredients; bring to a boil. Add shrimp. Reduce heat; simmer, uncovered, until shrimp turn pink, 4-5 minutes.
2. Drain shrimp and immediately rinse in cold water. Refrigerate until cold, 2-3 hours. In a small bowl, combine the sauce ingredients. Refrigerate until serving.
3. Arrange shrimp on a serving platter; serve with sauce. If desired, serve with lemon wedges.

1 OZ. COOKED SHRIMP WITH ABOUT 2 TSP. SAUCE 59 cal., 1g fat (0 sat. fat), 66mg chol., 555mg sod., 4g carb. (2g sugars, 0 fiber), 9g pro.

SHRIMP COCKTAIL WITH HOMEMADE DIPPING SAUCE

CHICKEN & SAUSAGE TORTELLINI ALFREDO CASSEROLE

3. Meanwhile, unroll the crescent dough; press perforations to seal. Spread pesto on top. Roll up jelly-roll style, starting with short side; pinch seam to seal. Using a serrated knife, cut crosswise into 8 slices.
4. Remove casserole from oven; arrange slices over casserole, cut side up. Bake, uncovered, until rolls are golden brown, 15-20 minutes longer. Sprinkle with cheese. If desired, top with torn basil leaves.
1 SERVING 523 cal., 27g fat (12g sat. fat), 101mg chol., 1176mg sod., 38g carb. (4g sugars, 2g fiber), 32g pro.

CHICKEN & SAUSAGE TORTELLINI ALFREDO CASSEROLE

Pesto pinwheel rolls top this golden-crusted casserole. With its spicy Italian sausage, sun-dried tomatoes, plump cheese tortellini and velvety Alfredo sauce, this dish makes a thoroughly satisfying meal.
—*Jeanne Holt, Mendota Heights, MN*

PREP: 15 min. • **BAKE:** 45 min.
MAKES: 8 servings

- 1 pkg. (9 oz.) refrigerated cheese tortellini
- 1 jar (15 oz.) Alfredo sauce
- 1 can (14 oz.) water-packed quartered artichoke hearts, drained
- 1 pkg. (12 oz.) fully cooked Italian chicken sausage links, cut into ½-in. slices
- 2 cups shredded cooked chicken breast
- 1 cup shredded Italian cheese blend
- ½ cup oil-packed sun-dried tomatoes, chopped

TOPPING
- 1 pkg. (8 oz.) refrigerated crescent rolls
- ⅓ cup prepared pesto
- ¼ cup shredded Italian cheese blend
  Torn fresh basil leaves, optional

1. Preheat oven to 350°. In a 6-qt. stockpot, cook tortellini according to package directions, reducing cook time to 5 minutes. Drain; return to pot. Add the Alfredo sauce, artichoke hearts, sausage, chicken, cheese and tomatoes; toss gently to combine.
2. Transfer mixture to a greased 2-qt. baking pan, spreading evenly. Bake, covered, 30 minutes.

PRETTY DELICIOUS

Infused water makes a lovely addition to the party table—so much nicer than plain ice water! Combine the ingredients with 2 qt. cold water, and refrigerate 12-24 hours. Strain before serving.

RASPBERRY & LEMON
1 cup fresh raspberries
3 lemon slices

ROSEMARY & GINGER
3 fresh rosemary sprigs
1 Tbsp. minced fresh gingerroot

TANGERINE & THYME
2 tangerines, sliced
3 fresh thyme sprigs

9 ESSENTIAL TIPS THAT MAKE TRAVELING WITH FOOD SO MUCH EASIER

Consider these ingenious hacks the next time you're transporting food.

KEEP YOUR SLOW COOKER'S LID ON TIGHT

Wrap a small bungee cord around (or thread it through) the lid's top handle; hook each end onto the slow cooker's side handles. Give it a wiggle to make sure it's good to go.

KEEP CAKES INTACT

Before assembling a cake, place a dab of frosting in the middle of the cake plate or cake board. The frosting acts as a glue to prevent the cake from slipping as you decorate, and helps the cake stay put in the car. For insurance, bring along decorating tools in an emergency cake toolkit so you can fix up smudges.

PREVENT FOOD FROM SLIDING IN THE BACKSEAT

Yoga mats and drawer liners are no-slip by design, so they make a great liner for your trunk or backseat to keep your food from slipping and sliding during travel. You can trust that even elaborate layer cakes will be safe with this simple setup.

MAKE ASSEMBLY EASY WITH A TO-GO SALAD KIT

To ensure your salad won't get soggy before you get to the party, prep all your ingredients separately in reusable containers and place them in a large serving bowl along with a bag of greens, a bottle of dressing and your serving tools. When you reach your destination, simply toss everything together and serve.

KEEP COOKIES IN PLACE

Line your cookie plate with a pretty kitchen towel or linen napkin and place your baked goods on top. Cover with plastic wrap, and your cookies and other baked goods won't budge.

KEEP HEAVY BAKES IN FOIL PANS FROM CAVING IN

Disposable foil pans are useful and convenient, but are prone to caving in when filled heavy ingredients. Slide a baking sheet underneath the foil pan for support. This will also make handling easier if the foil pan is hot out of the oven.

GIVE COLD DISHES AN EXTRA LAYER OF INSULATION

News flash: Newspaper makes a good insulator. To keep something extra cold, line a cooler with some newspaper and tuck it around and over your chilled dish.

KEEP LIDS IN PLACE

Painter's tape will keep lids in place without leaving a residue—so there won't be any marks on Grandma's vintage baking dish. Peel off the tape before serving.

TRANSPORT HOMEMADE SAUCES SAFELY

The best way to transport salsas and other homemade sauces is to pour them in a soup canister, Mason jar or large water bottle, and then place in your cupholder for the ride.

MINI MUFFULETTA

Mediterranean meets comfort food when French rolls are slathered with olive spread and stuffed with layers of salami and cheese. You can make these muffulettas the night before and cut them into appetizer-sized slices just before serving.

—*Gareth Craner, Minden, NV*

PREP: 25 min. + chilling • **MAKES:** 3 dozen

- 1 cup pimiento-stuffed olives, drained and chopped
- 1 can (4¼ oz.) chopped ripe olives
- 1 Tbsp. balsamic vinegar
- 1½ tsp. red wine vinegar
- 1½ tsp. olive oil
- 1 garlic clove, minced
- ½ tsp. dried basil
- ½ tsp. dried oregano
- 6 French rolls, split
- ½ lb. thinly sliced hard salami
- ¼ lb. sliced provolone cheese
- ½ lb. thinly sliced cotto salami
- ¼ lb. sliced part-skim mozzarella cheese

1. In a large bowl, combine the first 8 ingredients; set aside. Hollow out tops and bottoms of rolls, leaving ¾-in. shells (discard removed bread or save for another use).
2. Spread the olive mixture over tops and bottoms of rolls. On roll bottoms, layer hard salami, provolone cheese, cotto salami and mozzarella cheese. Replace tops.
3. Wrap tightly. Refrigerate overnight. Cut each into 6 wedges; secure sandwiches with toothpicks.

1 WEDGE 119 cal., 8g fat (3g sat. fat), 16mg chol., 537mg sod., 7g carb. (0 sugars, 0 fiber), 6g pro.

CARAMEL-PECAN MONKEY BREAD

Everyone will get a kick out of pulling off gooey pieces of this delectable monkey bread. It's hard to resist the caramel-coated treat.
—Taste of Home *Test Kitchen*

PREP: 20 min. + chilling
BAKE: 30 min. + cooling
MAKES: 20 servings

- 1 pkg. (¼ oz.) active dry yeast
- ¼ cup warm water (110° to 115°)
- 5 Tbsp. plus ½ cup butter, divided
- 1¼ cups warm 2% milk (110° to 115°)
- 2 large eggs, room temperature
- 1¼ cups sugar, divided
- 1 tsp. salt
- 5 cups all-purpose flour
- 1 tsp. ground cinnamon

CARAMEL
- ⅔ cup packed brown sugar
- ¼ cup butter, cubed
- ¼ cup heavy whipping cream
- ¾ cup chopped pecans, divided

GLAZE (OPTIONAL)
- 4 oz. cream cheese, softened
- ¼ cup butter, softened
- 1½ cups confectioners' sugar
- 3 to 5 Tbsp. 2% milk

1. Dissolve yeast in warm water. Melt 5 Tbsp. butter. Add milk, eggs and the melted butter; stir in ¼ cup sugar, salt and 3 cups flour. Beat on medium speed for 3 minutes. Stir in enough of the remaining flour to form a firm dough.

2. Turn dough onto a floured surface; knead until smooth and elastic, 6-8 minutes. Place in a greased bowl, turning once to grease the top. Refrigerate, covered, overnight.

3. Punch dough down; shape into 40 balls (about 1¼ in. diameter). Melt remaining ½ cup butter. In a shallow bowl, combine cinnamon and the remaining 1 cup sugar. Dip balls in the butter, then roll in the sugar mixture.

4. For caramel, in a small saucepan over medium heat, bring brown sugar, butter and cream to a boil. Cook and stir for 3 minutes. Pour half the caramel into a greased 10-in. fluted tube pan; layer with half the pecans and half the dough balls; repeat. Cover and let rise until doubled, about 45 minutes.

5. Preheat oven to 350°. Bake until golden brown, 30-40 minutes. (Cover loosely with foil for last 10 minutes if top browns too quickly.) Cool 10 minutes before inverting onto a serving plate.

6. For glaze (if desired), beat cream cheese and butter until blended; gradually beat in confectioners' sugar. Add enough milk to reach desired consistency. Drizzle glaze over warm bread.

2 PIECES 334 cal., 15g fat (8g sat. fat), 52mg chol., 207mg sod., 45g carb. (21g sugars, 1g fiber), 5g pro.

MARINATED
SAUSAGE
KABOBS

MARINATED SAUSAGE KABOBS

These flavorful and colorful appetizers are so fun, they'll be the talk of the party. And they're so easy. Simply assemble the day before and forget about them! Your guests will love the marinade flavor.
—*Joanne Boone, Danville, OH*

- -

PREP: 20 min. + marinating
MAKES: 3 dozen

- ¼ cup olive oil
- 1 Tbsp. white vinegar
- ½ tsp. minced garlic
- ½ tsp. dried basil
- ½ tsp. dried oregano
- 8 oz. cheddar cheese, cut into ¾-in. cubes
- 1 can (6 oz.) pitted ripe olives, drained
- 8 oz. hard salami, cut into ¾-in. cubes
- 1 medium sweet red pepper, cut into ¾-in. pieces
- 1 medium green pepper, cut into ¾-in. pieces

1. In a large shallow dish, combine the first 5 ingredients; add the remaining ingredients. Stir to coat; refrigerate at least 4 hours. Drain, discarding marinade.
2. For kabobs, thread cheese, olives, salami and peppers onto toothpicks.
1 KABOB 69 cal., 6g fat (2g sat. fat), 12mg chol., 165mg sod., 1g carb. (0 sugars, 0 fiber), 3g pro.

PINEAPPLE CHEESE BALL

PINEAPPLE CHEESE BALL

Pineapple lends a fruity tang to this fun and tasty appetizer.
—*Anne Halfhill, Sunbury, OH*

- -

PREP: 20 min. + chilling
MAKES: 1 cheese ball (3 cups)

- 2 pkg. (8 oz. each) cream cheese, softened
- 1 can (8 oz.) unsweetened crushed pineapple, drained
- ¼ cup finely chopped green pepper
- 2 Tbsp. finely chopped onion
- 2 tsp. seasoned salt
- 1½ cups finely chopped walnuts
  Optional: Assorted crackers and fresh vegetables

1. In a small bowl, beat the softened cream cheese, pineapple, green pepper, onion and seasoned salt until blended. Refrigerate, covered, for 30 minutes.
2. Shape into a ball (mixture will be soft); coat in walnuts. Refrigerated, covered, overnight. Serve with crackers and vegetables if desired.
2 TBSP. 87 cal., 8g fat (2g sat. fat), 10mg chol., 155mg sod., 3g carb. (1g sugars, 1g fiber), 3g pro.

#GIRLDINNER

Instead of making 1 large cheese ball, make 2 smaller balls—1 to take to the party and 1 for home! Cheese balls keep for up to 2 weeks in the fridge, so this is nice to have on hand to add to a plate with fresh fruit, vegetables and crackers or flatbread, such as pita or naan.

BLUEBERRY PAN-CAKE WITH MAPLE FROSTING

This cake is a fun and appropriate contribution to a brunch potluck—the batter is made with pancake mix!
—*Matthew Hass, Ellison Bay, WI*

PREP: 10 min. • **BAKE:** 15 min. + cooling
MAKES: 12 servings

- 3 cups complete buttermilk pancake mix
- 1¾ cups water
- 1 cup fresh blueberries
- 2 tsp. all-purpose flour

FROSTING
- 2 cups confectioners' sugar
- ⅓ cup maple syrup
- ¼ cup butter, softened

1. Stir pancake mix and water just until moistened. In another bowl, toss blueberries with flour. Fold into batter.
2. Transfer to a greased 13x9-in. baking pan. Bake at 350° until a toothpick inserted in center comes out clean, 15-18 minutes. Cool in pan on a wire rack.
3. Beat frosting ingredients until smooth; spread over completely cooled cake.
1 PIECE 257 cal., 5g fat (2g sat. fat), 10mg chol., 449mg sod., 51g carb. (30g sugars, 1g fiber), 3g pro.

CRAB WONTON CUPS

CRAB WONTON CUPS

Add these tasty little crab tarts to your list of special-occasion finger foods. They're excellent served warm and crispy from the oven.
—*Connie McDowell, Greenwood, DE*

TAKES: 30 min. • **MAKES:** 32 appetizers

- 32 wonton wrappers
  Cooking spray
- 1 pkg. (8 oz.) cream cheese, softened
- ½ cup heavy whipping cream
- 1 large egg, room temperature
- 1 Tbsp. Dijon mustard
- 1 tsp. Worcestershire sauce
- 5 drops hot pepper sauce
- 1 cup lump crabmeat, drained
- ¼ cup thinly sliced green onions
- ¼ cup finely chopped sweet red pepper
- 1 cup grated Parmesan cheese
  Minced chives, optional

1. Preheat oven to 350°. Press the wonton wrappers into miniature muffin cups coated with cooking spray. Spritz wrappers with cooking spray. Bake until lightly browned, 8-9 minutes.
2. Meanwhile, in a small bowl, beat cream cheese, cream, egg, mustard, Worcestershire sauce and pepper sauce until smooth. Stir in crab, green onions and red pepper; spoon into the wonton cups. Sprinkle with grated Parmesan cheese.
3. Bake until filling is heated through, 10-12 minutes. Serve warm. If desired, garnish with minced chives. Refrigerate leftovers.
1 WONTON CUP 77 cal., 5g fat (3g sat. fat), 26mg chol., 153mg sod., 5g carb. (0 sugars, 0 fiber), 3g pro.

CHEESEBURGER
BOMBS

CHEESEBURGER BOMBS

Instead of enjoying your cheeseburger on a bun, have it in one! These bundles are a perfect take-along option.
—Taste of Home *Test Kitchen*

PREP: 25 min. • **BAKE:** 20 min.
MAKES: 8 servings

- ½ lb. ground beef
- ¼ cup chopped onion
- ¼ cup crumbled cooked bacon
- ¼ cup ketchup
- 2 Tbsp. prepared mustard
- 2 Tbsp. chopped dill pickle or pickle relish
- 1 tube (16.3 oz.) large refrigerated buttermilk biscuits
- ½ cup shredded cheddar cheese
- 1 large egg, beaten
- ½ tsp. sesame seeds

1. Preheat oven to 350°. In a large skillet, cook beef and onion over medium heat until the beef is no longer pink and the onion is tender, 3-4 minutes, breaking up beef into crumbles; drain. Stir in bacon, ketchup, mustard and pickles; cool slightly.
2. On a lightly floured surface, roll each biscuit into a 5-in. circle. Add 1 Tbsp. cheese in the center of each biscuit; top with 2 Tbsp. of the meat mixture. Bring biscuit dough over filling to center; pinch to seal.
3. Place rolls seam side down on a parchment-lined baking sheet. Brush tops with beaten egg; sprinkle with sesame seeds. Bake until golden brown, 18-20 minutes. Serve warm.
1 CHEESEBURGER BOMB 276 cal., 13g fat (5g sat. fat), 27mg chol., 897mg sod., 28g carb. (5g sugars, 1g fiber), 12g pro.

CREAMY MAKE-AHEAD MASHED POTATOES

My recipe takes mashed potatoes to the next level with a savory topping of cheese, onions and bacon.
—JoAnn Koerkenmeier, Damiansville, IL

PREP: 35 min. + chilling • **BAKE:** 40 min.
MAKES: 10 servings

- 3 lbs. potatoes (about 9 medium), peeled and cubed
- 6 bacon strips, chopped
- 8 oz. cream cheese, softened
- ½ cup sour cream
- ½ cup butter, cubed
- ¼ cup 2% milk
- 1½ tsp. onion powder
- 1 tsp. salt
- 1 tsp. garlic powder
- ½ tsp. pepper
- 1 cup shredded cheddar cheese
- 3 green onions, chopped

1. Place potatoes in a Dutch oven; cover with water. Bring to a boil. Reduce heat; cook, uncovered, for 10-15 minutes or until tender.
2. Meanwhile, in a skillet, cook bacon over medium heat until crisp. Remove to paper towels with a slotted spoon; drain.
3. Drain potatoes; return to pan. Mash potatoes, gradually adding cream cheese, sour cream and butter. Stir in milk and seasonings. Transfer to a greased 13x9-in. baking dish; sprinkle with cheese, green onions and bacon. Refrigerate, covered, up to 1-2 days.
4. Preheat oven to 350°. Remove potatoes from refrigerator and let stand while the oven heats. Bake, covered, 30 minutes. Uncover; bake 10 minutes longer or until heated through.
¾ CUP 419 cal., 24g fat (15g sat. fat), 74mg chol., 544mg sod., 41g carb. (4g sugars, 4g fiber), 11g pro.

JAZZED-UP FRENCH BREAD

This is a perfect dish to take to a cookout—it's easy to make, and who doesn't love cheesy bread? Prepare it at home and wrap it in foil, then put it on the grill when you arrive.
—*Lori LeCroy, East Tawas, MI*

PREP: 10 min. • **GRILL:** 25 min.
MAKES: 10 servings

- 2 cups shredded Colby-Monterey Jack cheese
- ⅔ cup mayonnaise
- 6 green onions, chopped
- 1 loaf (1 lb.) French bread, halved lengthwise

1. In a small bowl, combine the cheese, mayonnaise and onions. Spread over cut sides of bread and reassemble loaf. Wrap in a double thickness of heavy-duty foil (about 28x18 in.); seal tightly.
2. Grill, covered, over indirect medium heat for 25-30 minutes or until cheese is melted, turning once. Let stand for 5 minutes before cutting into slices.

1 PIECE 313 cal., 19g fat (7g sat. fat), 25mg chol., 491mg sod., 25g carb. (2g sugars, 1g fiber), 10g pro.

MUSHROOM CHEESE BREAD Combine 1 cup shredded mozzarella cheese, a 4-oz. can of drained mushroom stems and pieces, ⅓ cup mayonnaise and 2 Tbsp. each shredded Parmesan cheese and chopped green onion. Proceed as directed.

BACON GARLIC BREAD Combine ⅓ cup each mayonnaise and softened butter. Stir in 1 cup shredded Italian cheese blend, 4 crumbled cooked bacon strips and 5 minced garlic cloves. Proceed as directed.

JAZZED-UP
FRENCH
BREAD

COLORFUL DEVILED EGGS

CHOCOLATE LAVA CAKE

Individual lava cakes are a guaranteed crowd pleaser at dinner parties, but they're hard to take on the road. This rich, decadent slow-cooker version solves that! Everyone just loves it.
—*Latona Dwyer, Palm Beach Gardens, FL*

PREP: 15 min. • **COOK:** 3 hours
MAKES: 12 servings

- 1 pkg. devil's food cake mix (regular size)
- 1⅔ cups water
- 3 large eggs, room temperature
- ⅓ cup canola oil
- 2 cups cold 2% milk
- 1 pkg. (3.9 oz.) instant chocolate pudding mix
- 2 cups semisweet chocolate chips
  Whipped cream, optional

1. In a large bowl, combine cake mix, water, eggs and oil; beat on low speed for 30 seconds. Beat on medium for 2 minutes. Transfer to a greased 4-qt. slow cooker.
2. In another bowl, whisk milk and pudding mix for 2 minutes. Let stand until soft-set, about 2 minutes. Spoon over cake batter; sprinkle with chocolate chips. Cook, covered, on high until a toothpick inserted in the cake portion comes out with moist crumbs, 3-4 hours. Serve warm, with whipped cream if desired.

¾ CUP 215 cal., 10g fat (4g sat. fat), 28mg chol., 254mg sod., 32g carb. (22g sugars, 2g fiber), 3g pro.

TEST KITCHEN TIP
Use a slow-cooker liner to make cleanup a breeze.

COLORFUL DEVILED EGGS

These eye-catching classics bring a pop of color to baby showers, spring brunches and bridal get-togethers.
—*Taste of Home Test Kitchen*

TAKES: 20 min. • **MAKES:** 1 dozen

- 6 hard-boiled large eggs, peeled
- ¼ cup mayonnaise
- ½ tsp. ground mustard
- ¼ tsp. garlic powder
- ⅛ tsp. salt
- ⅛ tsp. pepper
  Assorted food coloring
- ⅛ tsp. paprika

1. Cut eggs in half lengthwise; remove yolks and set aside egg whites. Mash yolks. Mix in mayonnaise, mustard, garlic powder, salt and pepper. Cover and refrigerate while preparing egg whites.
2. Prepare food coloring according to package directions for egg dyeing. Dye egg whites to desired colors. Drain on paper towels. Spoon or pipe filling into egg whites; sprinkle with paprika. Refrigerate until serving.

1 STUFFED EGG HALF 70 cal., 6g fat (1g sat. fat), 95mg chol., 79mg sod., 0 carb. (0 sugars, 0 fiber), 3g pro.

PARTIES

HONEY
CHAMPAGNE
FONDUE
P. 167

MANGO
BELLINI
P. 170

CHAMPAGNE
BLONDIES
P. 171

NEW YEAR'S EVE

There's no better way to kick off another trip around the sun than with a party with your best friends. Who needs to go out and fight traffic and crowds when you can offer all the bubbles, bling and the best bites at home? So load up your plate, toss some confetti and raise your glass to the most epic party yet!

GREEK SHRIMP CANAPES

FRUIT & CHEESE BOARD

Who says cheese and charcuterie get to have all the fun? Make this a party favorite with any fruits that are in season.
—Taste of Home *Test Kitchen*

- -

TAKES: 25 minutes • **MAKES:** 14 servings

10	fresh strawberries, halved
8	fresh or dried figs, halved
2	small navel oranges, thinly sliced
12	oz. seedless red grapes (about 1½ cups)
1	medium mango, halved and scored
½	cup fresh blueberries
1	cup fresh blackberries
½	cup dried banana chips
2	large kiwifruit, peeled, halved and thinly sliced
12	oz. seedless watermelon (about 6 slices)
½	cup unblanched almonds
8	oz. Brie cheese
8	oz. mascarpone cheese
½	cup honey

On a large platter or cutting board, arrange fruit, almonds and cheeses. Place honey in a small jar; tuck jar among fruit.

1 SERVING 304 cal., 17g fat (8g sat. fat), 36mg chol., 116mg sod., 36g carb. (30g sugars, 4g fiber), 7g pro.

#GIRLDINNER

A fruit and cheese board can be dressed up to make a party spread dazzle, or a scaled-down version can provide a simple and fresh at-home dinner for one. See our Boards chapter (p. 68) for more ideas and tips for how to construct a showstopping board.

GREEK SHRIMP CANAPES

I grew up by the ocean and then moved to a land-locked state. I wanted to show people in my area how to easily cook seafood, and this is the recipe I came up with. It's become a neighborhood favorite.
—Amy Harris, Springville, UT

- -

PREP: 15 min. + marinating
COOK: 65 min. • **MAKES:** 2½ dozen

1½	cups olive oil
¾	cup lemon juice
⅔	cup dry white wine
¼	cup Greek seasoning
4	garlic cloves, minced
1	lb. uncooked shrimp (31-40 per lb.), peeled and deveined
2	large cucumbers
1	pkg. (8 oz.) cream cheese, softened Minced fresh parsley

1. In a large bowl, whisk the first 5 ingredients until blended. Pour 1½ cups marinade into a large bowl. Add shrimp and stir to coat. Cover and refrigerate 45 minutes.
2. Meanwhile, pour the remaining marinade into a 4- or 5-qt. slow cooker. Cook, covered, on high for 45 minutes.
3. Drain shrimp, discarding the marinade in bowl. Add shrimp to slow cooker. Cook, covered, on high until the shrimp turn pink, about 20 minutes longer, stirring once; drain.
4. Cut each cucumber into ¼-in.-thick slices. Scoop out centers, leaving bottoms intact. Pipe or spread cream cheese onto each cucumber slice; top with shrimp and parsley.

HEALTH TIP Slim down this appetizer further by using reduced-fat cream cheese.

1 CANAPE 68 cal., 6g fat (2g sat. fat), 26mg chol., 139mg sod., 1g carb. (1g sugars, 0 fiber), 3g pro.

FRUIT &
CHEESE
BOARD

FONDUE-MAKING TIPS

- Cheese melts more quickly and easily if it is shredded, grated or cut into small cubes. Cooking spray keeps the cheese from sticking to the cheese grater, making cleanup easy.

- Add a little cornstarch to the shredded cheese to help it bind with the wine or broth.

- Reduce the heat to low before beginning to add the cheese into hot liquids one handful at a time. Keep the heat at low while the cheese melts.

- Cheese fondues are often made with white wine. If you don't wish to use wine, substitute vegetable or chicken broth.

HONEY CHAMPAGNE FONDUE

HONEY CHAMPAGNE FONDUE

This special champagne fondue has wonderful flavor from Swiss cheese and a hint of sweetness from honey. It clings well to any kind of dipper.
—*Shannon Copley, Upper Arlington, OH*

TAKES: 30 min. • **MAKES:** 4 cups

- 1 Tbsp. cornstarch
- 1 tsp. ground mustard
- ¼ tsp. white pepper
- 1¼ cups champagne
- 1 tsp. lemon juice
- 2 Tbsp. finely chopped shallot
- 1 garlic clove, minced
- 1½ lbs. Swiss cheese, shredded
- 2 Tbsp. honey
  Pinch ground nutmeg
  Toasted French bread, asparagus, tart apple slices, endive spears or cooked shrimp

1. In a large saucepan, combine cornstarch, ground mustard and white pepper. Whisk in champagne and lemon juice until smooth. Add shallot and garlic; bring to a boil. Reduce heat to medium-low; cook and stir until thickened, about 1 minute. Gradually stir in cheese until melted. Stir in honey. Sprinkle with nutmeg.
2. Keep warm in a fondue pot or small slow cooker. Serve with toasted bread, asparagus, apple slices, endive or cooked shrimp as desired.

¼ CUP 256 cal., 18g fat (10g sat. fat), 53mg chol., 107mg sod., 5g carb. (3g sugars, 0 fiber), 15g pro.

MUSHROOM & OLIVE BRUSCHETTA

I tried this delicious bruschetta toast at a party and knew I had to make it myself. Since I couldn't find the person who brought the dish, I began trying to duplicate it on my own. The original was made on an English muffin, but party rye or baguette slices work as well.
—*Lynne German, Buford, GA*

PREP: 15 min. • **BAKE:** 10 min.
MAKES: 4 dozen

- 1½ cups finely shredded cheddar cheese
- ½ cup canned mushroom stems and pieces, drained and chopped
- ½ cup chopped green onions
- ½ cup chopped pitted green olives
- ½ cup chopped ripe olives
- ½ cup mayonnaise
- ¼ tsp. curry powder
- 2 French bread baguettes (10½ oz. each)
  Julienned green onions, optional

1. Preheat oven to 400°. In a large bowl, combine the first 7 ingredients. Cut each baguette into 24 slices; place on ungreased baking sheets. Bake until lightly toasted, about 5 minutes.
2. Top toasted baguette slices with cheese mixture. Bake until cheese is melted, 4-5 minutes. If desired, top with julienned green onions.

FREEZE OPTION Cover and freeze toasted, topped and unbaked baguette slices on a parchment-lined baking sheet until firm. Transfer to a freezer container; return to freezer. To use, bake baguette slices on ungreased baking sheets in a preheated 400° oven until heated through, 8-10 minutes.

1 APPETIZER 66 cal., 3g fat (1g sat. fat), 4mg chol., 161mg sod., 7g carb. (0 sugars, 0 fiber), 2g pro.

BUDGET-FRIENDLY CHAMPAGNE ALTERNATIVES

A bottle of bubbly is an iconic marker of special occasions and always a solid choice for a party. However, if your budget doesn't allow for a premium Champagne, don't despair!

By definition, Champagne comes only from the Champagne region in France. Other sparkling wines must officially go by other names (but consumers often still call them "champagne"). Many of those will have lower price tags.

If you're looking for non-French Champagne-style wine, check the label for the words *méthode Champenoise* or *méthode traditionnelle*. This indicates the wine was made using the same double-fermentation method used to make Champagne. Spanish cavas as well as many California sparkling wines fall in this category.

Other sparkling wines use a faster, single-fermentation method. Italian Proseccos and lambruscos both use this "tank" method and deliver a fresh, drinkable wine that will not break your budget.

CRUDITE DIP

To bring out the best in this tangy dip, chill it before serving. This will allow the flavors time to blend.
—Taste of Home *Test Kitchen*

PREP: 5 min. + chilling • **MAKES:** 1½ cups

1 cup sour cream
½ cup mayonnaise
2 green onions, finely chopped
1 Tbsp. lemon juice
1 Tbsp. minced fresh parsley
1 tsp. dill weed
1 garlic clove, minced
½ tsp. seasoned salt
⅛ tsp. pepper
  Assorted fresh vegetables

Combine the first 9 ingredients; mix well. Cover and refrigerate at least 2 hours. If desired, sprinkle with additional parsley. Serve with vegetables.
2 TBSP. 102 cal., 11g fat (3g sat. fat), 5mg chol., 117mg sod., 1g carb. (1g sugars, 0 fiber), 1g pro.

POINSETTIA

Mixing festive red cranberry juice, Triple Sec and champagne creates a fun cocktail for Christmas parties, a New Year's Eve bash or any get-together during the fall and winter seasons. Garnish with a few fresh berries and enjoy.
—Taste of Home *Test Kitchen*

TAKES: 5 min. • **MAKES:** 1 serving

1 oz. cranberry juice
½ oz. Triple Sec, optional
4 oz. chilled champagne or other sparkling wine
  Optional: Fresh cranberries and fresh rosemary sprigs

Pour cranberry juice into a champagne flute or wine glass. Add Triple Sec if desired. Top with champagne. If desired, garnish with cranberries and rosemary.
1 SERVING 95 cal., 0 fat (0 sat. fat), 0 chol., 1mg sod., 5g carb. (4g sugars, 0 fiber), 0 pro.

SPICY CRAB SALAD TAPAS

I served these at a party and everyone went wild! These delicious morsels have a crispy flaky outside filled with creamy sweet crab that has a little kick. I used scalloped-edge cookie cutters to cut my pastry, but you can use a small biscuit cutter.
—Vanessa Mason, Summerdale, AL

PREP: 35 min. + chilling
BAKE: 20 min. + cooling
MAKES: about 2 dozen

1 can (16 oz.) lump crabmeat, drained
¼ cup finely chopped sweet red pepper
¼ cup finely chopped sweet yellow pepper
¼ cup finely chopped green onions
1 jalapeno pepper, seeded and finely chopped
1 Tbsp. minced fresh cilantro
1 Tbsp. lemon juice
2 garlic cloves, minced
1 tsp. ground mustard
½ cup mayonnaise
½ tsp. salt
¼ tsp. pepper
1 pkg. (17.3 oz.) frozen puff pastry, thawed
1 large egg
1 Tbsp. water
  Optional: Minced fresh parsley and seafood seasoning

1. Combine the first 12 ingredients. Refrigerate, covered, at least 1 hour.
2. Meanwhile, on a lightly floured surface, unfold puff pastry. Roll each pastry into a 10-in. square; cut each into twenty-five 2-in. squares. Using a round 1½-in. cookie cutter, cut out the centers of half the puff pastry squares. Whisk egg and water; brush over pastry. Place cutout squares on top of solid squares; transfer to parchment-lined baking sheets.
3. Bake at 375° until golden brown, about 18 minutes. Cool to room temperature.
4. Once cool, spoon 1 heaping Tbsp. of crab salad into center of each cooked pastry. If desired, top with minced parsley and seasoning. Serve tapas immediately.
NOTE Wear disposable gloves when cutting hot peppers; the oils can burn skin. Avoid touching your face.
1 APPETIZER 145 cal., 9g fat (2g sat. fat), 25mg chol., 240mg sod., 11g carb. (0 sugars, 2g fiber), 5g pro.

TEST KITCHEN TIPS

• The puff pastry shells can be made ahead of time and filled right before your guests arrive.

• To keep your pastry from bending over while baking, make sure you cut them straight up and down without twisting the knife.

SERVING CHAMPAGNE & FIZZY COCKTAILS

• If you're serving it straight, a quality Champagne is worth the money. But for mixed drinks, a less expensive brand or a sparkling wine is fine. Go for a drier instead of a sweeter wine—the additions you'll be making to create the cocktail will make it sweet enough.

• Any drink made with fizzy ingredients should be stirred, not shaken. Just like shaking a soda can, vigorous shaking can lead to a messy carbonation explosion.

• When serving sparkling wine, let the bottle sit in the refrigerator for 2-3 hours or chill it in an ice bucket for 30 minutes. The target temperature is between 39° and 48°. And remember—chill the champagne, never the glass.

• If mixing cocktails in batches, as with a pitcher of sangria, add ice to the glasses when serving, not before. Melting ice can dilute any cocktail, but it's even worse for sparkling cocktails—they'll go flat.

• For cold drinks, add the fizzy bit last. Whether it's wine, soda or tonic, add the sparkling ingredient just before serving to keep the effervescence alive for your guests.

• Some experts say a traditional tall, slender flute makes sparkling wine taste better; others say a tulip-shaped glass is better for bringing out the aromas. So choose the glasses you like best ... you'll have an expert in your corner either way!

MANGO BELLINI

MANGO BELLINI

Simple yet delicious, this mango Bellini is made with fresh mango puree and your favorite sparkling wine—I usually choose Prosecco for mine. You can easily turn it into a mocktail by using sparkling water in place of the wine.
—*Ellen Folkman, Crystal Beach, FL*

- -

TAKES: 5 min. • **MAKES:** 6 servings

- ¾ cup mango nectar or fresh mango puree, chilled
- 1 bottle (750 ml) champagne or other sparkling wine, chilled

Add 2 Tbsp. mango nectar to each of 6 champagne glasses. Top with champagne; gently stir to combine.
1 BELLINI 101 cal., 0 fat (0 sat. fat), 0 chol., 1mg sod., 6g carb. (4g sugars, 0 fiber), 0 pro.

ORANGE CRANBERRY SPLASH

I created this citrusy cocktail while tending bar on the Jersey Shore. For a festive finishing touch during the holiday season, garnish each glass with fresh cranberries.
—*Ralph Florio, New York, NY*

- -

TAKES: 10 min. • **MAKES:** 6 servings

- 3 cups lemon-lime soda
- ¾ cup orange-flavored vodka
- ½ cup cranberry juice
- 6 Tbsp. Triple Sec
  Ice cubes
GARNISH
  Fresh cranberries

In a pitcher, combine the soda, vodka, cranberry juice and Triple Sec. Serve over ice. Garnish with cranberries.
1 SERVING 177 cal., 0 fat (0 sat. fat), 0 chol., 15mg sod., 22g carb. (21g sugars, 0 fiber), 0 pro.

CHAMPAGNE
BLONDIES

CHAMPAGNE BLONDIES

After searching in vain for a fun champagne recipe to take to a friend's bridal shower, I came up with this twist on blondies. The recipe calls for white chocolate chips, but sometimes I like to use butterscotch or even semisweet chocolate instead.

—Heather Karow, Burnett, WI

PREP: 25 min. • **BAKE:** 25 min. + cooling
MAKES: 16 servings

- ½ cup butter, softened
- 1 cup packed light brown sugar
- 1 large egg, room temperature
- ¼ cup champagne
- 1¼ cups all-purpose flour
- 1 tsp. baking powder
- ¼ tsp. salt
- ½ cup white baking chips
- ½ cup chopped hazelnuts, optional

GLAZE
- 1 cup confectioners' sugar
- 2 Tbsp. champagne

1. Preheat oven to 350°. Line an 8-in. square baking pan with parchment, letting ends extend up sides. In a large bowl, beat butter and brown sugar until crumbly, about 2 minutes. Beat in egg and champagne (batter may appear curdled). In another bowl, whisk flour, baking powder and salt; gradually add to the butter mixture. Fold in baking chips and, if desired, nuts.
2. Spread mixture into prepared pan. Bake until edges are brown and center is set (do not overbake), 25-30 minutes. Cool completely in pan on a wire rack.
3. Combine glaze ingredients; drizzle over blondies. Lifting with parchment, remove blondies from pan. Cut into bars. Store in an airtight container.

1 BLONDIE 203 cal., 8g fat (5g sat. fat), 28mg chol., 126mg sod., 32g carb. (24g sugars, 0 fiber), 2g pro.

A TOUCH OF GLITTER VASE

For a quick and easy bit of decor to make your home look dazzling, glitter up a plain glass vase to create a flower-filled centerpiece.

MATERIALS
- Vase
- Glitter
- Decoupage glue
- Masking tape

DIRECTIONS

Attach strips of masking tape around the bottom of a glass vase to mark the edge of your glitter design. Spread decoupage glue evenly on the vase below the tape; immediately sprinkle glitter over the entire glued section. Let the glue dry. Remove the tape and arrange a bouquet in the vase.

BUTTERMILK
PECAN WAFFLES
P. 179

HONEY
POPPY SEED
FRUIT SALAD
P. 176

FRESH
STRAWBERRY
SYRUP
P. 179

COTTON CANDY
CHAMPAGNE
COCKTAILS
P. 181

GALENTINE'S DAY

What's Galentine's Day? "Oh, it's only the BEST day of the year," according to Leslie Knope, overachieving deputy director of the Pawnee, Indiana, Parks and Recreation Department on TV's *Parks and Recreation*. "Every February 13th, my lady friends and I leave our husbands and boyfriends at home and we just come and kick it breakfast-style." Here's how to throw a fab Galentine's Day celebration of your own.

MINI SAUSAGE FRITTATAS

These are perfect for breakfast or brunch. While my gal pals love the spicy kick in hot sausage, I like using sage-flavored sausage and substituting Parmesan for cheddar.

—Courtney Wright, Birmingham, AL

- -

PREP: 15 min. • **BAKE:** 20 min.
MAKES: 1 dozen

- 1   lb. bulk pork sausage
- 1   large onion, finely chopped
- 6   large egg whites
- 4   large eggs
- ¼   cup 2% milk
- ¼   tsp. coarsely ground pepper
- ½   cup shredded sharp cheddar cheese
     Additional shredded cheddar cheese

1. Preheat oven to 350°. In a large skillet, cook sausage and onion over medium heat 6-8 minutes or until sausage is no longer pink and onion is tender, breaking sausage into crumbles; drain.

2. In a large bowl, whisk egg whites, eggs, milk and pepper; stir in sausage mixture and cheese. Fill greased muffin cups almost full; sprinkle with additional cheese.

3. Bake 20-25 minutes or until a knife inserted near the center comes out clean. Cool 5 minutes before removing from pans to wire racks.

2 MINI FRITTATAS 302 cal., 23g fat (8g sat. fat), 175mg chol., 629mg sod., 5g carb. (2g sugars, 0 fiber), 19g pro.

SUGARED DOUGHNUT HOLES

These tasty, tender doughnut bites are easy to make. Tuck them in a scalloped box and tie with a bow to give as a party favor.

—Judy Jungwirth, Athol, SD

- -

TAKES: 20 min. • **MAKES:** about 3 dozen

- 1½ cups all-purpose flour
- ⅓   cup sugar
- 2   tsp. baking powder
- ½   tsp. salt
- ½   tsp. ground nutmeg
- 1   large egg, room temperature
- ½   cup 2% milk
- 2   Tbsp. butter, melted
     Oil for deep-fat frying
     Confectioners' sugar

1. In a large bowl, combine the flour, sugar, baking powder, salt and nutmeg. Combine egg, milk and butter. Add to dry ingredients and mix well.

2. In an electric skillet or deep-fat fryer, heat oil to 375°. Drop dough by heaping teaspoonfuls, 5 or 6 at a time, into oil. Fry until browned, 1-2 minutes, turning once. Drain on paper towels. Roll warm doughnut holes in confectioners' sugar.

1 DOUGHNUT HOLE 47 cal., 2g fat (1g sat. fat), 7mg chol., 68mg sod., 6g carb. (2g sugars, 0 fiber), 1g pro.

HOW TO PLAN A GALENTINE'S DAY PARTY

This Feb. 13, make your girls feel special by throwing a Galentine's Day party that celebrates your cherished friendship.

ASSEMBLE THE SQUAD
This is a day to celebrate the women who make life wonderful, so be as inclusive as your budget allows. You could even ask each of your friends to invite a friend too.

MASTER THE MENU
If you're hosting, consider the menu offerings in this chapter or ask each friend to bring a dish to pass.

SERVE PINK DRINKS
A pink and frothy drink is so befitting of a Galentine's Day bash. You can bet Cotton Candy Champagne Cocktails (p. 181) will be a hit—or check out our Cocktails & Mocktails chapter (p. 46) for other options.

TURN ON GREAT MUSIC
Make a playlist that includes classic upbeat friendship-themed tunes like Cyndi Lauper's "Girls Just Wanna Have Fun," Sister Sledge's "We Are Family" and Queen's "You're My Best Friend."

BREAK OUT THE CHOCOLATE
Girlfriends and chocolate go together like chocolate and, well, everything. Serve chocolate desserts or set out a bowl with Hershey's Hugs and Kisses.

GIVE OUT VALENTINES
Since Valentine's Day is right around the corner, give each of your ladies a handwritten note saying why her friendship is meaningful to you.

PLAY GAL GAMES
Leslie Knope includes storytelling as part of her Galentine's Day tradition. You can do that, or play slumber party-esque games such as "Never Have I Ever," or organize a game of Pictionary or charades.

INSTAGRAM IT
Come up with an Instagram hashtag and notify your guests about it. Ask them to tag fun photos of themselves with friends, especially mutual friends. During the party, gather everyone around for a group selfie, and upload it to your Insta with the hashtag.

I donut know what i'd do without you

SUGARED DOUGHNUT HOLES

HONEY POPPY SEED FRUIT SALAD

The subtle honey sauce in this salad steals the show. It pairs well with any morning entree and takes just 10 minutes to assemble.
—*Dorothy Dinnean, Harrison, AR*

TAKES: 10 min. • **MAKES:** 8 servings

2 medium firm bananas, chopped
2 cups fresh blueberries
2 cups fresh raspberries
2 cups sliced fresh strawberries
5 Tbsp. honey
1 tsp. lemon juice
¾ tsp. poppy seeds

In a large bowl, combine the bananas and berries. In a small bowl, combine the honey, lemon juice and poppy seeds. Pour over fruit and toss to coat.

¾ CUP 117 cal., 1g fat (0 sat. fat), 0 chol., 2mg sod., 30g carb. (23g sugars, 5g fiber), 1g pro.

RASPBERRY SOUR CREAM COFFEE CAKE

RASPBERRY SOUR CREAM COFFEE CAKE

Coffee and cake are like a wink and a smile. You'll take one without the other but given a choice, you want both. This fresh and fruity breakfast pastry is perfect for brunch. A drizzle of icing adds a nice finishing touch.
—*Debbie Johnson, Centertown, MO*

PREP: 20 min. • **BAKE:** 30 min. + cooling
MAKES: 8 servings

1 cup fresh raspberries
3 Tbsp. brown sugar
1 cup all-purpose flour
⅓ cup sugar
½ tsp. baking powder
¼ tsp. baking soda
⅛ tsp. salt
1 large egg, room temperature
⅔ cup sour cream
3 Tbsp. butter, melted
1 tsp. vanilla extract
¼ cup sliced almonds
ICING
¼ cup confectioners' sugar
1½ tsp. 2% milk
¼ tsp. vanilla extract
   Additional raspberries, optional

1. Preheat oven to 350°. In a small bowl, toss raspberries with brown sugar.
2. In a large bowl, whisk flour, sugar, baking powder, baking soda and salt. In another bowl, whisk egg, sour cream, melted butter and vanilla until blended. Add to the flour mixture; stir just until moistened (batter will be thick).
3. Transfer half of the batter to a greased and floured 8-in. round baking pan. Top with the raspberry mixture. Spoon remaining batter over raspberries; sprinkle with almonds.
4. Bake until a toothpick inserted in center comes out clean, 30-35 minutes. Cool in pan 10 minutes before removing to a wire rack to cool.
5. In a small bowl, mix confectioners' sugar, milk and vanilla until smooth; drizzle over top. Serve warm. If desired, serve with additional raspberries.

1 PIECE 238 cal., 10g fat (5g sat. fat), 48mg chol., 154mg sod., 32g carb. (19g sugars, 2g fiber), 4g pro.

RASPBERRY
MERINGUE
HEARTS

4. For sauce, place raspberries in a food processor. Cover and process until blended. Strain, discarding the seeds. In a small saucepan, combine the cornstarch, pureed raspberries and jam until smooth. Bring to a boil over medium heat, stirring constantly. Cook and stir for 1 minute or until thickened. Cool.
5. To serve, spoon sauce into meringue hearts. Place scoop of sorbet on top. Sprinkle with sliced almonds. Garnish with fresh raspberries if desired.
1 MERINGUE WITH ½ CUP SORBET AND ¼ CUP SAUCE 423 cal., 7g fat (0 sat. fat), 0 chol., 53mg sod., 89g carb. (78g sugars, 6g fiber), 5g pro.

ZIPPY PRALINE BACON
I'm always looking for recipes to enhance the usual eggs and bacon, and this one is a surefire hit with the brunch crowd. Just be sure to make more than you think you might need because everybody will definitely want seconds!
—*Myrt Pfannkuche, Pell City, AL*

TAKES: 20 min. • **MAKES:** 20 pieces

- 1 lb. bacon strips
- 3 Tbsp. brown sugar
- 1½ tsp. chili powder
- ¼ cup finely chopped pecans

1. Preheat oven to 425°. Arrange bacon in a single layer in 2 foil-lined 15x10x1-in. pans. Bake 10 minutes; carefully pour off drippings.
2. Mix brown sugar and chili powder; sprinkle over bacon. Sprinkle with pecans. Bake until bacon is crisp, 5-10 minutes. Drain on paper towels.
1 PIECE 58 cal., 4g fat (1g sat. fat), 8mg chol., 151mg sod., 2g carb. (2g sugars, 0 fiber), 3g pro.

RASPBERRY MERINGUE HEARTS
Here's a lovely raspberry dessert that your guests will think is almost too pretty to eat! I love the way the meringue easily drapes into a heart shape.
—*Mary Lou Wayman, Salt Lake City, UT*

PREP: 30 min.
BAKE: 35 min. + cooling
MAKES: 6 servings

- 3 large egg whites
- ¼ tsp. cream of tartar
  Dash salt
- 1 cup sugar
- ⅓ cup finely chopped almonds, toasted
- 1 tsp. vanilla extract
SAUCE
- 3 cups fresh or frozen unsweetened raspberries, thawed
- 1 tsp. cornstarch
- ½ cup seedless raspberry jam
- 3 cups raspberry or lemon sorbet
- ⅓ cup sliced almonds, toasted
  Additional fresh raspberries, optional

1. Place egg whites in a small mixing bowl; let stand at room temperature for 30 minutes.
2. Preheat oven to 300°. Beat egg whites, cream of tartar and salt on medium speed until soft peaks form. Add sugar 1 Tbsp. at a time, beating on high until stiff peaks form and sugar is dissolved. Fold in chopped almonds and vanilla.
3. Drop meringue into 6 mounds on a parchment-lined baking sheet. Shape into 4-in. hearts with the back of a spoon, building up the edges slightly. Bake for 35 minutes. Turn oven off; leave meringues in the oven for 1-1½ hours.

PAIRS
WITH

SPARKLING
COCONUT GRAPE
JUICE, P. 54

BUTTERMILK
PECAN WAFFLES

BUTTERMILK PECAN WAFFLES

These golden waffles are a favorite for breakfast, so we enjoy them often. They're as easy to prepare as regular waffles, but their unique taste makes them exceptional.
—Edna Hoffman, Hebron, IN

PREP: 10 min. • **COOK:** 5 min./batch
MAKES: 7 waffles

- 2 cups all-purpose flour
- 1 Tbsp. baking powder
- 1 tsp. baking soda
- ½ tsp. salt
- 2 cups buttermilk
- 4 large eggs, room temperature
- ½ cup butter, melted
- 3 Tbsp. chopped pecans

1. In a large bowl, whisk flour, baking powder, baking soda and salt. In another bowl, whisk buttermilk and eggs until blended. Add to dry ingredients; stir just until moistened. Stir in butter.
2. Pour about ¾ cup batter onto a lightly greased, preheated waffle maker. Sprinkle with a few pecans. Bake according to the manufacturer's directions until golden brown. Repeat with remaining batter and pecans.
NOTE To substitute for each cup of buttermilk, use 1 Tbsp. white vinegar or lemon juice plus enough milk to measure 1 cup. Stir, then let stand 5 minutes. Or, use 1 cup plain yogurt or 1¾ tsp. cream of tartar plus 1 cup milk.
1 WAFFLE 337 cal., 19g fat (10g sat. fat), 159mg chol., 762mg sod., 31g carb. (4g sugars, 1g fiber), 10g pro.

FRESH STRAWBERRY SYRUP

FRESH STRAWBERRY SYRUP

One summer our garden yielded about 80 quarts of strawberries! We preserved a good portion of that as strawberry syrup. We treat ourselves to this sweet, warm mixture over waffles or pancakes.
—Heather Biedler, Martinsburg, WV

TAKES: 15 min. • **MAKES:** 2 cups

- ¼ cup sugar
- 2 tsp. cornstarch
  Dash salt
- 2 cups chopped fresh strawberries
- ½ cup water
- ½ tsp. lemon juice

In a small saucepan, combine sugar, cornstarch and salt. Stir in strawberries, water and lemon juice until blended. Bring to a boil. Reduce heat; simmer, uncovered, until mixture is thickened and strawberries are tender, 2-3 minutes.
¼ CUP 40 cal., 0 fat (0 sat. fat), 0 chol., 19mg sod., 10g carb. (8g sugars, 1g fiber), 0 pro.

PEANUT BUTTER MALLOW TOPPING

This might just be the perfect topping— it's fabulous drizzled over ice cream, brownies, pancakes and waffles, or sliced apples and bananas.
—Sandy DeCosta, Vineland, NJ

TAKES: 10 min. • **MAKES:** 2 cups

- 1 jar (7 oz.) marshmallow creme
- ½ cup chunky peanut butter
- ¼ cup hot water
- 1 Tbsp. chocolate syrup

In a mixing bowl, combine all ingredients; beat until blended.
2 TBSP. 93 cal., 4g fat (1g sat. fat), 0 chol., 49mg sod., 10g carb. (9g sugars, 1g fiber), 2g pro.

MARBLED MERINGUE HEARTS

HOW TO MAKE A NAPKIN ENVELOPE

Give your table setting some love with this easy envelope napkin fold.

1. Fold a napkin in half diagonally, with the point facing up. Then take the bottom corners and fold to meet in the middle.

2. Fold the outer edges in once again so they meet in the middle.

3. Fold the bottom half up until it meets the base of the triangle.

4. Fold down the triangle flap. Top with a meringue heart.

MARBLED MERINGUE HEARTS

Pretty pastel cookies are a fun way to brighten any special occasion. For a change of flavor, replace the vanilla with a different extract, such as almond or raspberry.
—Laurie Herr, Westford, VT

- -

PREP: 25 min. • **BAKE:** 20 min. + cooling
MAKES: about 2 dozen

- 3 large egg whites
- ½ tsp. vanilla extract
- ¼ tsp. cream of tartar
- ¾ cup sugar
  Red food coloring

1. Place egg whites in a large bowl; let stand at room temperature for 30 minutes. Line baking sheets with parchment.
2. Preheat oven to 200°. Add vanilla and cream of tartar to egg whites; beat on medium speed until soft peaks form. Gradually beat in sugar, 1 Tbsp. at a time, on high until stiff peaks form. Remove ¼ cup and tint pink, using red food coloring. Lightly swirl pink mixture into remaining meringue. Fill pastry bag with meringue. Pipe 2-in. heart shapes 2 in. apart onto prepared baking sheets.
3. Bake 20 minutes or until set and dry. Turn oven off; leave meringues in oven until oven has completely cooled. Store in an airtight container.
1 MERINGUE 27 cal., 0 fat (0 sat. fat), 0 chol., 7mg sod., 6g carb. (6g sugars, 0 fiber), 0 pro.

TEST KITCHEN TIP

For the greatest volume, place egg whites in a clean metal or glass mixing bowl. Even a drop of fat from the egg yolk or a film sometimes found on plastic bowls will prevent egg whites from foaming. For this reason, be sure to use clean beaters as well.

BITTERSWEET DOUBLE CHOCOLATE TRUFFLES

Milk chocolate chips enhance the bittersweet flavor in these decadent treats. Tie a few in pretty ribbons for an easy gift.
—Taste of Home Test Kitchen

- -

PREP: 30 min. + chilling
MAKES: 1½ dozen

- 1 cup 60% cacao bittersweet chocolate baking chips
- ¾ cup whipped topping
- ¼ tsp. ground cinnamon
- 1 cup milk chocolate chips
- 1 tsp. shortening
  Optional toppings: Crushed peppermint candies, sprinkles and chopped nuts

1. In a small saucepan, melt bittersweet chips over low heat. Transfer to a bowl; cool to lukewarm, about 7 minutes.
2. Beat in the whipped topping and cinnamon. Place in the freezer for 15 minutes or until firm enough to form into balls. Shape mixture into 1-in. balls.
3. In a microwave, melt milk chocolate chips and shortening; stir until smooth. Dip truffles in chocolate and place on waxed paper-lined baking sheets. Immediately sprinkle with toppings of your choice. Refrigerate until firm. Store in an airtight container in the refrigerator.
1 TRUFFLE 105 cal., 6g fat (4g sat. fat), 2mg chol., 8mg sod., 12g carb. (10g sugars, 1g fiber), 1g pro.

COTTON CANDY CHAMPAGNE COCKTAILS

You'll love these whimsical champagne cocktails. The cotton candy melts away, leaving behind its sweetness and its pretty pink color.
—Taste of Home Test Kitchen

- -

TAKES: 5 min. • **MAKES:** 6 servings

- 6 Tbsp. raspberry-flavored vodka
- 1 bottle (750 ml) champagne, chilled
- 1½ cups pink cotton candy

Add 1 Tbsp. vodka to each of 6 champagne flutes. Top with champagne; create a garnish for each glass by threading a puff of cotton candy on a cocktail toothpick. To serve, stir in cotton candy.
1 COCKTAIL 125 cal., 0 fat (0 sat. fat), 0 chol., 0 sod., 4g carb. (2g sugars, 0 fiber), 0 pro.

COGNAC
CHAMPAGNE
COCKTAIL
P. 184

RED VELVET
CUPCAKES
WITH COCONUT
FROSTING
P. 189

ASPARAGUS
PASTRY PUFFS
P. 185

HOLLYWOOD AWARDS SHOW PARTY

Invite your movie- and TV-loving peeps over for a night of posh noshes, fun games and glam embellishments while you rate the fashion, critique the speeches and predict the winners.

HOW TO HOST AN AWARDS SHOW BASH THAT'S A REAL WINNER

Use these clever ideas to throw a star-studded viewing party your friends won't soon forget!

SET THE DRESS CODE

When it comes to what you and your guests wear, go one of two ways. Let the celebs on the small screen inspire everyone to go full-on glam. Or keep things ultra casual for comfy viewing from the couch—even donning PJs!

GO FOR GOLD
(AND BLACK AND RED)

The unofficial color palette of La-La Land is black, gold and deep red. Incorporate the quintessential colors any way you can with popcorn boxes, serving trays, napkins and decorations. If you're getting together for the Grammys, spray-paint old vinyl records to create a DIY serving platter!

TURN UP THE TUNES

Create a playlist that's an ode to the awards show you're watching. For the Oscars, include songs from the soundtracks of nominated films or ones inspired by their plots. For the Grammys, cue up music from every category.

SERVE FANCY STARTERS

It's only fitting to serve chic refreshments to match the glamour of the awards shows. Start guests off with champagne cocktails and upscale apps.

ROLL OUT THE RED DESSERTS

As a wink to the famous walkway, whip up a red velvet delicacy, such as cupcakes, cake pops, cookies or cheesecake.

COGNAC CHAMPAGNE COCKTAIL

COGNAC CHAMPAGNE COCKTAIL

Celebrate the new year or any special occasion with this festive champagne cocktail. Not only is it fruity and refreshing, but it also packs a punch!
—Francine Lizotte, Langley, BC

- -

TAKES: 10 min. • **MAKES:** 8 servings

- 1 cup pulp-free orange juice, chilled
- 1 can (7½ oz.) lemon-lime soda, chilled
- 1 can (6 oz.) unsweetened pineapple juice, chilled
- ⅓ cup Cognac or brandy
- ¼ cup simple syrup, chilled
- 1 bottle (750 ml) champagne or other sparkling wine, chilled

In a large pitcher or punch bowl, combine the first 5 ingredients. Stir in champagne. Serve immediately.
¾ CUP 309 cal., 0 fat (0 sat. fat), 0 chol., 7mg sod., 38g carb. (32g sugars, 0 fiber), 1g pro.

GO FOR GOLD

At this glitzy party, it's gold everything, and even the smallest details add to the overall glamour! Add extra sparkle to your glasses of champagne with glittery swizzle sticks.

ASPARAGUS
PASTRY PUFFS

ASPARAGUS PASTRY PUFFS

When the first asparagus of the season appears, we serve it rolled inside puff pastry with a yummy cheese filling. Our guests always compliment these lovely treats.

—*Cindy Jamieson, Tonawanda, NY*

PREP: 30 min. **BAKE:** 25 min.
MAKES: 16 servings

- 1   lb. fresh asparagus, trimmed
- 4   oz. cream cheese, softened
- ¼   cup grated Parmesan cheese
- 1   Tbsp. stone-ground mustard
- 2   tsp. lemon juice
- ¼   tsp. salt
- ¼   tsp. pepper
- 1   pkg. (17.3 oz.) frozen puff pastry, thawed
- 1   large egg
- 2   Tbsp. water

1. Preheat oven to 400°. In a large skillet, bring 1½ in. water to a boil. Add asparagus; cook, uncovered, until crisp-tender, 1-3 minutes. Remove asparagus and immediately drop into ice water. Drain and pat dry.
2. In a small bowl, mix cream cheese, Parmesan cheese, mustard, lemon juice, salt and pepper until blended. Unfold puff pastry sheets; cut each sheet in half to make a total of 4 rectangles. Spread each rectangle with a fourth of the cream cheese mixture to within ¼ in. of edges. Arrange asparagus over top, allowing tips to show at each end; roll up jelly-roll style. Using a serrated knife, cut each roll crosswise into 4 sections.
3. Place on a parchment-lined baking sheet, seam side down. In a small bowl, whisk egg and water until blended; brush lightly over tops.
4. Bake until pastry is golden brown, 25-30 minutes. Remove from pan to a wire rack to cool slightly; serve warm.
1 PASTRY PUFF 188 cal., 11g fat (4g sat. fat), 21mg chol., 211mg sod., 18g carb. (1g sugars, 3g fiber), 4g pro.

HIP POP

This glitzy spectacle calls for 'corn!
Liven up the sweet or salty snack
with creative and delicious stir-ins.

PARMESAN RANCH POPCORN

*Mix ¼ cup grated Parmesan cheese, 2 Tbsp. dry
ranch salad dressing mix, 1 tsp. dried parsley flakes
and ¼ tsp. onion powder. Drizzle ⅓ cup melted
butter over 3½ qt. popped popcorn; toss with the
cheese mixture. Store in airtight containers.*

ITALIAN CHEESE POPCORN

*Mix ⅓ cup grated Romano cheese, 2¼ tsp. Italian
seasoning and ¾ tsp. garlic salt. Drizzle ⅓ cup
melted butter over 3½ qt. popped popcorn; toss
with cheese mixture. Store in airtight containers.*

PEPPERMINT POPCORN

*Drizzle 8 oz. melted white candy coating over 3½ qt.
popped popcorn; sprinkle with ⅓ cup crushed
peppermint candies and toss. Immediately spread
onto waxed paper; let stand until set. Break into
pieces. Store in airtight containers.*

*PARMESAN
RANCH
POPCORN*

*ITALIAN
CHEESE
POPCORN*

*PEPPERMINT
POPCORN*

WHITE CHOCOLATE TRUFFLES

These beautiful white candies are irresistible on a party tray—and also make a gorgeous little takeaway present when nestled in a gift box, wrapped in a ribbon and given to guests at the end of an evening.
—*Gloria Nolan, Peoria, PA*

PREP: 20 min. + chilling • **MAKES:** 5 dozen

- 8 Tbsp. butter, cubed
- 2 Tbsp. heavy whipping cream
- 18 oz. white candy coating, coarsely chopped
- ¼ cup confectioners' sugar
  Coarse or confectioners' sugar

1. In top of a double boiler or a metal bowl over barely simmering water, melt butter into cream; remove from heat. Gradually add candy coating, stirring continuously with a rubber spatula until the candy coating begins to melt. Return to heat; stir constantly until mixture is smooth. Stir in confectioners' sugar. (If mixture separates, beat with a mixer for 30 seconds.) Pour into an 8-in. square pan. Chill until slightly hardened, about 20 minutes.
2. Using a melon baller or spoon, scoop out and shape into 1-in. balls. Roll in coarse sugar. Store in an airtight container in the refrigerator.
NOTE: White confectionery coating is found in the baking section of most grocery stores. It is sometime labeled almond bark or candy coating and is often sold in bulk packages of 1-1½ pounds.
1 TRUFFLE 62 cal., 4g fat (3g sat. fat), 5mg chol., 12mg sod., 7g carb. (6g sugars, 0 fiber), 0 pro.

MARINATED OLIVE & CHEESE RING

MARINATED OLIVE & CHEESE RING

We love to make meals into celebrations, and an antipasto always kicks off the party. This one is almost too pretty to eat, especially when sprinkled with pimientos, fresh basil and parsley.
—*Patricia Harmon, Baden, PA*

PREP: 25 min. + chilling
MAKES: 16 servings

- 1 pkg. (8 oz.) cream cheese, cold
- 1 pkg. (10 oz.) sharp white cheddar cheese, cut into ¼-in. slices
- ⅓ cup pimiento-stuffed olives
- ⅓ cup pitted Greek olives
- ¼ cup balsamic vinegar
- ¼ cup olive oil
- 1 Tbsp. minced fresh parsley
- 1 Tbsp. minced fresh basil or 1 tsp. dried basil
- 2 garlic cloves, minced
- 1 jar (2 oz.) pimiento strips, drained and chopped
  Toasted French bread baguette slices

1. Cut cream cheese lengthwise in half; cut each half into ¼-in. slices. On a serving plate, arrange cheeses upright in a ring, alternating cheddar and cream cheese slices. Place olives in the center of the ring.
2. In a small bowl, whisk vinegar, oil, parsley, basil and garlic until blended; drizzle over cheeses and olives. Sprinkle with pimientos. Refrigerate, covered, at least 8 hours or overnight. Serve with baguette slices.
1 SERVING 168 cal., 16g fat (7g sat. fat), 34mg chol., 260mg sod., 2g carb. (1g sugars, 0 fiber), 6g pro.

SALMON SALAD-STUFFED ENDIVE LEAVES

Salmon creates an elegant appetizer in this vibrant recipe. It's simple to prepare and can even be made ahead of time.
—Melissa Carafa, Broomall, PA

TAKES: 15 min. • **MAKES:** 14 pieces

- 1 salmon fillet (6 oz.), cooked and flaked
- ¼ cup tartar sauce
- 2 tsp. capers
- 1 tsp. snipped fresh dill
- ¼ tsp. lemon-pepper seasoning
- 1 head Belgian endive (about 5 oz.), separated into leaves

In a small bowl, combine salmon, tartar sauce, capers, dill and lemon pepper. Spoon about 2 tsp. salmon salad onto each endive leaf. If desired, garnish with additional dill. Refrigerate until serving.

1 PIECE 42 cal., 3g fat (1g sat. fat), 9mg chol., 60mg sod., 2g carb. (0 sugars, 1g fiber), 3g pro.

#GIRLDINNER

This salad will last 3-4 days in the refrigerator—a couple of days longer than that if you used canned salmon instead of fresh. You can wrap it in lettuce leaves or spread it on crackers for a quick and easy light meal.

PAIRS WITH

SPARKLING BERRY PUNCH, P. 51

SALMON SALAD-STUFFED ENDIVE LEAVES

RED VELVET CUPCAKES WITH COCONUT FROSTING

1. Preheat oven to 350°. In a large bowl, cream butter and sugar until light and fluffy, 5-7 minutes. Add eggs, 1 at a time, beating well after each addition. Stir in food coloring and vanilla. Combine flour, cocoa, baking soda and salt. Combine buttermilk and vinegar. Add the dry ingredients to the creamed mixture alternately with buttermilk mixture, beating well after each addition.
2. Fill foil or paper-lined muffin cups two-thirds full. Bake until a toothpick inserted in center comes out clean, 18-22 minutes. Cool 10 minutes before removing from pans to wire rack to cool completely.
3. For frosting, in a large bowl, beat cream cheese and butter until fluffy, 3-5 minutes. Add confectioners' sugar and vanilla; beat until smooth. Stir in 1 cup coconut. Frost cupcakes.
4. Toast the remaining 1 cup coconut; sprinkle over cupcakes. Store in the refrigerator.

1 CUPCAKE 296 cal., 18g fat (12g sat. fat), 59mg chol., 260mg sod., 32g carb. (23g sugars, 1g fiber), 4g pro.

TEST KITCHEN TIP

If you're not a fan of coconut, you can simply omit the coconut and make a more traditional cream cheese frosting instead. You may need to add more confectioners' sugar to get your frosting to the right consistency, but the omission of the sweetened coconut means it won't be too sweet.

RED VELVET CUPCAKES WITH COCONUT FROSTING

Pay homage to the traditional red carpet with these richly colored treats! There's no better way to celebrate being together than with these fun-loving cupcakes.
—*Marie Rizzio, Interlochen, MI*

PREP: 25 min. • **BAKE:** 20 min. + cooling
MAKES: 2 dozen

¾ cup butter, softened
1½ cups sugar
2 large eggs, room temperature
1 Tbsp. red food coloring
1 tsp. vanilla extract
1¾ cups all-purpose flour
¼ cup baking cocoa
¾ tsp. baking soda
¾ tsp. salt
1 cup buttermilk
1 tsp. white vinegar
FROSTING
2 pkg. (8 oz. each) cream cheese, softened
¼ cup butter, softened
1½ cups confectioners' sugar
1 tsp. vanilla extract
2 cups sweetened shredded coconut, divided

CHAMPAGNE TRUFFLES

Who can resist champagne truffles? Especially when they are so very easy to make! Serve them in gold foil candy cups for a glamorous look.
—Deirdre Cox, Kansas City, MO

- -

PREP: 1 hour + chilling • **MAKES:** 7½ dozen

- 1 cup champagne or other sparkling wine
- 2 lbs. semisweet chocolate, chopped
- 1½ cups heavy whipping cream
- ½ cup unsalted butter, cubed
- 1 lb. dark chocolate candy coating, melted
  Edible gold paint, glitter or sprinkles

1. In a small saucepan, bring champagne to a boil. Cook until liquid is reduced to ⅓ cup, 15-20 minutes. Cool slightly.
2. Place semisweet chocolate in a small bowl. In another saucepan, heat cream just to a boil. Pour over chocolate; stir until smooth. Stir in butter and cooled champagne. Cool to room temperature, stirring occasionally. Refrigerate until firm, about 3 hours.
3. Shape into 1-in. balls. Place on baking sheets; cover and refrigerate for at least 1 hour.
4. Dip truffles in melted candy coating; allow excess to drip off. Place on waxed paper; let stand until set. Splatter with edible gold paint or sprinkle with glitter or sprinkles. Store in an airtight container in the refrigerator.
1 TRUFFLE 109 cal., 8g fat (5g sat. fat), 7mg chol., 3mg sod., 9g carb. (7g sugars, 1g fiber), 1g pro.

LEMON STARS

These little cookies have a light, crunchy texture and a citrusy zing. You can cut them into any shape you like—stars are perfect for a night of celeb-spotting!
—Jacqueline Hill, Norwalk, OH

- -

PREP: 45 min. + chilling
BAKE: 10 min./batch + cooling
MAKES: 9 dozen

- ½ cup butter-flavored shortening
- 1 cup sugar
- 1 large egg, room temperature
- 1½ tsp. lemon extract
- ½ cup sour cream
- 1 tsp. grated lemon zest
- 2¾ cups all-purpose flour
- ½ tsp. baking soda
- ½ tsp. salt

FROSTING
- 1½ cups confectioners' sugar
- 6 Tbsp. butter, softened
- ¾ tsp. lemon extract
- 3 drops yellow food coloring, optional
- 3 to 4 Tbsp. 2% milk
  Yellow colored sugar, optional

1. In a large bowl, cream shortening and sugar until light and fluffy, 5-7 minutes. Beat in egg and extract. Stir in sour cream and zest. Combine flour, baking soda and salt; gradually add to creamed mixture and mix well. Divide dough into 3 balls; cover and refrigerate for 3 hours or until easy to handle.
2. Preheat oven to 375°. Remove 1 portion of dough from the refrigerator at a time. On a lightly floured surface, roll out dough to ¼-in. thickness. Cut with a floured 2-in. star cookie cutter. Place 1 in. apart on ungreased baking sheets.
3. Bake until edges are lightly browned, 6-8 minutes. Remove to wire racks to cool completely.
4. For frosting, combine confectioners' sugar, butter, extract, food coloring if desired and enough milk to reach spreading consistency. Frost cookies; sprinkle with colored sugar if desired.
1 COOKIE 43 cal., 2g fat (1g sat. fat), 4mg chol., 23mg sod., 6g carb. (4g sugars, 0 fiber), 0 pro.

THE FAME GAMES

No matter which program is broadcasting on your tube, there's a way for you to interact and play! Try bingo, acceptance-speech Mad Libs, superlative assignments for your own squad (e.g., Best Dressed, Most Likely to Become Famous, etc.) and so much more.

CHAMPAGNE TRUFFLES

LEMON STARS

SWAG BAG

Celebs head home from an awards show with gifts, so why shouldn't your guests? Stuff paper bags with your favorite fancy things, such as iced sugar cookies, Champagne Truffles (recipe on opposite page), mini sparkling wine bottles, gold nail polish and confetti.

INDIVIDUAL
PIZZA CRUSTS
P. 195

PIZZA PARTY

Grab a handful of fresh ingredients and crank up the oven. It's time for a pizza party! Homemade crusts, two kinds of sauces and loads of tempting toppings deliver parlor-style fun from the comfort of your kitchen.

PIZZA PARTY

The best way to cater to your friends' varied pizza preferences is to have them make their own! Lay out a board of toppings and sauce, and let their imaginations run wild!

BUILD THE BOARD:

Base

- **Individual Pizza Crusts**
- **Homemade Pizza Sauce**
- **White Pizza Sauce**

Cheeses

- Mozzarella
- Parmesan

Meats

- Ham
- Bacon, cooked and chopped
- Pepperoni
- Sausage, cooked and crumbled

Toppings

- Crushed red pepper flakes
- Red onion
- Pepperoncini
- Pineapple
- Tomatoes
- Black olives
- Green peppers
- Mushrooms
- Fresh basil

HOMEMADE PIZZA SAUCE P. 197

PAIRS WITH

CHIANTI

INDIVIDUAL PIZZA CRUSTS

INDIVIDUAL PIZZA CRUSTS

This dough is simply perfect for parties. Everyone can pick their own toppings and it's always fun to do some cooking together. Or use the dough to make two 12-inch pizzas.

—*Beverly Anderson, Sinclairville, NY*

PREP: 10 min. + resting • **BAKE:** 15 min.
MAKES: 10 servings

- 2 pkg. (¼ oz. each) active dry yeast
- 2 cups warm water (110° to 115°)
- ¼ cup canola oil
- 2 tsp. sugar
- ½ tsp. salt
- 5 to 5½ cups all-purpose flour
  Cornmeal
  Pizza toppings of your choice

1. In a large bowl, dissolve yeast in warm water. Add oil, sugar, salt and 3 cups flour. Beat until smooth. Stir in enough remaining flour to form a firm dough. Turn onto a floured surface; cover and let rest for 10 minutes.
2. Divide dough into 10 pieces. Roll each portion into an 8-in. circle; prick each circle of dough several times with tines of a fork. Transfer dough to greased baking sheets lightly sprinkled with cornmeal, building up edges slightly. Do not let rise. Bake at 425° until lightly browned, 6-8 minutes. Add toppings as desired; bake 8-12 minutes longer.

1 CRUST 285 cal., 6g fat (1g sat. fat), 0 chol., 120mg sod., 49g carb. (1g sugars, 2g fiber), 7g pro.

5 TIPS FOR PIZZA-CRUST PERFECTION

Making your own pizza crust is far easier than you might think. Just keep these secrets in mind.

- Make sure to use the type of yeast called for in the pizza crust recipe.
- Use a thermometer to check the temperature of the water. If it's too cool, it won't activate the yeast; if it's too hot, it may kill the yeast.
- Don't use too much flour. Start with the minimum amount and add more only until the dough reaches the consistency indicated in the recipe.
- Use only enough flour on your work surface to keep the dough from sticking when you're kneading it.
- Continue kneading until the dough is no longer sticky, has a smooth, satiny texture and springs back when pressed with your fingers.

WHITE
PIZZA SAUCE

WHITE PIZZA SAUCE

If you prefer the rich flavor of white pizzas, this sauce will become your new favorite. Add more garlic or some fresh herbs for more flavor.
—Taste of Home *Test Kitchen*

TAKES: 15 min. • **MAKES:** 2 cups

- 2 Tbsp. butter
- 2 garlic cloves, minced
- 2 Tbsp. all-purpose flour
- 2 cups half-and-half cream
- ⅓ cup grated Parmesan cheese
- ½ tsp. Italian seasoning, optional

In a small saucepan, melt butter over medium heat. Add garlic; cook and stir 1 minute. Stir in flour until blended; gradually add cream. Bring to a boil; cook and stir until thickened, 1-2 minutes. Remove from heat. Stir in Parmesan cheese and, if desired, Italian seasoning.
¼ CUP 128 cal., 10g fat (6g sat. fat), 41mg chol., 113mg sod., 4g carb. (2g sugars, 0 fiber), 3g pro.

FRUIT ON A STICK

This fun finger food with its smooth, creamy dip makes a light and sweet companion to spicy pizza.
—Faye Hintz, Springfield, MO

TAKES: 15 min.
MAKES: 1 dozen (1½ cups dip)

- 1 pkg. (8 oz.) cream cheese, softened
- 1 jar (7 oz.) marshmallow creme
- 3 to 4 Tbsp. 2% milk
- 12 fresh strawberries, halved
- 24 cubes cantaloupe
- 3 medium kiwifruit, peeled and cut into eighths

Mix cream cheese, marshmallow creme and milk until smooth. Thread fruit onto 12 skewers. Serve with dip.
1 SKEWER WITH 2 TBSP. DIP 149 cal., 7g fat (4g sat. fat), 19mg chol., 77mg sod., 17g carb. (15g sugars, 1g fiber), 2g pro.

SUPER ITALIAN CHOPPED SALAD

Antipasto ingredients are sliced and diced to make this substantial salad. I like to buy sliced meat from the deli and chop it all so we can get a bit of everything in each bite.
—Kim Molina, Duarte, CA

TAKES: 25 min. • **MAKES:** 10 servings

- 3 cups torn romaine
- 1 can (15 oz.) garbanzo beans or chickpeas, rinsed and drained
- 1 jar (6½ oz.) marinated artichoke hearts, drained and chopped
- 1 medium green pepper, chopped
- 2 medium tomatoes, chopped
- 1 can (2¼ oz.) sliced ripe olives, drained
- 5 slices deli ham, chopped
- 5 thin slices hard salami, chopped
- 5 slices pepperoni, chopped
- 3 slices provolone cheese, chopped
- 2 green onions, chopped

DRESSING
- ¼ cup olive oil
- 2 Tbsp. red wine vinegar
- ¼ tsp. salt
- ⅛ tsp. pepper

TOPPINGS
- 2 Tbsp. grated Parmesan cheese Pepperoncini, optional

In a large bowl, combine the first 11 ingredients. For dressing, in a small bowl, whisk oil, vinegar, salt and pepper. Pour over salad; toss to coat. Sprinkle with cheese. Top with pepperoncini if desired.
NOTE Look for pepperoncini (pickled peppers) in the pickle and olive section of your grocery store.
¾ CUP 185 cal., 13g fat (3g sat. fat), 12mg chol., 444mg sod., 11g carb. (3g sugars, 3g fiber), 7g pro.

HOMEMADE PIZZA SAUCE

For years, I had trouble finding a pizza sauce my family liked, so I just started making my own. The evening I served it to company and they asked for my recipe, I knew I'd finally gotten it right! When I prepare my sauce, I usually fix enough for three to four pizzas and freeze it. Feel free to spice it up to suit your own tastes.
—Cheryl Kravik, Spanaway, WA

PREP: 10 min. • **COOK:** 70 min.
MAKES: about 4 cups

- 2 cans (15 oz. each) tomato sauce
- 1 can (12 oz.) tomato paste
- 1 Tbsp. Italian seasoning
- 1 Tbsp. dried oregano
- 1 to 2 tsp. fennel seed, crushed
- 1 tsp. onion powder
- 1 tsp. garlic powder
- ½ tsp. salt

In a large saucepan over medium heat, combine tomato sauce and paste. Add remaining ingredients; mix well. Bring to a boil, stirring constantly. Reduce heat; cover and simmer for 1 hour, stirring occasionally.
¼ CUP 26 cal., 0 fat (0 sat. fat), 0 chol., 189mg sod., 6g carb. (3g sugars, 2g fiber), 1g pro.

WONTON MOZZARELLA STICKS

You won't believe something this easy could taste so fantastic! Crunchy outside, gooey cheese inside, these mozzarella sticks are a treat all ages will love. Kids could help wrap them too.

—*Shirley Warren, Thiensville, WI*

- -

TAKES: 20 min. • **MAKES:** 1 dozen

12 pieces string cheese
12 large egg roll wrappers
    Oil for deep-fat frying
    Marinara or spaghetti sauce

1. Place a piece of string cheese near the bottom corner of 1 egg roll wrapper (keep remaining wrappers covered with a damp paper towel until ready to use). Fold bottom corner over cheese. Roll up halfway; fold sides toward center over cheese. Moisten remaining corner with water; roll up tightly to seal. Repeat with remaining wrappers and cheese.
2. In a deep cast-iron or electric skillet, heat ½ in. oil to 375°. Fry sticks, a few at a time, until golden brown, 30-60 seconds on each side. Drain on paper towels. Serve with marinara sauce.
1 MOZZARELLA STICK 241 cal., 14g fat (5g sat. fat), 23mg chol., 423mg sod., 19g carb. (0 sugars, 1g fiber), 10g pro.

TEST KITCHEN TIPS

- Look for egg roll wrappers in the produce section. Be sure to get wrappers labeled egg roll wrappers and not spring roll wrappers. Egg roll wrappers are soft and bendable while in the package. Spring roll wrappers are usually thin, stiff and call for a dip in water to soften them.

- For crispy fried foods, the key is having the oil hot enough. If your mozzarella sticks are soggy, kick your oil temp up a notch or two.

CANNOLI WAFER SANDWICHES

My family loves to visit a local Italian restaurant that has a wonderful dessert buffet. The cannoli is among our favorite choices, so I had to come up with my own simple version. These sandwiches are best served the same day they're made so the wafers remain nice and crisp.

—*Nichi Larson, Shawnee, KS*

- -

PREP: 35 min. + standing
MAKES: 3½ dozen

1 cup whole-milk ricotta cheese
¼ cup confectioners' sugar
1 Tbsp. sugar
¼ tsp. vanilla extract
1 pkg. (11 oz.) vanilla wafers
12 oz. white candy coating, melted
½ cup miniature semisweet chocolate chips
    Additional confectioners' sugar

1. In a small bowl, mix ricotta cheese, confectioners' sugar, sugar and vanilla until blended. Spread 1 scant tsp. filling on bottoms of half the wafers; cover with the remaining wafers.
2. Dip each sandwich cookie halfway into candy coating; allow excess to drip off. Place on waxed paper; sprinkle with chocolate chips. Let stand until set, about 10 minutes.
3. Serve within 2 hours or refrigerate until serving. Dust with additional confectioners' sugar just before serving.
1 SANDWICH COOKIE 93 cal., 5g fat (3g sat. fat), 4mg chol., 38mg sod., 13g carb. (10g sugars, 0 fiber), 1g pro.

BACON CAESAR SALAD

Family and friends always say my Caesar salad rivals any restaurant's version. The addition of bacon is a untraditional, but it lends a slightly smoky flavor and makes it distinctive. If I'm making this for a crowd, I'll prepare the croutons a day or so ahead of time and store them in an airtight container until the day of the party.

—*Sharon Tipton, Casselberry, FL*

- -

TAKES: 20 min. • **MAKES:** 12 servings

2 Tbsp. olive oil
2 cups cubed day-old bread
3 garlic cloves, sliced
DRESSING
½ cup olive oil
¼ cup lemon juice
1 Tbsp. Dijon mustard
3 garlic cloves, minced
1½ tsp. anchovy paste
    Dash pepper
SALAD
1 large bunch romaine, torn
4 bacon strips, cooked and crumbled
½ cup shredded Parmesan cheese

1. For croutons, in a large skillet, heat oil over medium heat. Add bread cubes; cook and stir until golden brown, 4-5 minutes. Add garlic; cook 1 minute longer. Remove to paper towels; cool.
2. For dressing, in a small bowl, whisk oil, lemon juice, mustard, garlic, anchovy paste and pepper.
3. In a serving bowl, combine romaine and bacon. Drizzle with dressing; toss to coat. Sprinkle with croutons and cheese.
¾ CUP 158 cal., 14g fat (3g sat. fat), 8mg chol., 229mg sod., 6g carb. (1g sugars, 1g fiber), 3g pro.
CHICKEN CAESAR SALAD Top salad with slices of grilled chicken breast.

CANNOLI WAFER SANDWICHES

BACON CAESAR SALAD

CARAMEL
BROWNIES

CARAMEL BROWNIES

I love to cook. My family can't possibly eat all the sweets I whip up, so my co-workers are more than happy to sample them—particularly these rich, chewy brownies full of gooey caramel, chocolate chips and crunchy walnuts.
—*Clara Bakke, Coon Rapids, MN*

PREP: 20 min. • **BAKE:** 50 min. + cooling
MAKES: 2 dozen

- 2 cups sugar
- 1 cup canola oil
- ¾ cup baking cocoa
- 4 large eggs, room temperature
- ¼ cup 2% milk
- 1½ cups all-purpose flour
- 1 tsp. salt
- 1 tsp. baking powder
- 1 cup semisweet chocolate chips
- 1 cup chopped walnuts, divided
- 1 pkg. (11 oz.) caramels
- ⅓ cup sweetened condensed milk

1. Preheat oven to 350°. In a large bowl, beat sugar, oil, cocoa, eggs and milk. In another bowl, combine flour, salt and baking powder; gradually add to the egg mixture until well blended. Fold in chocolate chips and ½ cup walnuts.
2. Spoon two-thirds of the batter into a greased 13x9-in. baking pan. Bake for 12 minutes.
3. Meanwhile, in a large saucepan, heat caramels and condensed milk over low heat until the caramels are melted. Pour over baked brownie layer. Sprinkle with the remaining ½ cup walnuts.
4. Drop remaining batter by teaspoonfuls over the caramel layer. Carefully swirl brownie batter with a knife.
5. Bake until a toothpick inserted in center comes out with moist crumbs (do not overbake), 35-40 minutes longer. Cool completely on a wire rack.
1 BROWNIE 325 cal., 17g fat (3g sat. fat), 34mg chol., 170mg sod., 42g carb. (32g sugars, 1g fiber), 4g pro.

CRUNCHY ITALIAN SNACK MIX

Every time my son visits, he asks me to make a batch of my snack mix. It has become a requirement when we all sit down to play board games.
—*Sheryl Little, Cabot, AR*

PREP: 10 min. • **BAKE:** 30 min. + cooling
MAKES: 2½ qt.

- 4 cups Rice Chex
- 4 cups Corn Chex
- 1 pkg. (5 oz.) miniature sesame breadsticks
- 2 cups Goldfish cheddar crackers
- ½ cup mixed nuts
- ½ cup butter, melted
- ¼ cup grated Parmesan cheese
- 3 Tbsp. Italian salad dressing
- 1½ tsp. Italian seasoning
- ½ tsp. garlic salt

1. Preheat oven to 300°. In a large bowl, combine cereals, breadsticks, crackers and nuts. In a small bowl, mix butter, cheese, salad dressing, Italian seasoning and garlic salt. Drizzle over cereal mixture; toss to coat.
2. Spread the mixture into 2 greased 15x10x1-in. baking pans. Bake for 30 minutes, stirring every 10 minutes. Cool completely in pans on wire racks. Store in an airtight container.
¾ CUP 292 cal., 16g fat (6g sat. fat), 22mg chol., 542mg sod., 34g carb. (3g sugars, 3g fiber), 6g pro.

BASIL-GARLIC CHEESE BREAD

Here's a crusty, crunchy bread that goes together in minutes and is fantastic with all kinds of pasta dishes!
—*Deni Adkins, Scottsboro, AL*

TAKES: 10 min. • **MAKES:** 10 servings

- ½ cup butter, softened
- 2 Tbsp. grated Parmesan cheese
- 2 Tbsp. olive oil
- 1 Tbsp. lemon juice
- 2 tsp. minced garlic
- 1 to 2 tsp. dried basil
- 1 loaf (1 lb.) unsliced French bread, halved lengthwise

In a small bowl, combine the first 6 ingredients; spread over cut sides of bread. Place on an ungreased baking sheet. Broil 4-6 in. from the heat until lightly browned, 2-3 minutes. Cut into 2-in. slices.
2 PIECES 241 cal., 13g fat (7g sat. fat), 25mg chol., 375mg sod., 26g carb. (1g sugars, 1g fiber), 6g pro.

UPCYCLING IDEA

Instead of tossing out cans from tomato products, wash and dry them, then use them as vases for fresh herbs or fill them with utensils and breadsticks!

BUCKWHEAT
BRUNCH
CREPES
P. 209

LADIES' BRUNCH

Bring a touch of France to your table with a plate stacked high with delicate, buttery crepes your friends will love. Crepes can be simple or extravagant, hot or cold, sweet or savory, and filled and shaped to suit any occasion. Look here for fresh ideas on how to dress up the humble crepe with endless fillings, toppings and garnishes.

BASIC CREPES

CREPE TOPPERS

Sweet ideas: Fresh fruit, berries, jam, honey, marmalade, maple syrup, lemon curd, nut butters, chocolate chips, whipped cream, pie filling, hot fudge, caramel sauce, chopped nuts, ice cream, shaved chocolate.

Savory ideas: Shredded cheese, mushrooms, grape tomatoes, mixed greens, ham, salami, prosciutto, pesto, bacon, avocado.

BASIC CREPES

This is our favorite simple crepe recipe. It's best to make the batter at least 30 minutes ahead so the flour can absorb all the moisture before you start cooking the crepes. You can use this recipe as the starting point for other crepes in this chapter if you wish.
—Taste of Home *Test Kitchen*

PREP: 10 min. + chilling • **COOK:** 20 min.
MAKES: 20 crepes

- 4 large eggs
- 1½ cups 2% milk
- 1 cup all-purpose flour
- 1½ tsp. sugar
- ⅛ tsp. salt
- 8 tsp. butter

1. In a small bowl, whisk eggs and milk. In another bowl, mix flour, sugar and salt; add to egg mixture and mix well. Refrigerate, covered, 1 hour.
2. Melt 1 tsp. butter in an 8-in. nonstick skillet over medium heat. Stir batter. Fill a ¼-cup measure halfway with batter; pour into center of pan. Quickly lift and tilt pan to coat bottom evenly. Cook until top appears dry; turn crepe over and cook until bottom is cooked, 15-20 seconds longer. Remove to a wire rack. Repeat with remaining batter, adding butter to skillet as needed. When cool, stack crepes between pieces of waxed paper or paper towels.
1 CREPE 61 cal., 3g fat (2g sat. fat), 43mg chol., 50mg sod., 6g carb. (1g sugars, 0 fiber), 3g pro.

#GIRLDINNER

Crepes can be made in advance; once stacked between layers of waxed paper, they can keep in the fridge for several days, or can be frozen for several months. That makes it super easy to prepare for a party, or just to fix 1 or 2 crepes for nights when you're on your own and want something quick, light and a little bit fancy.

BUCKWHEAT BRUNCH CREPES

My husband and I enjoy these delicious crepes with sweet berry sauce and cream on Saturday mornings or even at supper time with sausage and eggs. They're considered a delicacy here, especially with a drizzle of maple syrup.
—*Sharon Dyck, Roxton Falls, QC*

PREP: 20 min. + chilling • **COOK:** 15 min.
MAKES: 3 servings

- 5 Tbsp. heavy whipping cream
- ½ cup sour cream

CREPES

- 2 large eggs
- ½ cup 2% milk
- ⅓ cup all-purpose flour
- 3 Tbsp. buckwheat flour or whole wheat flour
- ½ tsp. salt

BERRY SAUCE

- ½ cup sugar
- 1 Tbsp. cornstarch
  Dash salt
- ½ cup water
- ⅓ cup fresh blueberries
- ⅓ cup fresh raspberries
- 4½ tsp. butter, divided
- 1 tsp. lemon juice

1. In a small bowl, beat whipping cream until stiff peaks form; fold into sour cream. Cover and refrigerate.
2. For the crepe batter, in a large bowl, whisk eggs and milk. In another bowl, mix flours and salt; add to the egg mixture and mix well. Refrigerate, covered, 1 hour.
3. Meanwhile, for the sauce, in a small saucepan, combine sugar, cornstarch and salt; whisk in water until smooth. Bring to a boil; cook and stir until thickened, 1-2 minutes. Add berries; cook over medium-low heat until the berries pop. Stir in 1½ tsp. butter and lemon juice until butter is melted. Set aside and keep warm.
4. Heat 1 tsp. remaining butter in an 8-in. nonstick skillet over medium heat. Stir crepe batter. Fill a ¼-cup measure halfway with batter; pour into center of pan. Quickly lift and tilt pan to coat bottom evenly. Cook until top appears dry; turn crepe over and cook until bottom is cooked, 15-20 seconds longer. Remove to a wire rack. Repeat with remaining batter, adding butter to skillet as needed. When cool, stack crepes between pieces of waxed paper or paper towels. Serve crepes with berry sauce and cream mixture.
2 CREPES 516 cal., 27g fat (16g sat. fat), 180mg chol., 577mg sod., 60g carb. (40g sugars, 2g fiber), 10g pro.

SALMON & GOAT CHEESE CREPES

Homemade crepes filled with a fabulous goat cheese cream and topped with smoked salmon add a real wow factor to a brunch table. The flavors will impress your guests.
—*Amy Burton, Fuquay-Varina, NC*

PREP: 20 min. + chilling • **COOK:** 10 min.
MAKES: 5 servings

- 3 large eggs
- 1¼ cups 2% milk
- ½ cup water
- 1 cup whole wheat pastry flour
- 1 cup all-purpose flour
- ¾ tsp. salt

FILLING

- 12 oz. fresh goat cheese
- ¾ cup roasted sweet red peppers
- 1 Tbsp. plus 1½ tsp. lemon juice
- 1½ tsp. smoked paprika
- 1 garlic clove, peeled and halved
- 1 lb. smoked salmon fillets
- 2 cups fresh baby spinach
- 3 Tbsp. capers, drained
- 1 Tbsp. snipped fresh dill

1. In a large bowl, whisk eggs, milk and water. In another bowl, mix flours and salt; add to egg mixture and mix well. Refrigerate, covered, 1 hour.
2. Meanwhile, in a food processor, combine goat cheese, red peppers, lemon juice, paprika and garlic; cover and process until blended, 2-3 minutes. Refrigerate until ready to use.
3. Heat a lightly greased 8-in. skillet over medium heat. Stir batter. Pour ¼ cup batter into center of pan. Quickly lift and tilt the pan to coat bottom evenly. Cook until top appears dry; turn crepe over and cook until bottom is cooked, 15-20 seconds longer. Remove to a wire rack. Repeat with remaining batter, greasing pan as needed. When cool, stack crepes between pieces of waxed paper or paper towels.
4. Spread 2 Tbsp. cheese mixture down center of each crepe. Top with salmon, spinach, capers and dill; roll up. If desired, garnish with additional cheese.
2 CREPES 235 cal., 8g fat (4g sat. fat), 91mg chol., 837mg sod., 21g carb. (2g sugars, 2g fiber), 17g pro. **DIABETIC EXCHANGES** 2 medium-fat meat, 1½ starch.

SUNSHINE CREPES

We wanted something light to go with coffee for a special breakfast, so I whipped up these sweet and fruity crepes. They were a big hit! Fill them with whatever canned or fresh fruit you have available.

—Mary Hobbs, Campbell, MO

- -

PREP: 15 min. + chilling • **COOK:** 15 min.
MAKES: 6 servings

- 2   large eggs, room temperature
- ⅔   cup 2% milk
- 1   Tbsp. canola oil
- ½   cup all-purpose flour
- 1   tsp. sugar
- ¼   tsp. salt

FILLING
- 1   can (20 oz.) crushed pineapple, drained
- 1   can (11 oz.) mandarin oranges, drained
- 1   tsp. vanilla extract
- 1   carton (8 oz.) frozen whipped topping, thawed
      Confectioners' sugar

1. In a large bowl, whisk eggs, milk and oil. In another bowl, mix flour, sugar and salt; add to egg mixture and mix well. Refrigerate, covered, 1 hour.

2. Heat a lightly greased 8-in. nonstick skillet over medium heat. Stir batter. Fill a ¼-cup measure halfway with batter; pour into center of pan. Quickly lift and tilt pan to coat bottom evenly. Cook until top appears dry; turn crepe over and cook until bottom is cooked, 15-20 seconds longer. Remove to a wire rack. Repeat with remaining batter, greasing pan as needed. When cool, stack crepes between pieces of waxed paper or paper towels.

3. For filling, in a large bowl, combine pineapple, oranges and vanilla; fold in whipped topping. Spread ⅓ cup over each crepe; fold into quarters. Dust with confectioners' sugar.

2 CREPES 299 cal., 11g fat (7g sat. fat), 64mg chol., 139mg sod., 43g carb. (31g sugars, 1g fiber), 5g pro.

BROCCOLI CHEESE CREPES

This recipe is perfect to prepare for a special brunch or light dinner for two—plus, it's easy to double or triple the recipe. I tuck a cheesy broccoli mixture into tender homemade crepes with delicious results.

—Jane Shapton, Irvine, CA

- -

PREP: 25 min. + chilling • **BAKE:** 5 min.
MAKES: 2 servings

- 2   large eggs
- ¼   cup water
- 6   Tbsp. all-purpose flour
- ½   tsp. salt

FILLING
- 1   Tbsp. butter
- 2   Tbsp. chopped onion
- 1   Tbsp. all-purpose flour
- 1   cup 2% milk
- 1   cup shredded cheddar cheese, divided
- 1   to 1½ tsp. Dijon mustard
- 1   tsp. Worcestershire sauce
- ¼   tsp. pepper
- ⅛   tsp. salt
- 2   cups frozen chopped broccoli, thawed

1. For batter, combine eggs, water, flour and salt in a blender. Cover and process until blended. Refrigerate, covered, 30 minutes.

2. Meanwhile, in a small saucepan, melt butter over medium heat; add onion. Cook and stir until tender, 1-2 minutes. Stir in flour until blended. Gradually whisk in milk. Bring to a boil, stirring constantly; cook and stir until slightly thickened, about 2 minutes. Reduce heat to low. Stir in ½ cup cheese, mustard, Worcestershire sauce, pepper and salt until cheese is melted. Stir in broccoli. Cover; keep warm.

3. Preheat oven to 350°. Heat a lightly greased 8-in. nonstick skillet over medium heat. Stir batter. Fill a ¼-cup measure halfway with batter; pour into center of the pan. Quickly lift and tilt pan to coat bottom evenly. Cook until top appears dry; turn crepe over and cook until bottom is cooked, 15-20 seconds longer. Remove to a wire rack. Repeat with remaining batter, greasing pan as needed.

4. Spoon about ½ cup filling down the center of each crepe; roll up. Place seam side down in an ungreased 11x7-in. baking dish. Sprinkle with remaining ½ cup cheese. Bake, uncovered, until cheese is melted, 5-7 minutes.

3 CREPES 586 cal., 34g fat (18g sat. fat), 269mg chol., 1412mg sod., 40g carb. (10g sugars, 7g fiber), 32g pro.

BROCCOLI
CHEESE
CREPES

CREAMY
STRAWBERRY
CREPES

PAIRS
WITH

CLASSIC MIMOSA,
P. 47

CREAMY STRAWBERRY CREPES

Wrap summer-ripe strawberries and creamy filling into these delicate crepes for an elegant brunch entree.
—*Kathy Kochiss, Huntington, CT*

PREP: 15 min. + chilling • **COOK:** 35 min.
MAKES: 7 servings

4   large eggs, room temperature
1   cup 2% milk
1   cup water
2   Tbsp. butter, melted
2   cups all-purpose flour
¼   tsp. salt
FILLING
1   pkg. (8 oz.) cream cheese, softened
1¼ cups confectioners' sugar
1   Tbsp. lemon juice
1   tsp. grated lemon zest
½   tsp. vanilla extract
4   cups fresh strawberries, sliced, divided
1   cup heavy whipping cream, whipped

1. In a large bowl, whisk eggs, milk, water and butter. In another bowl, mix flour and salt; add to egg mixture and mix well. Refrigerate, covered, 1 hour.
2. Heat a lightly greased 8-in. nonstick skillet over medium heat. Stir batter. Fill a ¼-cup measure halfway with batter; pour into center of pan. Quickly lift and tilt pan to coat bottom evenly. Cook until top appears dry; turn crepe over and cook until bottom is cooked, 15-20 seconds longer. Remove to a wire rack. Repeat with remaining batter, greasing pan as needed. When cool, stack crepes between pieces of waxed paper or paper towels.

3. For filling, in a small bowl, beat cream cheese, confectioners' sugar, lemon juice and zest, and vanilla until smooth. Fold in 2 cups berries and the whipped cream.
4. Spoon about ⅓ cup filling down the center of each crepe; roll up. Garnish with remaining berries and, if desired, additional confectioners' sugar. Cover and refrigerate or freeze remaining crepes in an airtight container, unfilled, for another use.

2 CREPES 415 cal., 26g fat (16g sat. fat), 115mg chol., 163mg sod., 40g carb. (28g sugars, 2g fiber), 7g pro.

TEST KITCHEN TIPS

My rolled crepes are a mess! If you're having a hard time rolling up your crepes, try folding them instead. Fill and fold in half, fold again and then fold again once more to create a triangular-shaped crepe. Then, you can stack them without smearing the filling. (This is a great technique for storing them in the fridge!)

Can I use frozen strawberries instead of fresh? We recommend using fresh strawberries for this recipe for their texture.

How can I make strawberry crepes my own? There are many tasty ways to level up these crepes! Drizzle chocolate sauce, add Nutella to the filling, top with powdered sugar or serve with a dollop of homemade whipped cream.

TIPS FOR HOSTING THE PERFECT BRUNCH

PLAN A MIX OF DISHES
Offer both savory and sweet items. Supplement homemade dishes with bakery delicacies.

OFFER DRINK CHOICES
Offer either a morning cocktail or straight juice. A mimosa—a mix of champagne and orange juice—is classic and convenient (see our suggestions for different mimosas on p. 47). Have other juices on hand, too.

SET UP A COFFEE STATION
A coffee station lets everyone fix their coffee just how they like it. Stock with essentials like sugar and cream, then add flavored syrups and spices like cinnamon and nutmeg.

DECORATE LIGHTLY
This quote from the 1964 *Joy of Cooking* holds true: "Don't make your effects so stagy that your guests' reactions will be 'She went to a lot of trouble.' Make them rather say, 'She had a lot of fun doing it.'"

SET UP THE NIGHT BEFORE
Lay out the place settings, decorate, and make sure there are enough seats. Jot down reminders about reheating muffins, brewing coffee, cleaning last-minute dishes and more.

RELAX!
Remember, the whole point of a party is to enjoy the company of your loved ones. Everything else is just details.

CREAMY BANANA CREPES

My husband and I enjoy taking turns fixing weekend breakfasts. These crepes are frequently on our menus. The sweet-and-sour banana filling is delicious. You'll want to serve them for lunch, dinner and dessert!
—Parrish Smith, Lincoln, NE

PREP: 15 min. + chilling • COOK: 15 min.
MAKES: 6 servings

- 2 large eggs
- ¾ cup water
- ¾ cup 2% milk
- 2 Tbsp. butter, melted
- ½ tsp. vanilla extract
- 1 cup all-purpose flour
- 1 Tbsp. sugar
- ½ tsp. salt

BANANA FILLING
- 3 Tbsp. butter
- 3 Tbsp. brown sugar
- 3 medium firm bananas, cut into ¼-in. slices

SOUR CREAM FILLING
- 1 cup sour cream
- 2 Tbsp. confectioners' sugar
- ½ cup slivered almonds, toasted

1. In a small bowl, whisk eggs, water, milk, butter and vanilla. In another bowl, mix flour, sugar and salt; add to the egg mixture and mix well. Refrigerate, covered, 1 hour.
2. Heat a lightly greased 8-in. skillet over medium heat. Stir batter. Fill a ¼-cup measure three-fourths full with batter; pour into center of pan. Quickly lift and tilt pan to coat bottom evenly. Cook until top appears dry; turn crepe over and cook until bottom is cooked, 15-20 seconds longer. Remove to a wire rack. Repeat with remaining batter, greasing pan as needed. When crepes are cool, stack them between pieces of waxed paper or paper towels.
3. For banana filling, in a small skillet, heat butter and brown sugar over medium heat until sugar is dissolved. Add bananas; toss to coat. Remove from heat; keep warm.
4. For sour cream filling, in a small bowl, combine sour cream and confectioners' sugar. Spread over half of each crepe. Top with banana filling and almonds; fold crepe over filling. If desired, sprinkle with additional confectioners' sugar and almonds.

2 CREPES 429 cal., 25g fat (12g sat. fat), 99mg chol., 327mg sod., 46g carb. (22g sugars, 3g fiber), 9g pro.

ASPARAGUS CREPES

I love serving these tender crepes with their light lemony sauce in spring. But my husband likes them anytime. In fact, it's the only way he'll eat asparagus!
—Carol Hemker, Phenix City, AL

PREP: 25 min. + chilling • BAKE: 10 min.
MAKES: 2 servings

- ½ cup 2% milk
- 1 large egg
- ⅓ cup plus 2 tsp. all-purpose flour
- 24 asparagus spears, cooked and drained

SAUCE
- 2 large egg yolks
- ¼ cup water
- 1 Tbsp. butter, melted
- 1 Tbsp. lemon juice
- ⅛ tsp. salt
  Dash cayenne pepper
  Paprika

1. For batter, combine milk and egg in a blender; cover and process until blended. Add flour; cover and process until blended. Refrigerate, covered, 1 hour.
2. Preheat oven to 350°. Heat a lightly greased 8-in. skillet over medium heat. Stir batter. Pour ¼ cup batter into center of pan. Quickly lift and tilt pan to coat bottom evenly. Cook until top appears dry; turn crepe over and cook until bottom is cooked, 15-20 seconds longer. Remove to a wire rack. Repeat with remaining batter, greasing pan as needed.
3. Place 6 asparagus spears on 1 side of each crepe; roll up. Place in a greased 11x7-in. baking dish. Bake, uncovered, until heated through, 10-15 minutes.
4. In a saucepan, whisk egg yolks and water. Cook over low heat, stirring constantly, until mixture is thickened and coats the back of a metal spoon and a thermometer reads at least 160°. Whisk in the butter, lemon juice, salt and cayenne. Pour over warm crepes; sprinkle with paprika. Serve immediately.

2 CREPES 299 cal., 15g fat (7g sat. fat), 298mg chol., 291mg sod., 30g carb. (6g sugars, 4g fiber), 15g pro.

ASPARAGUS
CREPES

PAIRS
WITH

CHARDONNAY

MEXICAN
STEAK
FAJITAS
P. 217

ZESTY
GREEN
TOMATO
SALSA
P. 214

TAJIN
LIMEADE
P. 215

SPRING FIESTA

Whether you're celebrating Cinco de Mayo or are just in the mood for a Mexican-style spread, here's a lineup bursting with flavors. Make your fiesta unforgettable with sizzling fajitas, fruity margaritas, tres leches cake, homemade guac and other zesty, spicy and cheesy favorites. Que deliciosos!

PATIO PINTOS

Any time Mom had the gang over for dinner, she made these pinto beans. Once, she made a batch for my cousin's birthday and he ate the entire thing.
—*Joan Hallford, Fort Worth, TX*

PREP: 25 min. • **BAKE:** 1 hour
MAKES: 10 servings

- ½ lb. bacon strips, chopped
- 1 large onion, chopped
- 2 garlic cloves, minced
- 6 cans (15 oz. each) pinto beans, rinsed and drained
- 4 cans (8 oz. each) tomato sauce
- 2 cans (4 oz. each) chopped green chiles
- ⅓ cup packed brown sugar
- 1 tsp. chili powder
- ¾ tsp. salt
- ½ tsp. dried oregano
- ¼ tsp. pepper

1. Preheat oven to 350°. In a Dutch oven, cook bacon over medium heat until crisp, stirring occasionally. Remove with a slotted spoon; drain on paper towels. Discard drippings, reserving 2 Tbsp. in pan.
2. Add onion to drippings; cook and stir over medium heat 6-8 minutes or until tender. Add garlic; cook 1 minute longer. Stir in beans, tomato sauce, green chiles, brown sugar and seasonings. Sprinkle top with bacon. Bake, covered, 60-70 minutes or until heated through.

FREEZE OPTION Freeze cooled bean mixture in freezer containers. To use, partially thaw in refrigerator overnight. Heat through in a saucepan, stirring occasionally; add water if necessary.

¾ CUP 349 cal., 8g fat (2g sat. fat), 11mg chol., 1183mg sod., 55g carb. (13g sugars, 12g fiber), 17g pro.

ZESTY GREEN TOMATO SALSA

ZESTY GREEN TOMATO SALSA

I came up with this fresh salsa to use up all the green tomatoes from the garden when it started to get cold.
—*Vanessa Moon, Tucson, AZ*

PREP: 20 min. + standing • **COOK:** 10 min.
MAKES: 6 cups

- 1 medium green pepper
- 1 serrano pepper
- 5 medium green tomatoes or 5 large tomatillos, husked
- 1 medium onion, chopped
- 2 garlic cloves, minced
- ⅓ cup lime juice
- 2 Tbsp. olive oil
- 4 tsp. agave nectar
- 1 tsp. coarsely ground pepper
- ½ tsp. salt
- 3 Tbsp. fresh cilantro leaves
- 1 medium ripe avocado, peeled, pitted and quartered
  Tortilla chips

1. Preheat broiler. Place peppers on a foil-lined baking sheet. Broil 3-4 in. from heat until skins blister, about 5 minutes. With tongs, rotate peppers a quarter turn. Broil and rotate until all sides are blistered and blackened. Immediately place in a bowl; let stand, covered, 20 minutes.
2. Using tongs, place tomatoes, a few at a time, in a pot of boiling water for 5 minutes. Remove tomatoes; cool slightly. Peel and finely chop tomatoes; place in a large bowl.
3. Remove skin, stems and seeds from charred peppers. Finely chop peppers; add to tomatoes. Stir in onion and garlic.
4. Place all remaining ingredients except chips in a blender; cover and process until smooth. Add to the tomato mixture, stirring to combine. Serve with chips.

NOTE Wear disposable gloves when cutting hot peppers; the oils can burn skin. Avoid touching your face.

¼ CUP SALSA 27 cal., 2g fat (0 sat. fat), 0 chol., 50mg sod., 2g carb. (1g sugars, 1g fiber), 0 pro. **DIABETIC EXCHANGES** 1 free food.

TAJIN LIMEADE

TAJIN LIMEADE

Tajin is a blend of chili peppers, salt and lime. I sprinkle it on a lot of food, but it's really delicious in limeade.
—*Amanda Phillips, Portland, OR*

PREP: 20 min. + freezing
MAKES: 8 servings

- 3 Tbsp. Tajin seasoning, divided
- 1 cup plus 1 Tbsp. sugar, divided
- 4 cups water, divided
- 3 cups fresh lime juice
  Lime wedges

1. Sprinkle 2 Tbsp. Tajin seasoning evenly in the bottom of 2 ice cube trays (16 ice cubes each). Fill with water and freeze.
2. In a saucepan, stir together 1 cup sugar and 1 cup water over medium-high heat. Bring to a boil, stirring frequently, until sugar dissolves. Remove from heat and let cool until room temperature.
3. In a large pitcher or bowl, stir together lime juice, sugar mixture and remaining 3 cups water. On a small plate, combine remaining 1 Tbsp. Tajin seasoning and 1 Tbsp. sugar. Moisten the rims of 8 tall glasses with lime wedges; dip rims in Tajin mixture. Place 3-4 ice Tajin-spiced cubes in each glass; fill with limeade. If desired, garnish with additional lime wedges.

1 CUP 126 cal., 0 fat (0 sat. fat), 0 chol., 749mg sod., 34g carb. (28g sugars, 0 fiber), 0 pro.

TALKING TAJIN

Tajin spice is a mix of dried chili peppers (chiles de arbol, guajillo and pasilla peppers), dehydrated lime and salt. With lime in the mix, it's great on the rim of drinks like margaritas (or this limeade). You can also use it as a spice rub for meats, or sprinkle it over fresh mango or cucumbers (with some added lime juice) to make a healthy, flavorful snack.

MEXICAN
STEAK
FAJITAS

MEXICAN STEAK FAJITAS

Strips of sirloin pick up plenty of spicy flavor from a marinade seasoned with cayenne pepper and cumin. These colorful fajitas are speedy and satisfying.
—Shirley Hilger, Lincoln, NE

TAKES: 30 min. • **MAKES:** 6 servings

- ¼ cup orange juice
- ¼ cup white vinegar
- 4 garlic cloves, minced
- 1 tsp. seasoned salt
- 1 tsp. dried oregano
- 1 tsp. ground cumin
- ¼ tsp. cayenne pepper
- 1 lb. beef top sirloin steak, cut into ¼-in. strips
- 1 medium onion, thinly sliced
- 1 medium green pepper, thinly sliced
- 1 medium sweet red pepper, thinly sliced
- 2 Tbsp. canola oil, divided
- 6 flour tortillas (10 in.)
  Optional: Shredded cheddar cheese, picante sauce and sour cream

SALSA CORN CAKES

1. In a large bowl, combine the orange juice, vinegar, garlic and seasonings; add the beef. Turn to coat; set aside. In a skillet, saute onion and peppers in 1 Tbsp. oil until crisp-tender; remove and set aside.
2. Drain and discard marinade from beef. In the same skillet, cook beef in remaining 1 Tbsp. oil until it reaches desired doneness, 2-4 minutes. Return vegetables to pan; heat through. Spoon meat and vegetables onto tortillas. If desired, top with cheese and serve with picante sauce and sour cream.
1 FAJITA 304 cal., 11g fat (2g sat. fat), 31mg chol., 425mg sod., 26g carb. (3g sugars, 5g fiber), 21g pro.

SALSA CORN CAKES

I whip up these patties to serve alongside nachos or tacos on summer evenings. The salsa is subtle but adds flavor. You can use fresh corn when it is in season.
—Lisa Boettcher, Rosebush, MI

TAKES: 20 min. • **MAKES:** 8 servings

- 6 oz. cream cheese, softened
- ¼ cup butter, melted
- 6 large eggs, room temperature
- 1 cup 2% milk
- 1½ cups all-purpose flour
- ½ cup cornmeal
- 1 tsp. baking powder
- 1 tsp. salt
- 1 can (15¼ oz.) whole kernel corn, drained
- ½ cup salsa, drained
- ¼ cup minced green onions
  Sour cream and additional salsa

1. In a large bowl, beat cream cheese and butter until smooth; add the eggs and mix well. Beat in the milk until smooth. Combine the flour, cornmeal, baking powder and salt; stir into the cream cheese mixture just until moistened. Fold in the corn, salsa and onions.
2. Pour batter by ¼ cupfuls into a large greased cast-iron skillet or hot griddle. Turn when bubbles form on top; cook until the second side is golden brown. Serve with sour cream and salsa.
1 SERVING 324 cal., 15g fat (8g sat. fat), 191mg chol., 715mg sod., 34g carb. (5g sugars, 3g fiber), 11g pro.

HEARTY CHICKEN ENCHILADAS

5. To use frozen enchiladas: Thaw in the refrigerator overnight. Remove from the refrigerator 30 minutes before baking. Bake as directed.
2 ENCHILADAS 577 cal., 20g fat (4g sat. fat), 83mg chol., 1541mg sod., 57g carb. (8g sugars, 8g fiber), 46g pro.

FIESTA CORN

Corn with tomatoes and jalapenos is one of the first dishes I cooked for my husband. Don't like heat? Use green bell peppers instead of jalapenos.
—*Cassandra Ramirez, Bardstown, KY*

TAKES: 25 min. • **MAKES:** 8 servings

- ¼ cup butter, cubed
- 1 small onion, chopped
- 2 to 3 jalapeno peppers, seeded and chopped
- 6 plum tomatoes, seeded and chopped
- 5 cups fresh or frozen corn
- 1½ tsp. salt
  Lime wedges, optional

1. In a 6-qt. stockpot, heat butter over medium heat. Add onion and jalapenos; cook and stir until onion is crisp-tender, 3-4 minutes. Stir in tomatoes; cook 3 minutes longer.
2. Add corn; cook, uncovered, until tender, stirring occasionally, 8-10 minutes. Stir in salt. If desired, serve with lime wedges.
NOTE Wear disposable gloves when cutting hot peppers; the oils can burn skin. Avoid touching your face.
¾ CUP 142 cal., 7g fat (4g sat. fat), 15mg chol., 505mg sod., 20g carb. (7g sugars, 3g fiber), 4g pro.

PAIRS WITH

CLASSIC MARGARITA, P. 56

HEARTY CHICKEN ENCHILADAS

My husband, Nathan, and I really like Mexican food, and this is our favorite dish. You can modify it to suit your taste by adding corn, rice or refried beans.
—*Jenny Miller, Raleigh, NC*

PREP: 6½ hours • **BAKE:** 25 min.
MAKES: 2 casseroles (2 servings each)

- 1 lb. boneless skinless chicken breasts
- 2 cans (15 oz. each) enchilada sauce
- 1 can (4 oz.) chopped green chiles
- 1 can (15 oz.) black beans, rinsed and drained
- 8 flour tortillas (6 in.), warmed
- 1 cup shredded Mexican cheese blend
  Optional: Sour cream, shredded lettuce, pico de gallo and sliced avocado

1. In a 3-qt. slow cooker, combine the chicken, enchilada sauce and chiles. Cook, covered, on low for 6-8 hours or until meat is tender.
2. Remove chicken and shred with 2 forks. Reserve 1⅔ cups cooking juices. Pour the remaining cooking juices into a large bowl; add the beans and shredded chicken. Coat 2 freezer-safe 8-in. square baking dishes with cooking spray; add ½ cup reserved juices to each.
3. Place about ⅓ cup chicken mixture down the center of each tortilla. Roll up and place seam side down in prepared dishes. Pour remaining reserved juices over top; sprinkle with cheese.
4. Cover 1 dish and freeze up to 3 months. Cover second dish and bake at 350° for 20 minutes. Uncover; bake until cheese is lightly browned, about 5 minutes longer. Serve with toppings as desired.

FIESTA
CORN

FRESAS CON CREMA

This refreshing dessert is wonderful when berries are in season. Media crema is a rich, unsweetened cream found in the baking aisle or ethnic food section of the grocery store. It's similar to creme fraiche and sour cream, although sour cream is quite a bit tangier.
—Taste of Home *Test Kitchen*

TAKES: 10 min. • **MAKES:** 4 servings

 1 can (7.6 oz.) media crema table cream
 3 Tbsp. sweetened condensed milk
 1 tsp. vanilla extract
 3 cups chopped fresh strawberries
    Fresh mint leaves, optional

In a small bowl, whisk crema, sweetened condensed milk and vanilla. Divide strawberries among 4 serving dishes. Top with milk mixture. Garnish with fresh mint if desired.

¾ CUP 241 cal., 17g fat (10g sat. fat), 43mg chol., 58mg sod., 21g carb. (14g sugars, 2g fiber), 2g pro.

MANGO & HABANERO GUACAMOLE

MORE GUACAMOLE RECIPES ON P.20-21

MANGO & HABANERO GUACAMOLE

For the ultimate sweet-spicy combo, pair mango with fresh habanero chili peppers. Depending on your preferred taste, you can control the guac's heat with the number of pepper seeds you use.
—Taste of Home *Test Kitchen*

TAKES: 15 min. • **MAKES:** 6 servings

 3 medium ripe avocados, peeled and cubed
 2 to 3 Tbsp. fresh lime juice
 ½ to 1 tsp. kosher salt
 1 medium mango, peeled and chopped
 ½ to 1 habanero pepper, seeded and chopped

In a bowl, mash avocados until almost smooth. Stir in lime juice and ½ tsp. salt. Let stand 10 minutes to allow flavors to blend. Adjust seasoning with additional lime juice and salt if desired. Top with mango and habanero.

NOTE Wear disposable gloves when cutting hot peppers; the oils can burn skin. Avoid touching your face.

¼ CUP 150 cal., 11g fat (2g sat. fat), 0 chol., 166mg sod., 15g carb. (8g sugars, 6g fiber), 2g pro. **DIABETIC EXCHANGES** 2 fat, 1 starch.

#GIRLDINNER

A plate of nachos makes a great light and easy dinner for one, as you can pick guac and other toppings to make sure you're getting the proper veggies and protein. See lots of nachos suggestions on p. 28-29.

MARGARITA
TRES LECHES
CAKE

MARGARITA TRES LECHES CAKE

The first time I ever had tres leches cake I felt like I was in heaven. I have made it at home using several techniques and flavors and this margarita twist on the classic is my favorite.
—Laurie Lufkin, Essex, MA

- -

PREP: 20 min. • **BAKE:** 20 min. + chilling
MAKES: 15 servings

- 4 large eggs, separated
- 1 cup sugar
- ½ cup tequila
- ½ cup butter, melted
- 6 Tbsp. Key lime juice, divided
- 1 tsp. vanilla extract
- 1¾ cups all-purpose flour
- 1 tsp. baking soda
- ½ tsp. salt
- ½ cup confectioners' sugar
- 1 tsp. cream of tartar
- 1 can (14 oz.) sweetened condensed milk
- 1 cup 2% milk
- ½ cup evaporated milk
- ½ cup heavy whipping cream
  Optional: Whipped cream and lime slices and zest

1. Place egg whites in a large bowl; let stand at room temperature for 30 minutes. Grease and flour a 13x9-in. baking pan.
2. Preheat oven to 375°. Beat sugar, tequila, butter, yolks, 3 Tbsp. lime juice and vanilla until well blended. Combine flour, baking soda and salt; gradually beat into the yolk mixture until blended.
3. Add confectioners' sugar and cream of tartar to the egg whites; beat with clean beaters until stiff peaks form. Fold into batter.
4. Transfer to prepared pan. Bake until a toothpick inserted in the center comes out clean, 18-20 minutes. Place pan on a wire rack. With a wooden skewer, poke holes in cake about ½ in. apart.
5. Beat condensed milk, 2% milk, evaporated milk, whipping cream and remaining 3 Tbsp. lime juice until blended. Drizzle over cake; let stand for 30 minutes. Refrigerate for 2 hours before serving.
6. Cut cake into squares. If desired, garnish with whipped cream, lime slices and zest.

1 PIECE 345 cal., 14g fat (8g sat. fat), 88mg chol., 282mg sod., 46g carb. (34g sugars, 0 fiber), 7g pro.

MARGARITA TRES LECHES CAKE TIPS:

What is the origin of tres leches cake? While most claim it's an authentic Mexican dessert, others believe it originated in a different country, like Nicaragua, Cuba or Puerto Rico. No matter where it originated, it's a favorite in many regions.

Can I use regular lime juice in this cake? Yes, it's fine —you'll hardly notice the difference between Key limes and regular limes when baked into a cake like this one.

How long does this cake last? This cake lasts about 4 days when stored in the fridge. So if you're making it in advance for a celebration, you can bake it the day before and be sure it will still taste fresh.

ROSEMARY
STRAWBERRY
DAIQUIRI
P. 58

LAVENDER
& LEMON
BISCOCHITOS
P. 229

LIME & DILL
CHIMICHURRI
SHRIMP
P. 224

SUMMER HERB PARTY

Ideal for entertaining members of your garden club—or just a bunch of friends with green thumbs—these recipes embrace the many flavorful herbs that grow in the summer. Arrange a plant swap so friends can share their favorite flavors, and get them involved in making their own herb butters and more!

MINTY MANGO SALSA

LIME & DILL CHIMICHURRI SHRIMP

Chimichurri is a popular condiment in Argentina and Uruguay and is most often used as a dipping sauce or a marinade for meats. My chimichurri shrimp incorporates dill and lime, which give it a brighter flavor and make it ideal for spring and summer entertaining.
—*Bonnie Landy, Castro Valley, CA*

PREP: 25 min. + standing • **GRILL:** 10 min.
MAKES: 4 servings

- ½ cup extra virgin olive oil
- ½ cup packed fresh parsley sprigs
- ¼ cup snipped fresh dill
- ¼ cup fresh cilantro leaves
- 3 Tbsp. lime juice
- 3 garlic cloves, halved
- ½ tsp. salt
- ¼ tsp. pepper
- 1 lb. uncooked shrimp (26-30 per lb.), peeled and deveined
- 1 medium red onion, cut into thick wedges
- 1 medium zucchini, cut into ½-in. pieces
- 1 medium yellow summer squash, cut into ½-in. pieces
- 8 cherry tomatoes
   Crusty bread

1. Place first 8 ingredients in a food processor; process until pureed. Reserve 6 Tbsp. mixture for serving. Place remaining mixture in a bowl; toss with shrimp and vegetables. Let stand 15 minutes.
2. Alternately thread shrimp and vegetables onto 8 metal or soaked wooden skewers. Grill, covered, over medium heat (or broil 4 in. from heat) until shrimp turn pink, 3-4 minutes per side. Serve on bed of additional herbs, with crusty bread and reserved sauce.
2 KABOBS 316 cal., 22g fat (3g sat. fat), 138mg chol., 371mg sod., 10g carb. (4g sugars, 2g fiber), 21g pro.

MINTY MANGO SALSA

I originally made this colorful mango salsa to garnish a smoked turkey my husband made. We have since tried it on chicken and fish. It also makes a fun snack or party appetizer scooped up with your favorite tortilla chips.
—*Diane Thompson, Nutrioso, AZ*

PREP: 10 min. + chilling
MAKES: about 2½ cups

- 1 large ripe mango, peeled and diced
- 1 medium sweet red pepper, diced
- 1 can (4 oz.) chopped green chiles
- ¼ cup chopped green onions
- 1 Tbsp. lime juice
- 2 tsp. minced fresh mint
- ¼ tsp. ground ginger
   Tortilla chips

In a small bowl, combine the mango, pepper, chiles, onions, juice, mint and ginger. Cover and refrigerate at least 8 hours. Serve with tortilla chips.
NOTE Wear disposable gloves when cutting hot peppers; the oils can burn skin. Avoid touching your face.
¼ CUP 27 cal., 0 fat (0 sat. fat), 0 chol., 46mg sod., 6g carb. (5g sugars, 1g fiber), 0 pro. **DIABETIC EXCHANGES** 1 free food.

TEST KITCHEN TIP

When buying mangos, look for ones that have a slight give to them but no soft spots. A ripe mango has a sweet fragrance; if it smells piney, let it ripen a few days before cutting.

LIME & DILL
CHIMICHURRI
SHRIMP

PAIRS
WITH

ROSEMARY
STRAWBERRY
DAIQUIRI, P. 58

TARRAGON BUTTER

This seasoned butter is a delicious way to add great flavor and a hint of color to your favorite breads and vegetables.

—*Connie Moore, Medway, OH*

TAKES: 5 min. • **MAKES:** 1 cup

- 1 cup butter, softened
- 2 Tbsp. minced fresh tarragon or 2 tsp. dried tarragon
- 2 Tbsp. minced fresh parsley
- 1 tsp. minced chives
- 1 garlic clove, minced
  Dash pepper

Beat all ingredients until blended. Shape into a log; wrap. Refrigerate up to 1 week or freeze up to several months

1 TBSP. 101 cal., 11g fat (7g sat. fat), 31mg chol., 116mg sod., 0 carb. (0 sugars, 0 fiber), 0 pro.

GIFTS TO GO

Invite guests to make their favorite herbs into flavored butters as a take-home treat. Snip, chop and mix into softened butter.

GREEN SALAD WITH TANGY BASIL VINAIGRETTE

GREEN SALAD WITH TANGY BASIL VINAIGRETTE

A tart and tangy dressing turns a basic salad into something special. It works for weeknight dining but is good enough for company and pairs perfectly with just about anything.

—*Kristin Rimkus, Snohomish, WA*

TAKES: 15 min. • **MAKES:** 4 servings

- 3 Tbsp. white wine vinegar
- 4½ tsp. minced fresh basil
- 4½ tsp. olive oil
- 1½ tsp. honey
- ¼ tsp. salt
- ⅛ tsp. pepper
- 6 cups torn mixed salad greens
- 1 cup cherry tomatoes, halved
- 2 Tbsp. shredded Parmesan cheese

In a small bowl, whisk the first 6 ingredients until blended. In a large bowl, combine salad greens and tomatoes. Drizzle with vinaigrette; toss to coat. Sprinkle with cheese.

1 CUP 89 cal., 6g fat (1g sat. fat), 2mg chol., 214mg sod., 7g carb. (4g sugars, 2g fiber), 3g pro. **DIABETIC EXCHANGES** 1 vegetable, 1 fat.

CHICKEN PICCATA WITH LEMON SAUCE

2. In a large nonstick skillet, brown 4 chicken breast halves in 1½ tsp. oil for 3-5 minutes on each side or until juices run clear. Remove and keep warm. Drain drippings. Repeat with remaining chicken and oil. Remove and keep warm.
3. In the same pan, melt butter. Add the remaining ¼ cup wine and 3 Tbsp. lemon juice. Bring to a boil. Boil, uncovered, until sauce is reduced by a fourth. Drizzle over chicken.

1 CHICKEN BREAST HALF 232 cal., 9g fat (4g sat. fat), 75mg chol., 346mg sod., 8g carb. (1g sugars, 0 fiber), 27g pro. **DIABETIC EXCHANGES** 3 lean meat, 1 fat, ½ starch.

THYMED ZUCCHINI SAUTE

Simple and flavorful, this recipe is a tasty and healthy way to use up all those zucchini that are taking over your garden. It's ready in no time!
—*Bobby Taylor, Ulster Park, NY*

TAKES: 15 min. • **MAKES:** 4 servings

- 1 Tbsp. olive oil
- 1 lb. medium zucchini, quartered lengthwise and halved
- ¼ cup finely chopped onion
- ½ vegetable bouillon cube, crushed
- 2 Tbsp. minced fresh parsley
- 1 tsp. minced fresh thyme or ¼ tsp. dried thyme

In a large skillet, heat oil over medium-high heat. Add zucchini, onion and bouillon; cook and stir 4-5 minutes or until zucchini is crisp-tender. Sprinkle with herbs.

¾ CUP 53 cal., 4g fat (1g sat. fat), 0 chol., 135mg sod., 5g carb. (2g sugars, 2g fiber), 2g pro. **DIABETIC EXCHANGES** 1 vegetable, ½ fat.

CHICKEN PICCATA WITH LEMON SAUCE

Once you've tried this tangy yet delicate entree, you won't hesitate to make it for company. Seasoned with Parmesan and parsley, the chicken cooks up golden brown, then is drizzled with a light lemon sauce.
—*Susan Pursell, Fountain Valley, CA*

PREP: 25 min. • **COOK:** 25 min.
MAKES: 8 servings

- 8 boneless skinless chicken breast halves (4 oz. each)
- ½ cup egg substitute
- 2 Tbsp. plus ¼ cup dry white wine or chicken broth, divided
- 5 Tbsp. lemon juice, divided
- 3 garlic cloves, minced
- ⅛ tsp. hot pepper sauce
- ½ cup all-purpose flour
- ½ cup grated Parmesan cheese
- ¼ cup minced fresh parsley
- ½ tsp. salt
- 3 tsp. olive oil, divided
- 2 Tbsp. butter

1. Flatten chicken to ¼-in. thickness. In a shallow dish, combine the egg substitute, 2 Tbsp. wine, 2 Tbsp. lemon juice, garlic and hot pepper sauce. In another shallow dish, combine the flour, Parmesan cheese, parsley and salt. Coat chicken with the flour mixture, dip in the egg substitute mixture, then coat again with the flour mixture.

LAVENDER
& LEMON
BISCOCHITOS

LAVENDER & LEMON BISCOCHITOS

Biscochitos are the state cookie of New Mexico, traditionally made with anise seeds. I substituted lavender and lemon to make my own intriguing and delicious version. I've also made these with lemon and thyme and they were scrumptious!
—Marla Clark, Albuquerque, NM

PREP: 30 min. + chilling
BAKE: 10 min./batch • **MAKES:** 6 dozen

- ½ cup unsalted butter, softened
- ⅔ cup sugar
- 1 large egg, room temperature
- 1 Tbsp. dried lavender flowers
- 1 Tbsp. grated lemon zest
- 1½ cups all-purpose flour
- 1 tsp. baking powder
- ¼ tsp. salt
  Optional: Lightly beaten egg white and fresh thyme sprigs

1. In a large bowl, cream butter and sugar until light and fluffy, 5-7 minutes. Beat in egg, lavender and lemon zest. In another bowl, whisk flour, baking powder and salt; gradually beat into creamed mixture. Divide dough in half. Shape each into a disk; cover and refrigerate 30 minutes or until firm enough to roll.
2. Preheat oven to 350°. On a lightly floured surface, roll each portion of dough to ¼-in. thickness. Cut with a floured 1-in. round cookie cutter. Place 1 in. apart on parchment-lined baking sheets. Sprinkle with additional sugar or, if desired, brush with egg white and press fresh thyme onto cookies.
3. Bake until bottoms are light brown, 9-11 minutes. Remove from pans to wire racks to cool. Store in airtight containers.
NOTE Look for dried lavender flowers in spice shops. If using lavender from the garden, make sure it hasn't been treated with chemicals.
1 COOKIE 29 cal., 1g fat (1g sat. fat), 6mg chol., 16mg sod., 4g carb. (2g sugars, 0 fiber), 0 pro.

CILANTRO PESTO

Feel free to make this simple pesto ahead of time and freeze it. This brightly colored condiment tastes as fresh as it looks!
—Karen Deaver, Babylon, NY

TAKES: 10 min. • **MAKES:** 1 cup

- 1 cup fresh cilantro leaves
- ¼ cup grated Parmesan cheese
- ¼ cup chopped walnuts
- 2 Tbsp. lime juice
- ½ cup olive oil
  Cooked jumbo shrimp, peeled and deveined

Place cilantro and cheese in a food processor; cover and pulse until chopped. Add walnuts and lime juice; cover and process until blended. While processing, gradually add oil in a steady stream. Serve with shrimp.
2 TBSP. 152 cal., 16g fat (2g sat. fat), 2mg chol., 40mg sod., 1g carb. (0 sugars, 0 fiber), 1g pro.

MARJORAM LENTILS

Providing 13 grams of fiber per serving, this delicious medley packs nutritional benefits! Enjoy the homey dish with a light meat entree or keep it meatless with a side of cornbread or rice.
—Mildred Sherrer, Fort Worth, TX

PREP: 30 min. • **COOK:** 45 min.
MAKES: 6 servings

- 4 medium carrots, chopped
- 2 medium onions, chopped
- 6 garlic cloves, minced
- 1 Tbsp. olive oil
- 1 can (14½ oz.) vegetable broth
- 1 cup dried lentils, rinsed
- 3 Tbsp. minced fresh marjoram or 1 Tbsp. dried marjoram
- 1½ tsp. rubbed sage
- 1 can (14½ oz.) diced tomatoes, undrained
- ¼ cup sherry or additional vegetable broth
- ¼ cup minced fresh parsley
- 3 Tbsp. shredded Swiss cheese

1. In a large nonstick saucepan, saute the carrots, onions and garlic in oil until tender. Stir in the broth, lentils, marjoram and sage. Bring to a boil. Reduce heat; cover and simmer for 30-45 minutes or until lentils are tender.
2. Stir in the tomatoes, sherry or additional broth and parsley; heat through. Sprinkle with cheese.
¾ CUP 216 cal., 4g fat (1g sat. fat), 3mg chol., 456mg sod., 34g carb. (9g sugars, 13g fiber), 11g pro. **DIABETIC EXCHANGES** 2 vegetable, 1½ starch, 1 lean meat, ½ fat.

FRESH HERBS AS DECOR

For a festive and aromatic touch, tuck fresh herbs through the napkin ring at each place setting. Go with a single herb for the whole table, or give different herbs to the guests—may we recommend parsley, sage, rosemary and thyme? Don't overdo it, or your place setting will look as if it contains a bouquet garni, but a single sprig is a lovely touch.

THE HERB SWAP BASICS

Assign your fellow green thumbs a type of herb to bring, let 'em swap and pot as they please, then send them on their way with a lush kitchen garden. From there, just add water!

Roll down brown paper bags and fill them with soil to contain the mess and add rustic flair to your table.

Spray-paint used veggie cans to make simple pots. Be sure to poke holes in the bottom for drainage.

Label clothespins with herb names and clip them to individual pots.

A portable bar cart doubles as a holder for finished planters, clearing table space. When the party's over, roll it to guests' cars for easy transferring.

BASIL

CILANTRO

DILL

THYME

HOW TO PRESERVE HERBS

As part of an herb swap, give your guests little information cards about each variety and how to keep their new herbs tasting best.

STORE FRESH HERBS

Wrap fresh herbs in a slightly damp paper towel and place in an airtight container. Store in the refrigerator for 5-7 days.

FREEZE FRESH HERBS

Chop fresh herbs and fill the empty sections of an ice cube tray with them. Carefully pour water into each herb-filled compartment and freeze.

DRY FRESH HERBS

Snip healthy branches and remove the leaves from the bottom inch of each stem. Bundle several stems together with string or a rubber band, and hang upside down in a warm, airy room. Check the herbs weekly until they're completely dry. Crumble the leaves into spice jars.

BASIL

Flavor: Depending on the variety, you'll notice hints of pepper, mint or anise.

How to use it: Pair with mild cheeses, fresh tomatoes and spicy flavors. It's most commonly used in Mediterranean, Asian and Indian dishes. For best results, add at the end of cooking.

CILANTRO
(AKA CORIANDER LEAF)

Flavor: Some find this herb bright and refreshing with a zesty flavor. Others detect a mild "soapy" taste for reasons that might be related to human genetics.

How to use it: Enjoy cilantro raw or cooked. Its invigorating flavor brings dull sauces to life. Cilantro is a staple of Latin American and Asian cooking.

DILL

Flavor: Delicate strands boast a strong clean, fresh earthiness, or a subtle flavor of licorice or fennel.

How to use it: Best used in small quantities—too much can overwhelm a dish—dill works well in spring salads and pairs well with vegetables like asparagus and peas. It's also a delicious addition to homemade salad dressings.

THYME

Flavor: This is a pungent herb with a slightly sweet and woodsy flavor. The leaves are aromatic and floral, strong but with an understated taste.

How to use it: A staple in French cooking, thyme works well with poultry dishes and strong cheeses. Or use it in breads, desserts and drinks.

CHEESE &
PIMIENTO
SPREAD
P. 234

WATERMELON &
CUCUMBER SALSA
P. 236

S'MORES
CUPCAKES
P. 241

FAVORITE
HOT CHOCOLATE
P. 239

BONFIRE PARTY

Summer is almost over, but there's still a warm breeze kissing your cheek. After soaking up the final days of swimming, hiking or lounging in a hammock, gather with friends around a backyard firepit. The cozy comfort and delicious food will turn any outdoor evening into a memorable night.

CHEESE & PIMIENTO SPREAD

MAC & CHEESE CUPS

I started making these for a close friend's daughter when she started eating solid food. She loves mac and cheese and could hold these in her tiny hands to feed herself. Now the adults like them more than the kids! They're always requested at potlucks.

—*Karen Lambert, Weaverville, NC*

PREP: 20 min. • **BAKE:** 25 min.
MAKES: 24 servings

- 1 lb. uncooked elbow macaroni
- 3 cups sharp cheddar cheese, finely shredded
- 5 Tbsp. butter, softened
- 3 large eggs
- 1 cup half-and-half cream
- ½ cup sour cream
- 1 tsp. salt
- ½ tsp. pepper

1. Preheat oven to 350°. Cook macaroni according to package directions, drain. Transfer to a large bowl. Stir in cheese and butter until melted.
2. In another bowl, whisk eggs, cream, sour cream, salt and pepper until blended. Add to macaroni mixture; stir until well blended.
3. Spoon macaroni into 24 well-greased muffin cups. Bake until golden brown, 25-30 minutes.

1 PIECE 178 cal., 10g fat (6g sat. fat), 50mg chol., 226mg sod., 15g carb. (1g sugars, 1g fiber), 7g pro.

#GIRLDINNER

These cute little mac and cheese cups can be kept in an airtight container in the refrigerator for 3-4 days, ready for a quick dinner. To reheat, pop them in the microwave for 1-2 minutes or bake them at 350° until heated through, 10-15 minutes.

CHEESE & PIMIENTO SPREAD

My mother made delicious pimiento cheese, but this is a spicy, modern version of her recipe. Serve it stuffed in celery or spread on crackers or a sandwich.

—*Elizabeth Hester, Elizabethtown, NC*

TAKES: 15 min. • **MAKES:** 2¾ cups

- 12 oz. sharp white cheddar cheese
- 8 oz. reduced-fat cream cheese, softened
- 2 tsp. Worcestershire sauce
- 2 tsp. white vinegar
- ¼ tsp. white pepper
- ¼ tsp. garlic powder
- ¼ tsp. cayenne pepper
- 1 jar (4 oz.) diced pimientos, undrained
    Assorted crackers and vegetables

Shred cheddar cheese; transfer to a large bowl. Add cream cheese, Worcestershire sauce, vinegar, pepper, garlic powder and cayenne; beat on low speed until blended. Drain pimientos, reserving 2 Tbsp. juice. Stir in pimientos and reserved juice. Serve with crackers and vegetables.

2 TBSP. 90 cal., 7g fat (4g sat. fat), 23mg chol., 150mg sod., 1g carb. (1g sugars, 0 fiber), 5g pro.

VEGGIE BACON SLAW

This crunchy salad is nutrient-dense and tasty too. Mix and match with your favorite dried fruit and nuts or whatever you have on hand.
—*Jeanne Larson,*
Rancho Santa Margarita, CA

PREP: 20 min. + chilling
MAKES: 12 servings

- 4 cups shredded fresh Brussels sprouts
- 4 large carrots, peeled and shredded
- 1 lb. bacon strips, cooked and crumbled
- 8 green onions, chopped
- ⅔ cup dried cranberries
- 1 cup sliced almonds, toasted

DRESSING
- 1 cup plain Greek yogurt
- ½ cup reduced-fat mayonnaise
- ½ cup cider vinegar
- ⅓ cup honey
- ½ tsp. garlic powder
- ½ tsp. sea salt

In a large bowl, combine the first 6 ingredients. In another bowl, whisk dressing ingredients until smooth; drizzle over salad and toss to coat. Refrigerate, covered, at least 2 hours before serving.
NOTE To toast nuts, bake in a shallow pan in a 350° oven for 5-10 minutes or cook in a skillet over low heat until lightly browned, stirring occasionally.
¾ CUP 269 cal., 16g fat (4g sat. fat), 22mg chol., 423mg sod., 25g carb. (18g sugars, 4g fiber), 9g pro.

SUMMER NIGHT SNUGGLES
Place rolled-up blankets in a basket for your guests to easily access. Spread the blankets on the grass (keeping a safe distance from the fire), or snuggle up in one if the night air gets chilly.

JALAPENO SLIDERS WITH CRISPY ONIONS

My husband and I love spicy foods, and this recipe was an excellent step up from a typical burger. It has just the right amount of flavor and spice for us, but it can be adjusted to suit your tastes.
—*Christy Addison, Clarksville, OH*

TAKES: 25 min. • **MAKES:** 8 servings

- 1 lb. ground beef
- ½ tsp. salt
- ¼ tsp. pepper
- 1 to 2 jalapeno pepper, seeded and thinly sliced
- 2 slices white American cheese, cut into 4 squares
- 8 slider buns, split and toasted
- 1 can (2.8 oz.) french-fried onions

Shape beef into eight ½-in.-thick patties; sprinkle with salt and pepper. In a large skillet, cook sliders over medium heat for 2-3 minutes. Turn and top with peppers and cheese. Continue cooking for 2-3 minutes or until a thermometer reads 160°. Serve on buns. Top with french-fried onions.
NOTE Wear disposable gloves when cutting hot peppers; the oils can burn skin. Avoid touching your face.
1 SLIDER 292 cal., 15g fat (5g sat. fat), 54mg chol., 517mg sod., 23g carb. (2g sugars, 1g fiber), 14g pro.

GRANDMA'S CLASSIC POTATO SALAD

4. Chop and refrigerate 1 hard-boiled egg; chop the remaining 3 hard-boiled eggs. In a large bowl, combine potatoes, celery, chopped onion and eggs; add dressing and stir until blended. Refrigerate until chilled. Garnish with reserved chopped egg and, if desired, sliced green onions.

¾ CUP 144 cal., 3g fat (1g sat. fat), 112mg chol., 402mg sod., 23g carb. (3g sugars, 2g fiber), 6g pro. **DIABETIC EXCHANGES** 1½ starch, ½ fat.

WATERMELON & CUCUMBER SALSA

The combo of watermelon and cucumber sounds unusual—but tastes amazing! Eat the salsa with chips, or serve it as a topper with hot dogs or chicken tacos for a refreshing change of pace.
—*Suzanne Curletto, Walnut Creek, CA*

- -

TAKES: 15 min. • **MAKES:** 3 cups

  1½ cups seeded chopped watermelon
  ¾ cup finely chopped cucumber
  ½ cup finely chopped sweet onion
  ¼ cup minced fresh cilantro
  1 jalapeno pepper, seeded and minced
  2 Tbsp. lime juice
  ¼ tsp. salt

In a small bowl, combine all ingredients; refrigerate until serving.
NOTE Wear disposable gloves when cutting hot peppers; the oils can burn skin. Avoid touching your face.
¼ CUP 10 cal., 0 fat (0 sat. fat), 0 chol., 50mg sod., 3g carb. (2g sugars, 0 fiber), 0 pro. **DIABETIC EXCHANGES** 1 free food.

#GIRLDINNER

This fresh salsa is a perfect combination of sweet and spicy—keep it in the fridge to eat with sandwiches or salads. Or it can stand in for fresh fruit on a charcuterie board, and you can scoop it up with crackers.

GRANDMA'S CLASSIC POTATO SALAD

When I asked my grandmother how old this recipe was, she told me that her mom used to make it when she was a little girl. It has definitely stood the test of time!
—*Kimberly Wallace, Dennison, OH*

- -

PREP: 25 min. • **COOK:** 20 min. + cooling
MAKES: 10 servings

  6 medium potatoes, peeled and cubed
  ¼ cup all-purpose flour
  1 Tbsp. sugar
  1½ tsp. salt
  1 tsp. ground mustard
  1 tsp. pepper
  ¾ cup water
  2 large eggs, beaten
  ¼ cup white vinegar
  4 hard-boiled large eggs, divided use
  2 celery ribs, chopped
  1 medium onion, chopped
     Sliced green onions, optional

1. Place potatoes in a large saucepan and cover with water. Bring to a boil. Reduce heat; cover and cook until tender, 15-20 minutes. Drain and cool to room temperature.
2. Meanwhile, in a small heavy saucepan, combine flour, sugar, salt, mustard and pepper. Gradually stir in water until smooth. Cook and stir over medium-high heat until thickened and bubbly. Reduce heat; cook and stir 2 minutes longer.
3. Remove from the heat. Stir a small amount of hot mixture into beaten eggs; return all to pan, stirring constantly. Bring to a gentle boil; cook and stir for 2 minutes longer. Remove from heat and cool completely. Gently stir in vinegar.

WATERMELON &
CUCUMBER SALSA

PAIRS
WITH

GEWURTZTRAMINER
OR ROSE

VANILLA CHAI TEA

An aromatic chai is comfort in a cup. It's extra special with a dollop of fresh whipped cream and a sprinkling of ground allspice on top. The whipped cream can be made a couple of hours in advance; keep it covered in the refrigerator until you're ready to serve.
—Taste of Home *Test Kitchen*

- -

TAKES: 25 min. • **MAKES:** 6 servings

  8 whole peppercorns
  ½ tsp. whole allspice
  2 cardamom pods
  1 cinnamon stick (3 in.)
  4 whole cloves
  8 tea bags
  1 Tbsp. honey
  4 cups boiling water
  2 cups 2% milk
  1 Tbsp. vanilla extract
  ½ cup heavy whipping cream
  1½ tsp. confectioners' sugar
     Ground allspice

1. Place first 5 ingredients in a large bowl. With the end of a wooden spoon handle, crush mixture until aromas are released. Add tea bags, honey and boiling water; steep, covered, 6 minutes.
2. In a small saucepan, heat milk. Strain tea into a heatproof pitcher; stir in milk and vanilla.
3. In a small bowl, beat cream until it begins to thicken. Add confectioners' sugar; beat until soft peaks form. Top individual servings with whipped cream; sprinkle with allspice.

1 CUP (WITH 2½ TBSP. TOPPING) 131 cal., 9g fat (6g sat. fat), 33mg chol., 48mg sod., 9g carb. (7g sugars, 0 fiber), 3g pro.

S'MORE BAR
It's not summer without everyone's favorite treat—s'mores! Pack a tray with Mason jars, a Thermos, cups and other accouterments to create an al fresco s'more or hot cocoa bar.

BUTTERSCOTCH PEANUT BUTTER SQUARES

These bars, which our family refers to as peanut butter brownies, are delicious! They slice and pack easily making them ideal for road trips and bake sales. I always double the recipe because a single batch is never enough!
—*Debbie Johnson, Centertown, MO*

- -

PREP: 20 min. + cooling
BAKE: 20 min. + cooling
MAKES: 16 squares

  1¼ cups all-purpose flour
  1 tsp. baking powder
  ½ tsp. salt
  1½ cups packed brown sugar
  ½ cup butter, cubed
  ½ cup chunky peanut butter
  2 large eggs, room temperature, lightly beaten
  1 tsp. vanilla extract

1. Preheat oven to 350°. In a small bowl, whisk flour, baking powder and salt.
2. In a large saucepan, combine brown sugar, butter and peanut butter; bring to a boil, stirring to blend. Remove from heat; cool slightly, about 10 minutes.
3. Stir eggs and vanilla into peanut butter mixture. Stir in flour mixture. Transfer to a greased 9-in. square baking pan. Bake for 20-25 minutes or until golden brown and a toothpick inserted in center comes out clean (do not overbake).
4. Cool completely in pan on a wire rack. Cut into squares. Store in an airtight container.

1 SQUARE 222 cal., 10g fat (4g sat. fat), 39mg chol., 203mg sod., 30g carb. (21g sugars, 1g fiber), 4g pro.

FAVORITE HOT CHOCOLATE

FAVORITE HOT CHOCOLATE

You need just a few basic ingredients to stir up this spirit-warming sipper. The comforting beverage is smooth and not too sweet, making it just right for a cozy chilly night.
—*Flo Snodderly, North Vernon, IN*

TAKES: 15 min. • **MAKES:** 8 servings

- 1 can (14 oz.) sweetened condensed milk
- ½ cup baking cocoa
- 6½ cups water
- 2 tsp. vanilla extract
  Optional: Sweetened whipped cream, marshmallows, chocolate syrup and Pirouette cookies

1. Place condensed milk and baking cocoa in a large saucepan; cook and stir over medium heat until blended. Gradually stir in water; heat through, stirring occasionally.
2. Remove from heat; stir in vanilla. Add toppings as desired.

1 CUP 177 cal., 5g fat (3g sat. fat), 17mg chol., 63mg sod., 30g carb. (27g sugars, 1g fiber), 5g pro.

SPICY SOUTHWESTERN FRUIT SALAD

This colorful fruit salad is special enough for company or to take to a potluck dinner. It's easy to double the recipe or swap in different fruits depending on what your group prefers.

—*Paula Marchesi, Lenhartsville, PA*

TAKES: 30 min. • **MAKES:** 8 servings

- 1 cup cubed peeled mango
- 1 cup cubed peeled papaya
- 1 cup cubed peeled fresh peaches
- 1 cup fresh blueberries
- 1 medium ripe avocado, peeled and cubed
- 1 cup frozen corn, thawed
- ⅓ cup chopped dried apricots
- ⅓ cup flaked coconut
- ¼ cup minced fresh cilantro
- 1 cup corn chips, lightly crushed

CHIPOTLE-COCONUT DRESSING

- ¼ cup coconut milk
- 2 Tbsp. lime juice
- 1 Tbsp. cider vinegar
- 1 chipotle pepper in adobo sauce, chopped
- 2 garlic cloves, minced
- ¼ tsp. cayenne pepper
- ¼ tsp. brown sugar
  Optional: Additional corn chips or flaked coconut

In a large bowl, combine the first 10 ingredients. In a small bowl, whisk coconut milk, lime juice, cider vinegar, chipotle, garlic, cayenne and brown sugar. Drizzle over fruit mixture; toss to coat. Sprinkle with additional corn chips or flaked coconut if desired. Serve immediately.

NOTE Wear disposable gloves when cutting hot peppers; the oils can burn skin. Avoid touching your face.

¾ CUP 161 cal., 7g fat (3g sat. fat), 0 chol., 65mg sod., 24g carb. (13g sugars, 4g fiber), 2g pro. **DIABETIC EXCHANGES** 1 starch, 1 fat, ½ fruit.

SPARKLER STATION

Use a galvanized metal bucket to house sparklers that guests can grab at their convenience. Then get ready to light up the night!

S'MORES CUPCAKES

TIN CAN LANTERN

Upcycle an empty tin can into a twinkling outdoor lantern. Using a drill or hammer and nails, drill or punch holes into the can. You can create a decorative design if you'd like. Place a votive candle inside for a warm glow. Be sure to place the can on a firesafe surface and do not leave a lit votive unattended.

S'MORES CUPCAKES

Marshmallow frosting puts these cupcakes over the top. Chocolate bar pieces and graham cracker crumbs on top make them extra indulgent and even more like the real thing—but better!
—*Erin Rachwal, Hartland, WI*

- -

PREP: 30 min.
BAKE: 20 min. + cooling
MAKES: 2 dozen

- ¾ cup water
- ¾ cup buttermilk
- 2 large eggs, room temperature
- 3 Tbsp. canola oil
- 1 tsp. vanilla extract
- 1½ cups all-purpose flour
- 1½ cups sugar
- ¾ cup baking cocoa
- 1½ tsp. baking soda
- ¾ tsp. salt
- ¾ tsp. baking powder

FROSTING
- 1½ cups butter, softened
- 2 cups confectioners' sugar
- ½ tsp. vanilla extract
- 2 jars (7 oz. each) marshmallow creme
- 2 Tbsp. graham cracker crumbs
- 2 milk chocolate candy bars (1.55 oz. each)
  Optional: Toasted marshmallows and graham cracker pieces

1. Preheat oven to 350°. In a large bowl, beat water, buttermilk, eggs, oil and vanilla until well blended. Combine flour, sugar, cocoa, baking soda, salt and baking powder; gradually beat into buttermilk mixture until blended.

2. Fill paper-lined muffin cups half full with batter. Bake for 16-20 minutes or until a toothpick inserted in center comes out clean. Cool in pans for 10 minutes before removing from pans to wire racks to cool completely.

3. For frosting, in a large bowl, beat butter until fluffy; beat in confectioners' sugar and vanilla until smooth. Add marshmallow creme; beat until light and fluffy. Spread or pipe frosting over cupcakes. Sprinkle with cracker crumbs. Break each candy bar into 12 pieces; garnish cupcakes. If desired, top with toasted marshmallows and graham cracker pieces.

1 CUPCAKE 330 cal., 15g fat (8g sat. fat), 47mg chol., 298mg sod., 43g carb. (35g sugars, 1g fiber), 3g pro.

JAM-TOPPED
MINI CHEESECAKES
P. 250

RUSTIC
CHOCOLATE
RASPBERRY TART
P. 249

CHOCOLATE-
CARAMEL
RUM COFFEE
P. 247

BOOK CLUB

Be it a classic work, a spicy new thriller or a celeb memoir bound to spur an invigorating debate, book clubs have long been a fun excuse to get friends together for good food, fun drinks and enlightening discussion. It's easy to create a warm setting that invites fellow bibliophiles to linger and relax over a glass of wine and a spread of amazing offerings.

CLASSIC COBB SALAD

Making this salad is a lot like putting in a garden. I plant everything in nice, neat sections, just as I do with seedlings.
—*Patricia Kile, Elizabethtown, PA*

TAKES: 20 min. • **MAKES:** 4 servings

- 6 cups torn iceberg lettuce
- 2 medium tomatoes, chopped
- 1 medium ripe avocado, peeled and chopped
- ¾ cup diced fully cooked ham
- 2 hard-boiled large eggs, chopped
- ¾ cup diced cooked turkey
- 1¼ cups sliced fresh mushrooms
- ½ cup crumbled blue cheese
  Salad dressing of choice
  Optional: Sliced ripe olives and lemon wedges

Place lettuce on a platter or in a large serving bowl. Arrange remaining ingredients in rows or sections as desired. Serve with dressing of choice; if desired, serve with sliced ripe olives and lemon wedges.

1 SERVING 260 cal., 15g fat (5g sat. fat), 148mg chol., 586mg sod., 10g carb. (5g sugars, 4g fiber), 23g pro. **DIABETIC EXCHANGES** 3 lean meat, 2 vegetable, 2 fat.

#GIRLDINNER

Cobb salad makes for a great impromptu single meal, with its combination of different food groups. You can mix and match the ingredients based on what you have in your fridge; green peppers and cooked chicken are great additions as well. To make things ultra convenient, keep hard-boiled eggs and a cooked meat—deli ham or rotisserie chicken—in your refrigerator.

CLASSIC COBB SALAD

LOADED TWICE-BAKED POTATO CASSEROLE

LOADED TWICE-BAKED POTATO CASSEROLE

Creamy, cheesy and loaded with bacon, this comforting casserole immediately makes guests feel at home. Twice-baked potatoes and potato skins make a scrumptious combination.
—*Cyndy Gerken, Naples, FL*

- -

PREP: 1½ hours • **BAKE:** 30 min.
MAKES: 8 servings

- 4   large baking potatoes (about 3¼ lbs.)
- 1   Tbsp. olive oil
- ¾   tsp. salt, divided
- ¾   tsp. pepper, divided
- ¼   cup butter, cubed
- ⅔   cup heavy whipping cream
- ¼   cup sour cream
- 2   cups shredded cheddar cheese, divided
- 6   bacon strips, cooked and crumbled, divided
- 2   green onions, sliced, divided
    Additional sour cream, optional

1. Preheat oven to 375°. Scrub potatoes; pierce several times with a fork. Brush with oil; sprinkle with ½ tsp. salt and ¼ tsp. pepper. Place in a foil-lined 15x10x1-in. baking pan; bake until tender, 1-1¼ hours. Cool slightly.
2. In a small saucepan, melt butter over medium heat. Whisk in whipping cream and ¼ cup sour cream. Add 1½ cups cheese; stir until melted. Remove from heat; cover to keep warm.
3. When potatoes are cool enough to handle, cut each potato lengthwise in half. Scoop out pulp and place in a large bowl. Cut 2 potato skin shells into 1-in. pieces; save remaining skins for another use.
4. Mash pulp with remaining ¼ tsp. salt and ½ tsp. pepper. Stir in cheese mixture, half the bacon and 2 Tbsp. green onion. Transfer to a greased 1½-qt. baking dish. Top with the cut-up potato skins. Sprinkle with remaining cheese and bacon.
5. Bake until heated through and lightly browned, 30-35 minutes. Sprinkle with remaining green onion. If desired, serve with additional sour cream.
½ CUP 367 cal., 27g fat (16g sat. fat), 84mg chol., 458mg sod., 20g carb. (2g sugars, 2g fiber), 12g pro.

SAVORY CRACKER SNACK MIX

After trying a snack mix with the flavors of my favorite Everything bagel seasoning, a friend suggested I make it even more versatile with something other than oyster crackers. Now it's a deliciously addictive snack!
—*Cyndy Gerken, Naples, FL*

- -

PREP: 15 min. • **BAKE:** 15 min. + cooling
MAKES: 4½ cups

- 1½   cups potato sticks
- 1½   cups cheddar-flavored snack crackers
- 1½   cups sourdough pretzel nuggets
- 3   Tbsp. butter
- ¼   cup grated Parmesan cheese
- 3   Tbsp. olive oil
- 1½   tsp. sesame seeds
- 1½   tsp. dried minced garlic
- 1½   tsp. dried minced onion
- 1½   tsp. poppy seeds
- ¼   tsp. kosher salt

1. Preheat oven to 350°. Combine potato sticks, crackers and pretzels. In a small saucepan, melt butter; stir in remaining ingredients. Drizzle over the cracker mixture; toss to coat.
2. Spread in a greased 15x10x1-in. baking pan. Bake until crisp and lightly browned, 10-15 minutes, stirring every 4 minutes. Cool completely in pan on a wire rack. Store in an airtight container.
¾ CUP 306 cal., 20g fat (7g sat. fat), 20mg chol., 468mg sod., 26g carb. (1g sugars, 1g fiber), 5g pro.

AT-HOME COFFEE BAR

Recreate the experience of visiting your favorite coffee shop by setting up a coffee bar stocked with all the essentials—coffee, teas, milk or cream, sugar or sweeteners and flavored syrups. Your guests can create their own perfect cuppa while the group talks over their favorite books.

DIY PAGE-TURNER TABLE RUNNER

Using a craft knife, carefully cut pages out of a discarded book. Use double-sided tape to randomly attach the pages to each other to the desired length and width.

CHOCOLATE-
CARAMEL
RUM COFFEE

ALMOND BISCOTTI

I've learned to bake a double batch of
these crisp dunking cookies, because
one batch goes too fast!
—*H. Michaelsen, St. Charles, IL*

PREP: 15 min. • **BAKE:** 35 min. + cooling
MAKES: 3 dozen

- ½ cup butter, softened
- 1¼ cups sugar, divided
- 3 large eggs, room temperature
- 1 tsp. anise extract
- 2 cups all-purpose flour
- 2 tsp. baking powder
  Dash salt
- ½ cup chopped almonds
- 2 tsp. 2% milk

1. Preheat oven to 375°. In a large bowl,
cream butter and 1 cup sugar until light
and fluffy, 5-7 minutes. Add eggs, 1 at a
time, beating well after each addition.
Beat in extract. Combine dry ingredients;
gradually add to creamed mixture and
mix well. Stir in almonds.
2. Line a baking sheet with foil and
grease foil. Divide dough in half; on
foil, shape each portion into a 12x3-in.
rectangle. Brush with milk; sprinkle
with remaining ¼ cup sugar.
3. Bake until golden brown and firm to
the touch, 15-20 minutes. Lift foil with
rectangles onto a wire rack; cool for
15 minutes. Reduce oven heat to 300°.
4. Transfer rectangles to a cutting board;
cut diagonally with a serrated knife into
½-in. slices. Place cut side down on
ungreased baking sheets.
5. Bake for 10 minutes. Turn and bake
until firm, 10 minutes longer. Remove
to wire racks to cool. Store in an airtight
container.
1 COOKIE 207 cal., 9g fat (4g sat. fat), 50mg
chol., 129mg sod., 29g carb. (16g sugars,
1g fiber), 4g pro.

CHOCOLATE-CARAMEL RUM COFFEE

This decadent drink can stand alone
as a final course or as a complement to
dessert. Our family loves it for sipping
in front of the fireplace.
—*Joyce Conway, Westerville, OH*

TAKES: 25 min. • **MAKES:** 8 servings

- 2 cans (12 oz. each) evaporated milk
- ¾ cup rum
- ½ cup chocolate syrup
- ½ cup caramel sundae syrup
- ¼ cup packed brown sugar
- 4 cups hot brewed coffee
- 2 Tbsp. coffee liqueur

COFFEE WHIPPED CREAM
- 1 cup heavy whipping cream
- 6 Tbsp. confectioners' sugar
- 2 Tbsp. coffee liqueur
  Instant espresso powder, optional

1. In a large saucepan, combine milk,
rum, syrups and brown sugar. Cook
over medium heat until hot (do not boil).
Stir in coffee and liqueur.
2. Meanwhile, for coffee whipped cream,
in a small bowl, beat cream until it
begins to thicken. Add confectioners'
sugar; beat until stiff peaks form. Fold
in liqueur until combined.
3. Pour coffee mixture into mugs.
Garnish with a dollop of coffee whipped
cream and, if desired, espresso powder.
**1 CUP COFFEE WITH ¼ CUP COFFEE
WHIPPED CREAM** 437 cal., 16g fat (11g sat.
fat), 68mg chol., 166mg sod., 50g carb.
(43g sugars, 0 fiber), 7g pro.

HOW TO PLAN A BOOK CLUB PARTY

If it's your turn to host your book club, turn to these creative ideas that will make your party the stuff of legends.

LITERARY-INSPIRED EATS

Draw menu inspiration from the day's book selection, basing your picks around the food or wine of the region where the plot is set or making the main character's favorite dish.

BOOKISH INVITATIONS

Remember the library check-out cards that used to be in a pocket inside every library book you checked out as a kid? Use those as inspiration for your book club party invitations.

A COZY SETTING

The setting of your party should be rich with detail. The easiest way to do this is by using what you already have—books. Set a stack of two or three books in the center of your coffee table. Top the stack with a vase of flowers or a candle safely tucked inside a jar.

Make sure your setting is warm and cozy. Give guests a selection of blankets to snuggle underneath while they share their favorite parts of the book you're discussing.

A HAPPY ENDING

Surprise guests with a parting gift such as a handmade bookmark or treat bags made out of old book pages.

To choose the club's next book, wrap 4-5 options in brown craft paper and have a guest choose at random. Oh, the suspense!

CHAI CUPCAKES

CHAI CUPCAKES

You'll get a double dose of the spicy blend that's frequently used to flavor tea in these tender single-size cakes. Both the cupcake and frosting use the sweet blend of spices.
—Taste of Home *Test Kitchen*

- -

PREP: 25 min. • **BAKE:** 25 min. + cooling
MAKES: 1 dozen

- ½ tsp. each ground ginger, cinnamon, cardamom and cloves
- ⅛ tsp. pepper
- ½ cup butter, softened
- 1 cup sugar
- 1 large egg, room temperature
- ½ tsp. vanilla extract
- 1½ cups cake flour
- 1½ tsp. baking powder
- ¼ tsp. salt
- ⅔ cup 2% milk

FROSTING
- 6 Tbsp. butter, softened
- 3 cups confectioners' sugar
- ¾ tsp. vanilla extract
- 3 to 4 Tbsp. 2% milk

1. In a small bowl, combine ginger, cinnamon, cardamom, cloves and pepper; set aside.

2. In a large bowl, cream butter and sugar until light and fluffy, 5-7 minutes. Beat in egg and vanilla. Combine flour, baking powder, salt and 1½ tsp. spice mixture. Gradually add to creamed mixture alternately with milk, beating well after each addition.

3. Fill 12 paper-lined muffin cups two-thirds full. Bake at 350° until a toothpick inserted in center comes out clean, 24-28 minutes. Cool for 10 minutes before removing from pans to wire racks to cool completely.

4. For frosting, in a large bowl, beat butter until fluffy; beat in confectioners' sugar, vanilla and remaining spice mixture until smooth. Add enough milk to reach desired consistency. Pipe frosting over cupcakes.

1 CUPCAKE 377 cal., 14g fat (9g sat. fat), 54mg chol., 209mg sod., 61g carb. (46g sugars, 0 fiber), 3g pro.

RUSTIC
CHOCOLATE
RASPBERRY
TART

RUSTIC CHOCOLATE RASPBERRY TART

Here's a delectable dessert that's simple but feels upscale. With its fresh raspberries and Nutella-covered homemade pastry crust, you and your guests won't be able to get enough.
—*Christina Seremetis, Rockland, MA*

- -

PREP: 20 min. + chilling
BAKE: 45 min. + cooling
MAKES: 8 servings

  5 oz. cream cheese, softened
  6 Tbsp. butter, softened
1½ cups all-purpose flour
FILLING
  2 cups fresh raspberries
  2 Tbsp. sugar
  1 tsp. cornstarch
⅓ cup Nutella

1. Process cream cheese and butter in a food processor until blended. Add flour; process just until a dough forms. Shape into a disk; wrap and refrigerate 1 hour or overnight.
2. Preheat oven to 350°. In a small bowl, toss raspberries, sugar and cornstarch with a fork, mashing some of the berries slightly.
3. On a lightly floured surface, roll dough into a 14x8-in. rectangle. Transfer to a parchment-lined baking sheet. Spread with Nutella to within 1 in. of edges. Top with the raspberry mixture. Fold pastry edges toward center of tart, pleating and pinching as needed.
4. Bake until crust is golden brown, 45-50 minutes. Transfer tart to a wire rack to cool.

1 PIECE 315 cal., 19g fat (10g sat. fat), 41mg chol., 130mg sod., 34g carb. (12g sugars, 3g fiber), 5g pro.

PAIRS
WITH

RUBY PORT

PAIRS WITH

BORDEAUX

FRENCH DIP
SANDWICH
WITH ONIONS

JAM-TOPPED MINI CHEESECAKES

Presto! We turned cheesecake into irresistible bite-sized snacks with these cute little treats. Feel free to use your favorite flavor of jam.
—Taste of Home *Test Kitchen*

PREP: 20 min. • **BAKE:** 15 min. + chilling
MAKES: 9 servings

- ⅔ cup graham cracker crumbs
- 2 Tbsp. butter, melted
- 1 pkg. (8 oz.) cream cheese, softened
- ⅓ cup sugar
- 1 tsp. vanilla extract
- 1 large egg, room temperature
- 3 Tbsp. assorted jams, warmed

1. Preheat oven to 350°. In a small bowl, combine graham cracker crumbs and butter. Press gently onto bottoms of 9 paper-lined muffin cups.
2. In another small bowl, beat cream cheese, sugar and vanilla until smooth. Add egg; beat on low speed just until combined. Spoon over crusts.
3. Bake 15-16 minutes or until centers are set. Cool for 10 minutes before removing from pan to a wire rack to cool completely. Refrigerate at least 1 hour.
4. Remove paper liners; top each cheesecake with 1 tsp. jam.
1 MINI CHEESECAKE 198 cal., 13g fat (7g sat. fat), 53mg chol., 141mg sod., 19g carb. (14g sugars, 0 fiber), 3g pro.

TEST KITCHEN TIP

Time is of the essence with many desserts, but cheesecake is one that actually tastes better the next day and has a shelf life of up to a few days. Cheesecake also freezes beautifully. All of this is good news for your party planning!

FRENCH DIP SANDWICH WITH ONIONS

When I want to impress company, these satisfying sandwiches are my first pick for the menu. I serve them au jus, with the cooking juices in individual bowls for dipping.
—Florence Robinson, Lenox, IA

PREP: 30 min. • **COOK:** 7 hours + standing
MAKES: 14 servings

- 2 large onions, cut into ¼-in. slices
- ¼ cup butter, cubed
- 1 beef rump roast or bottom round roast (3 to 4 lbs.)
- 5 cups water
- ½ cup soy sauce
- 1 envelope onion soup mix
- 1½ tsp. browning sauce, optional
- 1 garlic clove, minced
- 14 French rolls, split
- 2 cups shredded Swiss cheese

1. In a large skillet, saute onions in butter until tender. Transfer to a 5-qt. slow cooker. Cut roast in half; place over onions.
2. In a large bowl, combine water, soy sauce, soup mix, browning sauce if desired, and garlic; pour over roast. Cover and cook on low until meat is tender, 7-9 hours.
3. Remove roast with a slotted spoon and let stand for 15 minutes. Thinly slice meat across grain. Place on roll bottoms; sprinkle with Swiss cheese. Place on an ungreased baking sheet.
4. Broil 3-4 in. from heat until cheese is melted, about 1 minute. Replace tops. Skim fat from cooking juices; strain and serve as a dipping sauce if desired.
1 SANDWICH 399 cal., 15g fat (7g sat. fat), 81mg chol., 1099mg sod., 34g carb. (2g sugars, 2g fiber), 30g pro.

JAM-TOPPED
MINI CHEESECAKES

TRY BITTERSWEET
DOUBLE CHOCOLATE
TRUFFLES, P. 181

BLUE CHEESE
KALE SALAD
P. 256

BLACKBERRY
BALSAMIC
MANHATTAN
P. 48

HARVEST
PORK ROAST
P. 258

MURDER MYSTERY

You are cordially invited to a dinner to die for. We'll clue you in:
Macabre decor, scary-good food and a fun whodunit make
all the right ingredients for a killer party.

BACON-WRAPPED SCALLOPS WITH PEAR SAUCE

I enjoy cooking for my parents, and they definitely enjoy these bacon-wrapped scallops. If you prefer, replace the pear preserves with preserves or jam of a different flavor.
—*Ethan Hall, King, NC*

PREP: 25 min. • **COOK:** 10 min.
MAKES: 1 dozen

- 12 bacon strips
- ¾ cup pear preserves
- 2 Tbsp. reduced-sodium soy sauce
- 1 Tbsp. brown sugar
- ¼ to ½ tsp. crushed red pepper flakes
- 12 sea scallops (about ¾ lb.)
- ⅛ tsp. salt
- ⅛ tsp. pepper
- 1 tsp. olive oil

1. Preheat oven to 375°. Place bacon in an ungreased 15x10x1-in. baking pan. Bake for 7-10 minutes or until partially cooked but not crisp. Remove to paper towels to drain; keep warm.
2. Meanwhile, in a small saucepan, combine the preserves, soy sauce, brown sugar and pepper flakes. Bring to a boil. Reduce heat; simmer, uncovered, for 3-5 minutes or until thickened.
3. Wrap a bacon strip around each scallop; secure with toothpicks. Sprinkle with salt and pepper. In a large skillet, cook bacon-wrapped scallops in oil over medium-high heat for 5-7 minutes or until scallops are firm and opaque, turning once. Serve with pear sauce.
1 WRAPPED SCALLOP WITH 1 TBSP. SAUCE 400 cal., 6g fat (1g sat. fat), 121mg chol., 819mg sod., 21g carb. (11g sugars, 0 fiber), 60g pro.

THE BAR OF THE SHOW
Line a tiered cake stand with glasses, shakers, garnishes, bitters and more for a one-stop cocktail shop.

BRIE APPETIZERS WITH BACON-PLUM JAM

PAIRS WITH

BLACKBERRY BALSAMIC MANHATTAN, P. 48

BRIE APPETIZERS WITH BACON-PLUM JAM

Among my friends, I'm known as the Pork Master because I love to cook just about every cut of pork there is. These appetizers combine soft, mild Brie cheese with a sweet-sour bacon jam that has just a touch of Sriracha chili sauce.
—*Rick Pascocello, New York, NY*

PREP: 25 min. • **COOK:** 1¼ hours
MAKES: 2½ dozen

 1 lb. bacon strips, chopped
 1 cup thinly sliced sweet onion
 1 shallot, finely chopped
 5 garlic cloves, minced
 1 cup brewed coffee
 ½ cup water
 ¼ cup cider vinegar
 ¼ cup pitted dried plums (prunes), coarsely chopped
 3 Tbsp. brown sugar
 1 Tbsp. maple syrup
 1 Tbsp. Sriracha chili sauce
 ½ tsp. pepper
 30 slices Brie cheese (¼ in. thick)
 30 slices French bread baguette (¼ in. thick), toasted

1. In a large skillet, cook the bacon over medium heat until partially cooked but not crisp. Remove to paper towels with a slotted spoon; drain skillet, reserving 1 Tbsp. drippings.
2. Add onion and shallot to the drippings; cook and stir 5 minutes. Add the garlic; cook 2 minutes longer. Stir in coffee, water, vinegar, dried plums, brown sugar, maple syrup, chili sauce and pepper. Bring to a boil. Stir in the bacon. Reduce heat; simmer, uncovered, 1¼-1½ hours or until the liquid is syrupy, stirring occasionally. Remove from heat. Cool to room temperature.
3. Transfer mixture to a food processor; pulse until the jam reaches desired consistency. Place cheese slices on toasted baguette slices. Top each with 2 tsp. jam.
1 APPETIZER 91 cal., 5g fat (3g sat. fat), 17mg chol., 205mg sod., 6g carb. (3g sugars, 0 fiber), 4g pro.

SAUSAGE MUSHROOM APPETIZERS

These stuffed mushrooms are can't-stop-eating-them good. For variations, I sometimes substitute venison or crabmeat for the pork sausage in the stuffing.
—*Sheryl Siemonsma, Sioux Falls, SD*

PREP: 15 min. • **BAKE:** 20 min.
MAKES: 4 dozen

 48 large fresh mushrooms
 2 large eggs, lightly beaten
 1 lb. bulk pork sausage, cooked and crumbled
 1 cup shredded Swiss cheese
 ¼ cup mayonnaise
 3 Tbsp. butter, melted
 2 Tbsp. finely chopped onion
 2 tsp. spicy brown or horseradish mustard
 1 tsp. garlic salt
 1 tsp. Cajun seasoning
 1 tsp. Worcestershire sauce

1. Preheat oven to 350°. Remove mushroom stems (discard or save for another use); set caps aside. In a large bowl, combine remaining ingredients. Stuff into the mushroom caps.
2. Place the stuffed caps in 2 greased 13x9-in. baking dishes. Bake, uncovered, until heated through, 16-20 minutes.
1 STUFFED MUSHROOM 53 cal., 4g fat (2g sat. fat), 17mg chol., 129mg sod., 1g carb. (0 sugars, 0 fiber), 2g pro.

HOW TO HOST A KILLER MURDER MYSTERY PARTY

We'll clue you in on how to host a murder mystery party: Macabre decor, scary-good food and a fun whodunit add up to a dinner party that's to die for.

SELECT YOUR STORYLINE

A store-bought plot is the easiest route to take. Kits include all the pieces you'll need to decipher who among you is the mastermind behind a make-believe homicide. If you're feeling imaginative, craft your own crime from scratch!

GO ALL OUT ON GARNISHES

Get creative when it comes to dressing up your cocktails; "gothic" is a look to go for! We add extra spookiness—and smoky flavor—to the featured Blackberry Balsamic Manhattan (shown on p. 254, recipe on p. 48) with a charred sprig of rosemary. Let the herb burn for a few moments, blow it out and drop it into the beverage. Other add-ons include stirrers threaded with fresh berries and fresh orange pieces.

MAKE A MENU

Stick with doable yet elevated recipes for your dinner party, such as the pork roast, tossed kale salad and simple Brie appetizers in this chapter. Whatever you do, opt for recipes that have fresh, seasonal ingredients and that will satiate your guests for the duration of the game.

FINISH WITH A CONFECTION

Can you say "death by chocolate"? Rich chocolate—the darker the better—is a natural pairing for a murder mystery party.

BLUE CHEESE KALE SALAD

BLUE CHEESE KALE SALAD

Instead of your average dinner salad, try a kale salad. I didn't like kale until I made this one!
—*Kathryn Egly, Colorado Springs, CO*

- -

TAKES: 20 min. • **MAKES:** 12 servings

- ½ cup olive oil
- 3 Tbsp. lime juice
- 2 Tbsp. honey
- ¼ tsp. salt
- ⅛ tsp. pepper
- 1 bunch kale (about 12 oz.), trimmed and chopped (about 14 cups)
- ½ cup sliced almonds, toasted
- ½ cup dried cranberries
- ½ cup shredded Parmesan cheese
- ½ cup crumbled blue cheese

In a small bowl, whisk the first 5 ingredients. Place kale in a large bowl. Drizzle with dressing; toss to coat. Top with remaining ingredients.

1¼ CUPS 181 cal., 14g fat (3g sat. fat), 7mg chol., 183mg sod., 13g carb. (8g sugars, 1g fiber), 4g pro. **DIABETIC EXCHANGES** 3 fat, 1 vegetable, ½ starch.

TEST KITCHEN TIP

If you like your kale a little softer, you can massage it before adding the other ingredients. With your fingers, massage the trimmed and chopped kale for 2-3 minutes until the leaves become soft and darkened, then proceed with the recipe as directed.

FRENCH LOAVES

FRESH HERB BUTTER

I love impressing dinner guests with flavored butter. I mix up a big batch and freeze it. Then when company comes, this special spread is ready to go. Cut them in different shapes for a little fun.
—*Pam Duncan, Summers, AR*

PREP: 25 min. + freezing
MAKES: 24 servings

- 1 cup butter, softened
- 2 Tbsp. minced fresh chives
- 2 Tbsp. minced fresh parsley
- 1 Tbsp. minced fresh tarragon
- 1 Tbsp. lemon juice
- ¼ tsp. pepper

1. In a small bowl, beat all ingredients until blended. Spread onto a baking sheet to ½-in. thickness. Freeze, covered, until firm.
2. Cut butter with a 1-in. cookie cutter. Store, layered between waxed paper, in an airtight container in the refrigerator up to 1 week or in the freezer up to 3 months.

ABOUT 1 TBSP. 68 cal., 8g fat (5g sat. fat), 20mg chol., 61mg sod., 0 carb. (0 sugars, 0 fiber), 0 pro.

FRENCH LOAVES

My kids love to help me make this delicious bread. It's quite easy, and they enjoy the fact that they can be eating fresh bread in about two hours!
—*Denise Boutin, Grand Isle, VT*

PREP: 30 min. + rising • **BAKE:** 15 min.
MAKES: 2 loaves (12 pieces each)

- 2 Tbsp. active dry yeast
- 2 cups warm water (110° to 115°)
- 2 tsp. salt
- 1 tsp. sugar
- 4½ to 5 cups bread flour
- 1 tsp. cornmeal

1. In a large bowl, dissolve yeast in warm water. Add the salt, sugar and 2 cups flour. Beat until smooth. Stir in enough remaining flour to form a soft dough.

2. Turn dough onto a floured surface; knead until smooth and elastic, 6-8 minutes. Place in a greased bowl, turning once to grease the top. Cover and let rise in a warm place until doubled, about 1 hour.
3. Punch dough down. Turn onto a lightly floured surface; divide in half. Shape into two 12-in.-long loaves.
4. Place seam side down on a greased baking sheet. Cover and let rise until doubled, about 30 minutes.
5. Preheat oven to 450°. Sprinkle loaves with cornmeal. With a sharp knife, make 4 shallow slashes across the top of each loaf. Bake 15-20 minutes or until golden brown. Cool on a wire rack.
1 PIECE 97 cal., 1g fat (0 sat. fat), 0 chol., 198mg sod., 19g carb. (0 sugars, 1g fiber), 3g pro.

ROASTED GRAPE & SWEET CHEESE PHYLLO GALETTE

Faced with an abundant crop of grapes, I had to come up with a creative way to use them. It's fun to work with phyllo dough, and it bakes up golden and flaky. In this recipe, a layer of orange-kissed cream cheese is topped with roasted grapes. Then a bit of honey is drizzled on, and a sprinkle of coarse sugar is added to finish it off. You can use berries for this too.

—Kallee Krong-McCreery, Escondido, CA

PREP: 25 min. • **BAKE:** 35 min. + cooling
MAKES: 10 servings

- 1 pkg. (8 oz.) cream cheese, softened
- 2 Tbsp. orange marmalade
- 1 tsp. sugar
- 8 sheets phyllo dough (14x9-in. size)
- 4 Tbsp. butter, melted
- 1 cup seedless grapes
- 1 Tbsp. honey
- 2 tsp. coarse sugar

1. Preheat oven to 350°. In a large bowl, beat cream cheese, marmalade and sugar until smooth; set aside.
2. Place 1 sheet of phyllo on a parchment-lined baking sheet; brush with butter. Layer with remaining phyllo sheets, brushing each layer. (Keep remaining phyllo covered with a damp towel to prevent it from drying out.) Spread cream cheese mixture over phyllo to within 2 in. of edges. Arrange grapes over cream cheese.
3. Fold edges of phyllo over the filling, leaving center uncovered. Brush folded phyllo with any remaining butter; drizzle with honey and sprinkle with coarse sugar. Bake until phyllo is golden brown, 35-40 minutes. Transfer to a wire rack to cool completely. Refrigerate leftovers.
1 PIECE 177 cal., 13g fat (8g sat. fat), 35mg chol., 148mg sod., 15g carb. (9g sugars, 0 fiber), 2g pro.

WAX POETIC
For old-timey elegance, use wax to seal invitations or written clues in envelopes.

HARVEST PORK ROAST

I came up with this one evening when I had butternut squash, fresh picked apples and dried cranberries. I combined the ingredients into one succulent pork dish and everyone raved over it. This is also good with some added cinnamon or a garlic pepper rub.

—Shirley Tuttle-Malone, Glenfield, NY

PREP: 20 min.
BAKE: 70 min. + standing
MAKES: 12 servings

- 1 boneless pork loin roast (about 4 lbs.)
- 1 Tbsp. plus ¼ cup olive oil, divided
- 1 tsp. salt
- ½ tsp. pepper
- 3 garlic cloves, peeled and sliced
- 1 medium butternut squash (3 to 4 lbs.), peeled and cut into ¾-in. cubes
- 4 large apples, peeled and each cut into 8 wedges
- 1 cup dried cranberries
- ½ cup packed brown sugar
  Optional: 1 tsp. each minced fresh rosemary and minced fresh thyme

1. Preheat oven to 350°. If desired, tie pork with kitchen twine. Rub pork with 1 Tbsp. olive oil; sprinkle with salt and pepper. In a large skillet over medium-high heat, sear pork until browned on all sides, 7-9 minutes. Place in a large roasting pan; top pork with garlic slices. Bake, covered, for 30 minutes.
2. Meanwhile, combine the squash, apples, dried cranberries, brown sugar, remaining olive oil and, if desired, minced fresh rosemary and thyme; toss to coat.
3. Remove pork from oven; add squash mixture to roasting pan. Return pork to oven; roast, uncovered, for 40-50 minutes longer or until a thermometer inserted in the pork reads 145°.
4. Let pork stand 10 minutes before slicing. Drizzle pork with pan juices after slicing. Serve with the roasted squash mixture. If desired, top with additional fresh rosemary and thyme.
4 OZ. COOKED PORK WITH ¾ CUP VEGETABLES 395 cal., 13g fat (3g sat. fat), 75mg chol., 199mg sod., 41g carb. (28g sugars, 5g fiber), 31g pro.

HARVEST
PORK ROAST

CRIMSON COLLECTIBLES

Beguile guests by placing an assortment of eerie objects, such as a magnifying glass, blood-red flowers, black feathers and potions, within a clear cloche.

TURTLE TART WITH CARAMEL SAUCE

Between the creamy filling, crispy crust and gooey caramel sauce, there's a lot to love about this tart. Plus, you can make it two to three days in advance. One of my daughters even asks for this instead of cake on her birthday.
—*Leah Davis, Morrow, OH*

PREP: 15 min. + chilling
BAKE: 15 min. + cooling
MAKES: 12 servings

- 2 cups pecan halves, toasted
- ½ cup sugar
- 2 Tbsp. butter, melted

FILLING
- 2 cups semisweet chocolate chips
- 1½ cups heavy whipping cream
- ½ cup finely chopped pecans, toasted

CARAMEL SAUCE
- ½ cup butter, cubed
- 1 cup sugar
- 1 cup heavy whipping cream

1. Preheat oven to 350°. Place pecans and sugar in a food processor; pulse until finely ground. Add melted butter; pulse until combined. Press onto the bottom and up the side of a 9-in. fluted tart pan with removable bottom. Bake until golden brown, 12-15 minutes. Cool completely on a wire rack.
2. For filling, place chocolate chips in a small bowl. In a small saucepan, bring cream just to a boil. Pour over chocolate; stir with a whisk until smooth. Pour into cooled crust; cool slightly. Refrigerate until slightly set, about 30 minutes.
3. Sprinkle chopped pecans over filling. Refrigerate, covered, until set, about 3 hours.
4. For sauce, in a large heavy saucepan, melt butter over medium heat; stir in sugar until dissolved. Bring to a boil; cook for 10-12 minutes or until deep golden brown, stirring the mixture occasionally. Slowly whisk in cream until blended. Remove from heat; cool slightly. Serve with tart.
NOTE To toast nuts, bake in a shallow pan in a 350° oven for 5-10 minutes or cook in a skillet over low heat until lightly browned, stirring occasionally.
1 PIECE WITH 2 TBSP. CARAMEL SAUCE
632 cal., 51g fat (24g sat. fat), 82mg chol., 93mg sod., 47g carb. (43g sugars, 4g fiber), 5g pro.

MINI
CORN
DOGS
P. 264

LAKE
CHARLES
DIP
P. 267

CRAN &
CHERRY
PUNCH
P. 55

GAME NIGHT

We're not bluffing when we say a game night is the best way to spend quality time with friends. Gather your crew for a evening of card shufflin', dice rollin' and snack dunkin'. The rules? Everyone must come hungry and eager to play. Now get your game face on!

MINI CORN DOGS

Bring a county fair favorite into your home with these bite-sized corn dogs! I make my own by wrapping cornmeal dough around mini hot dogs. Kids and the young at heart love them.

—*Geralyn Harrington, Floral Park, NY*

TAKES: 30 min. • **MAKES:** 2 dozen

1⅔ cups all-purpose flour
⅓ cup cornmeal
3 tsp. baking powder
1 tsp. salt
3 Tbsp. cold butter
1 Tbsp. shortening
1 large egg, room temperature
¾ cup 2% milk
24 miniature hot dogs
HONEY MUSTARD SAUCE
⅓ cup honey
⅓ cup prepared mustard
1 Tbsp. molasses

1. In a large bowl, combine the first 4 ingredients. Cut in the butter and shortening until the mixture resembles coarse crumbs. Beat egg and milk. Stir into dry ingredients until a soft dough forms; dough will be sticky.
2. Turn dough onto a generously floured surface; knead 6-8 times or until smooth, adding additional flour as needed. Roll out to ¼-in. thickness. Cut with a 2¼-in. biscuit cutter. Fold each dough circle over a hot dog and press edge to seal. Place on greased baking sheets.
3. Bake at 450° until golden brown, 10-12 minutes. In a small bowl, combine sauce ingredients. Serve with corn dogs.

1 CORN DOG 109 cal., 5g fat (2g sat. fat), 18mg chol., 306mg sod., 14g carb. (5g sugars, 0 fiber), 3g pro.

MINI CORN DOGS

EASY
BACON
CHEESE
FONDUE

EASY BACON CHEESE FONDUE

When I'm looking for an appetizer with mass appeal but want a change from the usual cheese spread, this is the recipe I make. Everyone enjoys the rich flavor.
—*Bernice Morris, Marshfield, MO*

- -

TAKES: 30 min. • **MAKES:** 3¾ cups

- 4 to 5 bacon strips, diced
- ¼ cup chopped onion
- 2 Tbsp. all-purpose flour
- 1 lb. process Velveeta, cubed
- 2 cups sour cream
- 1 jalapeno pepper, seeded and chopped, optional
- 1 loaf (1 lb.) French bread, cubed
   Optional: Soft pretzel bites and halved miniature sweet peppers

1. In a large skillet, cook bacon over medium heat until crisp. Using a slotted spoon, remove to paper towels. In the drippings, saute onion until tender. Stir in flour until blended; cook and stir until thickened.
2. Reduce heat to low. Add cheese cubes; cook and stir until melted. Stir in sour cream, jalapeno if desired, and bacon; cook and stir just until heated through. Transfer to a fondue pot and keep warm. Serve with bread cubes and, if desired, pretzel bites and peppers.
NOTE Wear disposable gloves when cutting hot peppers; the oils can burn skin. Avoid touching your face.
4 TBSP. 305 cal., 18g fat (11g sat. fat), 48mg chol., 647mg sod., 21g carb. (4g sugars, 1g fiber), 11g pro.

HOW TO HOST A GAME NIGHT

With these ideas, your night will be fun- and food-filled ... with a little friendly competition, of course.

PICK WHAT TO PLAY

Picking a night that works for everyone is easy—agreeing on a game can be hard! Be sure to gear your selection toward your group. If you're short on games, try a local thrift store (just check to make sure all of the pieces are in place) or check the library—some lend board games as well as books.

SELECT YOUR SNACKS

We recommend small, mess-free munchies that can be grabbed, dunked and devoured in between rounds.

SET THE TABLE

First, place the game and its pieces on the table to ensure there's enough room, and set out your snacks in the remaining space. Serve small bites on a lazy Susan. That way everyone can reach the snacks, even as they're strategizing.

PLAY CLEAN

No, we don't mean playing by the rules! That's important, too, but so is keeping the table and game pieces tidy. Wet wipes, hand sanitizer, or finger bowls (p. 266) at each place setting helps when fingers get greasy from snacking.

GAME ON!

For optimal bonding, make game night a tech-free zone. Place phones in a separate room and turn off the TV. Now, it's time to snack—then attack!

MOZZARELLA STICKS

I'm particularly fond of these tasty mozzarella sticks because they're baked, not deep-fried. Cheese is one of my family's favorite foods. Being of Italian descent, I cook often with ricotta and mozzarella cheeses.
—*Mary Merchant, Barre, VT*

PREP: 15 min. + freezing • **BAKE:** 10 min.
MAKES: 6 servings

- 3 Tbsp. all-purpose flour
- 2 large eggs
- 1 Tbsp. water
- 1 cup dry bread crumbs
- 2½ tsp. Italian seasoning
- ½ tsp. garlic powder
- ⅛ tsp. pepper
- 12 sticks string cheese
  Cooking spray
- 1 cup marinara or spaghetti sauce, heated

1. Place flour in a shallow bowl. In another shallow bowl, beat eggs and water. In a third shallow bowl, combine bread crumbs, Italian seasoning, garlic powder and pepper. Coat cheese sticks with flour, then dip in the egg mixture and coat with the bread crumb mixture. Repeat egg and bread crumb coatings. Cover and freeze for at least 2 hours or overnight.
2. Place on a parchment-lined baking sheet; spray with cooking spray. Bake, uncovered, at 400° until heated through, 6-8 minutes. Allow to stand 3-5 minutes before serving. Serve with marinara or spaghetti sauce for dipping.
2 STICKS 312 cal., 17g fat (10g sat. fat), 116mg chol., 749mg sod., 22g carb. (4g sugars, 1g fiber), 20g pro.

HOT PIZZA DIP

You can assemble this effortless appetizer in a jiffy. The pizza-flavored dip goes very fast, so you may want to make two batches.
—*Stacie Morse, South Otselic, NY*

TAKES: 10 min.
MAKES: 24 servings (about 3 cups)

- 1 pkg. (8 oz.) cream cheese, softened
- 1 tsp. Italian seasoning
- 1 cup shredded part-skim mozzarella cheese
- ¾ cup grated Parmesan cheese
- 1 can (8 oz.) pizza sauce
- 2 Tbsp. chopped green pepper
- 2 Tbsp. thinly sliced green onion
  Breadsticks or tortilla chips

1. In a bowl, beat cream cheese and Italian seasoning. Spread in an ungreased 9-in. microwave-safe pie plate.
2. Combine mozzarella and Parmesan cheeses; sprinkle half over the cream cheese. Top with the pizza sauce, the remaining cheese mixture, green pepper and onion.
3. Microwave, uncovered, on high for 2-3 minutes or until cheese is almost melted, rotating a half-turn several times. Let stand for 1-2 minutes. Serve with breadsticks or tortilla chips.
2 TBSP. 62 cal., 5g fat (3g sat. fat), 15mg chol., 144mg sod., 2g carb. (1g sugars, 0 fiber), 3g pro.

LAKE CHARLES DIP

Italian salad dressing mix gives this simply delicious dip its wonderful flavor. Serve it with fresh veggies or crackers for an easy appetizer.
—*Shannon Copley, Upper Arlington, OH*

PREP: 15 min. + chilling • **MAKES:** 1½ cups

- 1 cup sour cream
- 2 Tbsp. reduced-fat mayonnaise
- 1 Tbsp. Italian salad dressing mix
- ⅓ cup finely chopped avocado
- 1 tsp. lemon juice
- ½ cup finely chopped seeded tomato
  Optional: Assorted crackers, cucumber slices, julienned sweet red pepper and carrot sticks

In a small bowl, combine the sour cream, mayonnaise and dressing mix. Toss avocado with lemon juice; stir into the sour cream mixture. Stir in tomato. Cover and refrigerate for at least 1 hour. Serve with crackers and assorted vegetables as desired.
¼ CUP 111 cal., 9g fat (5g sat. fat), 27mg chol., 216mg sod., 3g carb. (2g sugars, 1g fiber), 2g pro.

HAND 'EM LEMONS

Place slices of the puckery fruit and a shallow dish of warm water at each place setting. When fingers get greasy from snacking (no shame!), simply splash 'em in the water and rub with the lemon to freshen up quickly and keep your game pieces clean. We call that a win-win.

PAIRS WITH
CRAN & CHERRY
PUNCH, P. 55

LAKE
CHARLES
DIP

POPCORN NUT MIX

ONE-POT MAC & CHEESE

Who likes cleaning up after making mac and cheese? Not this girl. This one-pot mac and cheese is a family favorite, and my 3-year-old is thrilled to see it coming to the dinner table. We love to add sliced smoked sausage to this creamy mac!
—*Ashley Lecker, Green Bay, WI*

- -

PREP: 5 min. • **COOK:** 30 min.
MAKES: 10 servings

3½	cups whole milk
3	cups water
1	pkg. (16 oz.) elbow macaroni
4	oz. Velveeta, cubed
2	cups shredded sharp cheddar cheese
½	tsp. salt
½	tsp. coarsely ground pepper

In a Dutch oven, combine milk, water and macaroni; bring to a boil over medium heat. Reduce heat and simmer until macaroni is tender and almost all the cooking liquid has been absorbed, 12-15 minutes, stirring frequently. Reduce heat to low; stir in cheeses until melted. Season with salt and pepper.
1 CUP 344 cal., 14g fat (8g sat. fat), 42mg chol., 450mg sod., 39g carb. (6g sugars, 2g fiber), 16g pro.

#GIRLDINNER

To make your mac & cheese healthier—and a whole dinner—throw in some veggies and a source of protein such as chicken or turkey after the cheese is melted, then let it cook on low heat until the add-ins are heated through. You can also use whole wheat or a legume-based pasta to cut down on empty carbs and increase your daily protein intake.

POPCORN NUT MIX

Traditional popcorn nut mix gets a makeover with bright orange and cinnamon flavors.
—*Sandi Pichon, Memphis, TN*

- -

PREP: 10 min. • **BAKE:** 15 min. + cooling
MAKES: 9 cups

10	cups popped popcorn
1	cup mixed nuts
¼	cup honey
2	Tbsp. grated orange zest
2	Tbsp. orange juice
¼	tsp. ground cinnamon

1. Preheat oven to 350°. Place popcorn and nuts in a large bowl; set aside.
2. In a small saucepan, combine honey, orange zest, orange juice and cinnamon. Bring to a boil. Pour over the popcorn mixture; toss to coat. Transfer to an ungreased 13x9-in. baking pan.
3. Bake at 350° for 15 minutes, stirring twice. Cool completely on waxed paper. Store in an airtight container.
½ CUP 97 cal., 7g fat (1g sat. fat), 0 chol., 68mg sod., 9g carb. (4g sugars, 1g fiber), 2g pro.

BARBECUE CHICKEN SLIDERS

Thanks to rotisserie chicken, these cheesy, smoky sliders are a snap to make. The special barbecue sauce really takes it up a notch.
—*Nancy Heishman, Las Vegas, NV*

TAKES: 25 min. • **MAKES:** 4 servings

- ¾ cup beer or reduced-sodium chicken broth
- ½ cup barbecue sauce
- 1 Tbsp. bourbon
- 1 tsp. hot pepper sauce
- ¼ tsp. seasoned salt
- ¼ tsp. ground mustard
- 2 cups shredded rotisserie chicken
- 8 slider buns, split
- 1½ cups shredded smoked cheddar cheese

1. Preheat broiler. In a large saucepan, mix first 6 ingredients; bring to a boil. Reduce heat; simmer, uncovered, until slightly thickened, 8-10 minutes, stirring occasionally. Stir in the chicken; heat through.
2. Place buns on a baking sheet, cut side up. Broil 3-4 in. from heat until lightly toasted, 30-60 seconds.
3. Remove tops of buns from baking sheet. Top bottoms with chicken mixture; sprinkle with cheese. Broil 3-4 in. from heat until cheese is melted, 1-2 minutes. Add bun tops.
FREEZE OPTION Freeze cooled chicken mixture in freezer containers. To use, partially thaw in refrigerator overnight. Heat through in a saucepan, stirring occasionally; add water if necessary.
2 SLIDERS 529 cal., 23g fat (10g sat. fat), 106mg chol., 1023mg sod., 42g carb. (15g sugars, 1g fiber), 36g pro.

RASPBERRY WHITE CHOCOLATE BARS

RASPBERRY WHITE CHOCOLATE BARS

A co-worker's mother gave me this gem of a recipe a few years back. I can never decide what's more appealing—the attractive look of the bars or their incredible aroma while they're baking! Everyone who tries these asks for the recipe.
—*Mimi Priesman, Pace, FL*

PREP: 20 min. • **BAKE:** 45 min.
MAKES: 2 dozen

- ½ cup butter, cubed
- 1 pkg. (10 to 12 oz.) white baking chips, divided
- 2 large eggs
- ½ cup sugar
- 1 tsp. almond extract
- 1 cup all-purpose flour
- ½ tsp. salt
- ½ cup seedless raspberry jam
- ¼ cup sliced almonds

1. Preheat oven to 325°. In a small saucepan, melt butter. Remove from the heat; add 1 cup chips (do not stir). In a small bowl, beat eggs until foamy; gradually add sugar. Stir in the chip mixture and almond extract. Combine flour and salt; gradually add to the egg mixture just until combined.
2. Spread half the batter into a greased 9-in. square baking pan. Bake until golden brown, 15-20 minutes.
3. In a small saucepan, melt jam over low heat; spread over warm crust. Stir remaining chips into the remaining batter; drop by spoonfuls over the jam layer. Sprinkle with almonds.
4. Bake until a toothpick inserted in the center comes out clean, 30-35 minutes longer. Cool on a wire rack. Cut into bars.
1 BAR 162 cal., 9g fat (5g sat. fat), 30mg chol., 104mg sod., 20g carb. (8g sugars, 0 fiber), 2g pro.

CHOCOLATE CARAMEL COOKIES

CHOCOLATE CARAMEL COOKIES

This is my favorite recipe for bake sales and bazaars. Each delightfully sweet chocolate cookie has a fun caramel surprise in the middle.
—Melissa Vannoy, Childress, TX

- -

PREP: 25 min.
BAKE: 10 min./batch + cooling
MAKES: 5 dozen

- 1 cup butter, softened
- 1 cup plus 1 Tbsp. sugar, divided
- 1 cup packed brown sugar
- 2 large eggs, room temperature
- 2 tsp. vanilla extract
- 2½ cups all-purpose flour
- ¾ cup baking cocoa
- 1 tsp. baking soda
- 1 cup chopped pecans, divided
- 1 pkg. (13 oz.) Rolo candies

1. Preheat oven to 375°. In a large bowl, cream butter, 1 cup sugar and brown sugar. Beat in eggs and vanilla. Combine flour, cocoa and baking soda; gradually add to the creamed mixture just until combined. Stir in ½ cup pecans.
2. Shape dough by tablespoonfuls around each candy. In a small bowl, combine the remaining ½ cup pecans and sugar; dip each cookie halfway into the nut mixture.
3. Place the cookies with nut side up on ungreased baking sheets. Bake until tops are slightly cracked, 7-10 minutes. Cool for 3 minutes; remove to wire racks to cool completely.
1 COOKIE 121 cal., 6g fat (3g sat. fat), 15mg chol., 60mg sod., 16g carb. (11g sugars, 1g fiber), 1g pro.

CHUNKY MONKEY CUPCAKES

Peanut butter is a favorite of ours, and it brings a fun element to these cupcakes. They're good with or without garnishes.
—Holly Jones, Kennesaw, GA

- -

PREP: 30 min. • **BAKE:** 20 min. + cooling
MAKES: 2 dozen

- 2 cups mashed ripe bananas (about 5 medium)
- 1½ cups sugar
- 3 large eggs, room temperature
- ½ cup unsweetened applesauce
- ¼ cup canola oil
- 3 cups all-purpose flour
- 1 tsp. baking soda
- ½ tsp. baking powder
- ½ tsp. salt
- 1 cup semisweet chocolate chunks
  FROSTING
- 4 oz. reduced-fat cream cheese
- ¼ cup creamy peanut butter
- 3 Tbsp. butter, softened
- 1 to 1¼ cups confectioners' sugar
  Chopped salted peanuts, optional

1. Preheat oven to 350°. Line 24 muffin cups with paper liners.
2. Beat first 5 ingredients until well blended. In another bowl, whisk together flour, baking soda, baking powder and salt; gradually beat into the banana mixture. Fold in chocolate chunks.
3. Fill prepared cups three-fourths full. Bake until a toothpick inserted in center comes out clean, 20-25 minutes. Cool in pans 10 minutes before removing to wire racks to cool completely.
4. For frosting, beat cream cheese, peanut butter and butter until smooth. Gradually beat in enough confectioners' sugar to reach desired consistency. Spread over cupcakes. If desired, sprinkle with peanuts. Refrigerate leftovers.
1 CUPCAKE 250 cal., 9g fat (4g sat. fat), 30mg chol., 165mg sod., 40g carb. (25g sugars, 2g fiber), 4g pro.

CHAI TEA

Warm up a chilly December evening— or any day at all—with this inviting tea. The spices really come through, and it's even more delicious when stirred with a cinnamon stick.
—Kelly Pacowta, Danbury, CT

- -

TAKES: 20 min. • **MAKES:** 4 servings

- 4 whole cloves
- 2 whole peppercorns
- 4 tea bags
- 4 tsp. sugar
- ¼ tsp. ground ginger
- 1 cinnamon stick (3 in.)
- 2½ cups boiling water
- 2 cups 2% milk

1. Place cloves and peppercorns in a large bowl; with the end of a wooden spoon handle, crush the spices until their aromas are released.
2. Add the tea bags, sugar, ginger, cinnamon stick and boiling water. Cover; steep for 6 minutes. Meanwhile, in a small saucepan, heat the milk.
3. Strain tea, discarding spices and tea bags. Stir in hot milk. Pour into mugs.
1 CUP 92 cal., 4g fat (2g sat. fat), 12mg chol., 49mg sod., 10g carb. (10g sugars, 0 fiber), 4g pro.

TEST KITCHEN TIPS

Can I make a vegan version? To make this chai tea vegan, replace the milk with a dairy-free option. We recommend either an almond or coconut milk alternative. Using a milk alternative will make this chai a little thinner than when using 2% milk.

How should I store chai tea? We recommend serving chai right after making it. However, you can also store it in an airtight jar in the refrigerator for a few days.

AUTUMN
SURPRISE PIE
P. 281

BOURBON
SWEET POTATO PIE
P. 280

FRIENDSGIVING

Low-stress and low-key are the hallmarks of a Thanksgiving dinner spent with friends. Bring your favorite group of people together and make them part of the action with a casual potluck party. Delicious food, wine, laughter and fellowship—with everyone pitching in—will make the occasion one to remember. With a little planning and a selection of amazing dishes, your Friendsgiving party is one they'll all be grateful for.

PLACE OF GRACE UTENSIL HOLDERS

Set out these simple paper utensil holders with a pencil or pen at each place setting so your guests can reflect on the year's blessings.

MATERIALS
- 8½x11-in. writing or decorative paper
- Stamps (letter, numeral and optional decorative) and stamp pad

Note: Practice stamping on scrap paper to get the desired letter and number spacing, and to determine the pressure needed for a uniform impression. Then move on to the decorative paper.

DIRECTIONS (FOR EACH)

Step 1: Fold up one end of the paper about 5 in. so that the short end of the fold is on top.

Step 2: Measure 2¼ in. in from each side; mark lightly with pencil. Fold flaps back at measured marks, making a 4-in.-wide front pocket. Overlap the flaps at back and secure with tape or a sticker.

Step 3: Use letter stamps—or your best penmanship—to write "Count Your Blessings" near the top edge of the pocket. Add numerals to form a list.

Step 4: Using a ruler as guide, make dotted lines next to each numeral with a fine-tip marker. Stamp a decoration near the bottom of the pocket if desired.

PARMESAN-PRETZEL CRISPS

ROASTED RED PEPPER CHEESE PUFFS

These are as pretty as they are delicious. I came up with this recipe one day when I was planning on making lasagna. Instead, I used some of the ingredients to create these tasty bites.
—*Kelly Williams, Forked River, NJ*

PREP: 35 min. • **BAKE:** 20 min./batch
MAKES: 32 appetizers

- ¾ cup part-skim ricotta cheese
- ½ cup chopped roasted sweet red pepper, patted dry
- ¼ cup shredded provolone cheese
- 2 Tbsp. chopped ripe olives
- 1 Tbsp. minced fresh parsley
- 1 tsp. dried oregano
- ¼ tsp. pepper
- 3 Tbsp. grated Romano cheese, divided
- 1 pkg. (17.3 oz.) frozen puff pastry, thawed
- 1 tsp. 2% milk

1. Preheat oven to 375°. For filling, mix first 7 ingredients and 2 Tbsp. Romano cheese.
2. Unfold 1 pastry sheet; cut into 16 squares. Place 2 Tbsp. filling on half of each square. Brush edges of pastry with milk; fold over to form a rectangle. Seal edges with a fork; place 1 in. apart on a parchment-lined baking sheet. Repeat with the second pastry sheet and the remaining filling.
3. Cut slits in tops of pastries. Brush with milk; sprinkle with remaining 1 Tbsp. Romano cheese. Bake until golden brown, 20-22 minutes. Remove from pans to wire racks. Serve warm.
1 APPETIZER 91 cal., 5g fat (2g sat. fat), 3mg chol., 92mg sod., 9g carb. (0 sugars, 1g fiber), 2g pro.

PARMESAN-PRETZEL CRISPS

I love this recipe because I usually have the ingredients on hand and it is so easy to prepare. It's one of those snacks that makes guests think you've gone the extra mile.
—*Pauline Porterfield, Roxboro, NC*

PREP: 10 min. • **BAKE:** 10 min./batch
MAKES: about 3 dozen

- 1½ cups shredded Parmesan cheese
- ¼ cup finely crushed pretzels
- ⅛ tsp. crushed red pepper flakes
  Optional: Pizza sauce and sliced fresh basil

1. Preheat oven to 350°. Toss together cheese, pretzels and red pepper flakes. Place 2 tsp. mixture in each greased nonstick mini muffin cup.
2. Bake until golden brown, 10-15 minutes. If desired, serve with pizza sauce and basil.
1 CRISP 16 cal., 1g fat (1g sat. fat), 2mg chol., 66mg sod., 1g carb. (0 sugars, 0 fiber), 1g pro.

#GIRLDINNER

Keep these crisps in an airtight container, so you can pull them out at a moment's notice. They'd go well with fruit and cheese, or with a light dip or savory spread.

WHITE GRAPE JUICE BRINED TURKEY BREAST

I found this recipe many years ago in a holiday menu magazine. The turkey has just the right amount of spices and seasonings.
—Edie DeSpain, Logan, UT

PREP: 25 min. + chilling
BAKE: 2 hours + standing
MAKES: 12 servings

- 4 fresh rosemary sprigs
- 1 bottle (46 oz.) white grape juice
- ¼ cup kosher salt
- 6 bay leaves
- 4 garlic cloves, sliced
- 2 large oven roasting bags
- 1 bone-in turkey breast (5 to 6 lbs.)
- 1 Tbsp. butter, melted
- 2 garlic cloves, minced
- 1 tsp. paprika
- 1 tsp. dried thyme
- ½ tsp. rubbed sage
- ½ tsp. onion powder
- ¼ tsp. pepper

1. In a large saucepan, combine the first 5 ingredients; bring to a boil. Cook and stir until salt is dissolved. Cool completely.
2. Place 1 roasting bag inside the other. Place turkey breast inside both bags; pour in cooled brine. Seal bags, pressing out as much air as possible; turn to coat turkey. Place in a large dish. Refrigerate 8-24 hours, turning occasionally.
3. Place a rack in a foil-lined roasting pan. Mix remaining ingredients. Remove turkey from brine; rinse and pat dry. Discard brine. Place turkey in prepared pan; rub with butter mixture.
4. Roast at 325° until a thermometer reads 170°, 2-2½ hours. (Cover loosely with foil if turkey browns too quickly.) Remove from oven; tent with foil. Let stand 15 minutes before carving.

5 OZ. COOKED TURKEY 277 cal., 11g fat (4g sat. fat), 105mg chol., 257mg sod., 2g carb. (1g sugars, 0 fiber), 40g pro.

APPLE PROSCIUTTO BRUSCHETTA

This is a simple but delicious holiday appetizer. I use Honeycrisp apples, but you can use whatever apples you have handy. For adult parties, I add a splash of cream sherry wine for an extra special flavor.
—Nancy Heishman, Las Vegas, NV

PREP: 20 min. • **BAKE:** 10 min./batch
MAKES: 3 dozen

- 1 cup finely chopped peeled apple
- 1 cup grated Asiago cheese
- 2 oz. finely chopped prosciutto
- 1 tsp. minced fresh oregano
- 1 tsp. minced fresh thyme
- ¼ tsp. ground cinnamon
- ⅛ tsp. coarsely ground pepper
- 1 tsp. cream sherry or apple juice, optional
- 36 slices French bread baguette (¼ in. thick)

1. Preheat oven to 375°. For topping, combine first 7 ingredients and, if desired, sherry.
2. Place baguette slices on foil-lined baking sheets. Top each with 1 rounded Tbsp. topping. Bake until lightly browned and cheese is melted, 8-10 minutes.

1 APPETIZER 36 cal., 1g fat (1g sat. fat), 4mg chol., 88mg sod., 5g carb. (0 sugars, 0 fiber), 2g pro.

HARVEST BOW TIES

Spaghetti squash and bow ties make this meatless dish hearty and filling. Add a can of black beans if you'd like more protein, and switch up the tomatoes for variety. Try using Italian diced tomatoes or diced tomatoes with mild green chiles.
—Anne Lynch, Beacon, NY

PREP: 25 min. • **COOK:** 15 min.
MAKES: 6 servings

- 1 small spaghetti squash (about 1½ lbs.)
- 12 oz. uncooked bow tie pasta (about 4½ cups)
- 2 Tbsp. olive oil
- 1 lb. sliced fresh mushrooms
- 1 cup chopped sweet onion
- 2 garlic cloves, minced
- 1 can (14½ oz.) diced tomatoes, undrained
- 6 oz. fresh baby spinach (about 8 cups)
- ¾ tsp. salt
- ½ tsp. pepper
- 2 Tbsp. butter
- 2 Tbsp. sour cream

1. Halve squash lengthwise; discard seeds. Place squash on a microwave-safe plate, cut side down. Microwave, uncovered, on high until tender, 9-11 minutes. Cool slightly. Meanwhile, in a 6-qt. Dutch oven or stockpot, cook pasta according to package directions. Drain; return to pot.
2. In a large skillet, heat oil over medium-high heat; saute mushrooms and onion until tender. Add garlic; cook and stir 1 minute. Separate strands of squash with a fork; add to skillet. Stir in tomatoes, spinach, salt and pepper; cook until spinach is wilted, stirring occasionally. Stir in butter and sour cream until blended.
3. Add to pasta. Heat through, tossing to coat.

2 CUPS 349 cal., 11g fat (4g sat. fat), 14mg chol., 475mg sod., 54g carb. (8g sugars, 6g fiber), 12g pro.

HARVEST
BOW TIES

PAIRS
WITH

PINOT GRIGIO
OR SANGIOVESE

SWEET POTATO PANZANELLA

GREEN BEANS WITH SMOKED TURKEY BACON

I really like cooking with curry, and this is a wonderful slow-cooker favorite of mine. Made with fresh green beans, turkey bacon and garbanzo beans, it has loads of flavor. It can be a main dish or a side dish. For vegetarians, just eliminate the bacon.

—*Nancy Heishman, Las Vegas, NV*

PREP: 25 min. • **COOK:** 5 hours
MAKES: 10 servings

- 2 lbs. fresh green beans, trimmed
- 1 can (15 oz.) garbanzo beans or chickpeas, rinsed and drained
- 1 large red onion, chopped
- 1 large sweet red pepper, chopped
- 8 turkey bacon strips, chopped
- 1 can (15 oz.) crushed tomatoes
- ¼ cup lemon juice
- 2 Tbsp. minced fresh parsley
- 3 garlic cloves, minced
- 3 tsp. curry powder
- 1 tsp. freshly ground pepper
- ¾ tsp. salt
- ¼ cup minced fresh basil
- 1½ cups crumbled feta cheese

1. Place first 4 ingredients in a 6-qt. slow cooker. In a large nonstick skillet, cook bacon over medium heat until crisp, stirring occasionally. Add to slow cooker.
2. In a small bowl, mix tomatoes, lemon juice, parsley, garlic, curry, pepper and salt. Pour over bean mixture.
3. Cook, covered, on low until green beans are tender, 5-6 hours. Stir in basil. Top with cheese before serving.
¾ CUP 168 cal., 6g fat (3g sat. fat), 21mg chol., 633mg sod., 21g carb. (7g sugars, 7g fiber), 9g pro. **DIABETIC EXCHANGES** 1 starch, 1 vegetable, 1 medium-fat meat.

SWEET POTATO PANZANELLA

This is my favorite lunch dish during the fall season. Every bite is filled with flavor and texture, but it isn't too high in calories.

—*Mary Leverette, Columbia, SC*

TAKES: 30 min. • **MAKES:** 8 servings

- 2 cups cubed peeled sweet potatoes
- 4 cups cubed French bread
- 4 Tbsp. olive oil, divided
- ⅛ tsp. salt
- ⅛ tsp. pepper
- 4 cups fresh baby spinach
- ½ small red onion, thinly sliced
- ¼ cup minced fresh basil
- ¼ cup minced fresh cilantro
- ⅓ cup red wine vinegar

1. Preheat oven to 450°. Place the sweet potatoes in a large saucepan; add water to cover. Bring to a boil. Reduce heat; cook, covered, until just tender, 8-12 minutes. Drain; cool slightly.
2. Meanwhile, toss the bread cubes with 2 Tbsp. oil, salt and pepper. Spread evenly in an ungreased 15x10x1-in. pan. Bake until golden brown, about 5 minutes. Transfer to a large bowl; cool slightly.
3. Add spinach, red onion, herbs and sweet potatoes to toasted bread. In a small bowl, whisk together vinegar and remaining oil. Drizzle over salad; toss gently to combine.
¾ CUP 142 cal., 7g fat (1g sat. fat), 0 chol., 150mg sod., 17g carb. (3g sugars, 2g fiber), 2g pro. **DIABETIC EXCHANGES** 1½ fat, 1 starch.

APPLE
QUINOA
SPOON
BREAD

APPLE QUINOA SPOON BREAD

My cousin is a strict vegetarian, so creating satisfying veggie dishes is my yearly challenge. This spoon bread can act as an amazing Thanksgiving side, but the addition of hearty, healthy quinoa and vegetables make it a well-rounded casserole. Pair it with a seasonal salad to make a filling vegetarian meal.
—*Christine Wendland, Browns Mills, NJ*

PREP: 25 min. • **BAKE:** 25 min.
MAKES: 9 servings

- ⅔ cup water
- ⅓ cup quinoa, rinsed
- 1 Tbsp. canola oil
- 1 small apple, peeled and diced
- 1 small onion, finely chopped
- 1 small parsnip, peeled and diced
- ½ tsp. celery seed
- 1¼ tsp. salt, divided
- 1 Tbsp. minced fresh sage
- ¾ cup yellow cornmeal
- ¼ cup all-purpose flour
- 1 Tbsp. sugar
- 1 tsp. baking powder
- 1 large egg, room temperature
- 1½ cups 2% milk, divided

1. Preheat oven to 375°. In a small saucepan, bring water to a boil. Add quinoa. Reduce heat; simmer, covered, until liquid is absorbed, 12-15 minutes. Fluff with a fork; cool slightly.
2. Meanwhile, in a large skillet, heat oil over medium heat; saute apple, onion and parsnip with celery seed and ½ tsp. salt until softened, 4-5 minutes. Remove from heat; stir in sage.
3. In a large bowl, whisk together cornmeal, flour, sugar, baking powder and remaining ¾ tsp. salt. In another bowl, whisk together egg and 1 cup milk. Add to cornmeal mixture, stirring just until moistened. Fold in quinoa and the apple mixture.
4. Transfer to a greased 8-in. square baking dish. Pour remaining ½ cup milk over the top.
5. Bake, uncovered, until the edges are golden brown, 25-30 minutes. Let stand 5 minutes before serving. If desired, sprinkle with additional minced sage.
1 SERVING 153 cal., 4g fat (1g sat. fat), 24mg chol., 412mg sod., 26g carb. (6g sugars, 2g fiber), 5g pro. **DIABETIC EXCHANGES** 1½ starch, 1 fat.

PUMPKIN-COCONUT SOUP

Thai food lovers will go crazy for this soup. It has a deep flavor from the combination of onion, coconut milk and spices.
—*Susan Hein, Burlington, WI*

PREP: 20 min. • **COOK:** 25 min.
MAKES: 12 servings (3 qt.)

- 2 Tbsp. butter
- 1 large onion, chopped
- 2 Tbsp. minced fresh gingerroot
- 2 cartons (32 oz. each) chicken stock
- 2 cans (15 oz. each) pumpkin
- 1 tsp. salt
- ¾ tsp. ground cinnamon
- ½ tsp. ground nutmeg
- ½ tsp. pepper
- 2 cups light coconut milk
  Optional toppings: Sour cream, pepitas and minced fresh parsley

1. In a large saucepan, heat butter over medium-high heat; saute onion and ginger until tender. Add stock, pumpkin and seasonings; whisk until blended. Bring to a boil. Reduce heat; simmer, covered, until flavors are blended, about 15 minutes.
2. Puree soup using an immersion blender, or cool slightly and puree soup in batches in a blender; return to pan. Stir in coconut milk; heat through. Serve with toppings as desired.
1 CUP 91 cal., 5g fat (3g sat. fat), 5mg chol., 556mg sod., 9g carb. (4g sugars, 2g fiber), 4g pro. **DIABETIC EXCHANGES** 1 fat, ½ starch.

TOP TIPS FOR A FABULOUS FRIENDSGIVING PARTY

A holiday potluck party is the low-stress alternative to a fancy feast, so keep things simple, and don't be afraid to ask for help. From setup to serving to cleanup, this party is about sharing, and everyone has something to bring to the table. Keep these tips in mind:

- The host makes the turkey and the gravy. The main course doesn't have to be turkey, but whatever it is, you should provide it.

- Make a plan for general food categories and the number of dishes, and include it with your invitations. Ask guests to RSVP with what they're bringing, so you don't end up with all desserts. If necessary, make specific requests.

- Assign appetizers to your most reliable friend, and ask her to arrive early.

- Ask that dishes are ready to go, or need only minimal reheating. You don't want a fight over kitchen space.

- Music helps set the mood. Have a party playlist, or ask a friend (who you know has good taste in music) to act as DJ.

- Let your guests help. Have a list of simple tasks they can do. Serving drinks, taking coats, stacking dishes—it all helps.

- Stock up on takeout cartons, and send guests home with leftovers. They (and your not-overloaded refrigerator) will love it!

BOURBON SWEET POTATO PIE

BOURBON SWEET POTATO PIE

There is nothing I don't love about this pie! I adore the flavors, and I like that I can sneak some whole grains into the crust. It belongs on every holiday dessert buffet.
—*Mary Leverette, Columbia, SC*

- -

PREP: 25 min. • **BAKE:** 40 min.
MAKES: 8 servings

- 1   cup quick-cooking oats
- ¾   cup packed dark brown sugar
- ¾   cup self-rising flour
- ½   cup butter, melted
- ⅔   cup chopped walnuts

FILLING

- 2   medium sweet potatoes (about 8 oz. each)
- 2   large eggs, lightly beaten
- ½   cup packed dark brown sugar
- ½   cup butter, melted
- ¼   cup self-rising flour
- 2   Tbsp. bourbon
     Sweetened whipped cream

1. Preheat oven to 325°. Mix the first 4 ingredients. Firmly press 1⅔ cups mixture onto bottom and up side of a well-greased 9-in. pie plate. Bake until light golden brown, 6-8 minutes. Cool on a wire rack.
2. Stir walnuts into the remaining oat mixture. Reserve for topping.
3. For filling, pierce potatoes with a fork; microwave on high until very tender, 10-13 minutes, turning once halfway. Cool slightly.
4. Peel potatoes and place in a large bowl; mash until smooth. Beat in eggs, brown sugar, melted butter, flour and bourbon until well blended. Add to crust.
5. Sprinkle with topping. Bake until golden brown and filling is set, 30-35 minutes. Cool on a wire rack; serve or refrigerate within 2 hours. Serve with whipped cream.
NOTE As a substitute for 1 cup of self-rising flour, place 1½ tsp. baking powder and ½ tsp. salt in a measuring cup. Add all-purpose flour to measure 1 cup.
1 PIECE 570 cal., 31g fat (16g sat. fat), 108mg chol., 403mg sod., 67g carb. (40g sugars, 4g fiber), 7g pro.

AUTUMN SURPRISE PIE

THE GRATEFUL PUMPKIN

A white pumpkin is the canvas for thankful thoughts from all your guests. It's a happy display of the good things in life that last long after the leftovers head home.

AUTUMN SURPRISE PIE

What better way to welcome guests than with a homemade pie? This version calls for apples, pears and raisins flavored with rum extract.

—*Karen Gauvreau, Portage, MI*

PREP: 40 min. + chilling • **BAKE:** 45 min.
MAKES: 8 servings

- 1½ cups all-purpose flour
- 3 Tbsp. sugar
- ¼ tsp. plus ⅛ tsp. salt
- ¼ tsp. plus ⅛ tsp. baking powder
- 6 Tbsp. cold butter, cubed
- ⅓ cup fat-free milk
- 1½ tsp. cider vinegar

FILLING
- ½ cup sugar
- ¼ cup all-purpose flour
- 1 tsp. ground cinnamon
- ¼ tsp. ground nutmeg
- ¼ tsp. ground cloves
- 5 cups sliced peeled apples
- 2 cups sliced peeled ripe pears
- ⅓ cup raisins
- ¾ tsp. rum extract

TOPPING
- 1 large egg, lightly beaten
- 1 tsp. coarse sugar

1. Mix the first 4 ingredients; cut in butter until crumbly. Mix milk and vinegar; add gradually to the crumb mixture, tossing with a fork until dough holds together when pressed. Divide dough into 2 portions, 1 slightly larger than the other. Shape each into a disk; cover and refrigerate 1 hour or overnight.
2. Preheat oven to 425°. On a lightly floured surface, roll the larger portion of dough to a ⅛-in.-thick circle; transfer to a greased 9-in. pie plate. Trim crust even with rim. Refrigerate crust while preparing the filling.
3. Mix the first 5 filling ingredients. Place apples, pears and raisins in a large bowl. Add sugar mixture and extract; toss to combine. Spoon into crust.
4. Roll out the remaining portion of dough to a ⅛-in.-thick circle; cut into ¾-in.-wide strips. Arrange over filling in a lattice pattern. Trim and seal strips to edge of bottom crust; flute edge. Brush lattice with beaten egg. Sprinkle with coarse sugar.
5. Bake pie on a lower oven rack for 15 minutes. Reduce oven setting to 350°. Bake until crust is golden brown and filling is bubbly, 30-35 minutes. Cool on a wire rack.
1 PIECE 331 cal., 10g fat (6g sat. fat), 46mg chol., 217mg sod., 59g carb. (32g sugars, 3g fiber), 5g pro.

PROSCIUTTO-WRAPPED
ASPARAGUS WITH
RASPBERRY SAUCE
P. 285

HAM CROQUETTES
WITH MUSTARD SAUCE
P. 287

SPICY
BEEF SATAY
P.290

WINE & TAPAS

Make your party a masterpiece with a spread of dishes rich with Spanish and Mediterranean flavors. Tapas are traditionally served as small plates, so your guests can try them all!

HOST A WINE TASTING PARTY LIKE A PRO

Bring together all your favorite people for an amazing wine tasting party, complete with food, games and, of course, great wine!

CHOOSE A THEME

Choose a theme for your lineup, whether it's a country or varietal. The Mediterranean-style apps in this chapter set the stage for out-of-the-ordinary wines from Spain, Greece and Italy. Ask wine-store staff to recommend hidden gems.

BUY YOUR WINE

Once you have your headcount, it's time to shop! One bottle yields 12 traditional 2-oz. tasting pours, so for fewer than 10 people, you'll be OK with one bottle of each wine. With more generous pours, you might get only six to eight glasses from each bottle.

GET THE NECESSARY SUPPLIES

Count on at least one wine glass per person—if you plan on comparing wines, you may need two glasses for each guest. Other supplies include water, spit buckets, palate cleansers such as crackers, and paper in case anyone wants to take notes.

PLAN THE MENU

Provide light finger foods so your guests aren't drinking on an empty stomach. A charcuterie board is a good option, but you can also put out an array of tasty apps.

HAVE INFOR MATION HANDY

No one expects you to lead the tasting like a sommelier, but chances are your guests will have questions. Do a bit of research in advance on the vineyards, grape varietals and so on.

MARINATED OLIVES

MARINATED OLIVES

These olives are nice to have for get-togethers because they're simple to make and they'll add a little zest to the buffet table offerings.
—*Marguerite Shaeffer, Sewell, NJ*

PREP: 10 min. + marinating
MAKES: 4 cups

- 2 cups large pimiento-stuffed olives, drained
- 1 cup pitted kalamata olives, drained
- 1 cup pitted medium ripe olives, drained
- ¼ cup olive oil
- 2 Tbsp. lemon juice
- 1 Tbsp. minced fresh thyme or 1 tsp. dried thyme
- 2 tsp. minced fresh rosemary or ½ tsp. dried rosemary, crushed
- 2 tsp. grated lemon zest
- 4 garlic cloves, slivered
  Pepper to taste

1. Place olives in a bowl. Combine the remaining ingredients; pour over olives and stir. Cover and refrigerate 1-2 days before serving, stirring several times each day.

2. Marinated olives may be refrigerated for up to 2 weeks. Serve them with a slotted spoon.

¼ CUP 98 cal., 10g fat (1g sat. fat), 0 chol., 572mg sod., 3g carb. (0 sugars, 0 fiber), 0 pro.

#GIRLDINNER

Marinated olives keep well in the refrigerator, so they're great to fill out a snack plate, a charcuterie board or a collection of savory items for a quick and light dinner for one.

PROSCIUTTO-WRAPPED ASPARAGUS WITH RASPBERRY SAUCE

Grilling the prosciutto with the asparagus gives this appetizer a salty crunch that's perfect for dipping into a sweet glaze. When a delicious appetizer is this easy to prepare, you owe it to yourself to try it! If the weather isn't right for grilling, you can also make these on the stovetop in an oiled grill pan or large skillet over medium heat.
—*Noelle Myers, Grand Forks, ND*

TAKES: 30 min. • **MAKES:** 16 appetizers

- ⅓ lb. thinly sliced prosciutto or deli ham
- 16 fresh asparagus spears, trimmed
- ½ cup seedless raspberry jam
- 2 Tbsp. balsamic vinegar

1. Cut prosciutto slices in half. Wrap a prosciutto piece around each asparagus spear; secure ends with toothpicks.
2. Grill asparagus, covered, on a greased rack over medium heat for 6-8 minutes or until prosciutto is crisp, turning once. Discard toothpicks.
3. In a small microwave-safe bowl, microwave jam and vinegar on high for 15-20 seconds or until jam is melted. Serve with asparagus.

1 ASPARAGUS SPEAR WITH 1½ TSP. SAUCE 50 cal., 1g fat (0 sat. fat), 8mg chol., 184mg sod., 7g carb. (7g sugars, 0 fiber), 3g pro. **DIABETIC EXCHANGES** ½ starch.

PROSCIUTTO-WRAPPED ASPARAGUS WITH RASPBERRY SAUCE

HAM CROQUETTES
WITH MUSTARD SAUCE

HAM CROQUETTES WITH MUSTARD SAUCE

Any leftover ham is set aside for these crispy croquettes. I shape them early in the day, then simply fry them at dinnertime. The mustard sauce is mild and pairs well with ham.
—*Kathy Vincek, Toms River, NJ*

PREP: 35 min. + chilling
COOK: 5 min./batch • **MAKES:** 1 dozen

- 2 cups finely chopped fully cooked ham
- 1 Tbsp. finely chopped onion
- 1 tsp. minced fresh parsley
- ¼ cup butter, cubed
- ¼ cup all-purpose flour
- ¼ tsp. salt
- ⅛ tsp. pepper
- 1 cup 2% milk
- 1 large egg
- 2 Tbsp. water
- ¾ cup dry bread crumbs
  Oil for deep-fat frying
  SAUCE
- 1½ tsp. butter
- 1½ tsp. all-purpose flour
- ¼ tsp. salt
  Dash pepper
- ½ cup 2% milk
- 4½ tsp. yellow mustard

1. In a small bowl, combine ham, onion and parsley.
2. In a small saucepan, melt butter. Stir in the flour, salt and pepper until smooth; gradually add milk. Bring to a boil; cook and stir 1 minute or until thickened. Stir into the ham mixture.
3. Spread mixture into an 8-in. square baking dish; cover and refrigerate at least 2 hours.
4. In a shallow bowl, combine egg and water. Place bread crumbs in a separate shallow bowl. Shape ham mixture into 12 balls (mixture will be soft); roll each ball in the egg mixture, then in the bread crumbs. Cover and refrigerate 2 hours longer.
5. In an electric skillet or deep fryer, heat oil to 375°. Fry croquettes, a few at a time, 2-3 minutes or until golden brown, turning once. Drain on paper towels.
6. Meanwhile, for the sauce, in a small saucepan, melt butter. Stir in the flour, salt and pepper until smooth; gradually add milk. Bring to a boil; cook and stir 2 minutes or until thickened. Stir in mustard. Serve with croquettes.

1 CROQUETTE WITH 2 TSP. SAUCE 188 cal., 14g fat (5g sat. fat), 44mg chol., 503mg sod., 8g carb. (2g sugars, 0 fiber), 7g pro.

HERBED FETA DIP

Guests can't get enough of this thick, zesty dip that bursts with fresh Mediterranean flavor. The feta cheese and fresh mint complement each other beautifully, creating the perfect sidekick for crunchy carrots, toasted pita chips, sliced baguettes or any other dipper you fancy.
—*Rebecca Ray, Chicago, IL*

TAKES: 25 min. • **MAKES:** 3 cups

- ½ cup packed fresh parsley sprigs
- ½ cup fresh mint leaves
- ½ cup olive oil
- 2 garlic cloves, peeled
- ½ tsp. pepper
- 4 cups (16 oz.) crumbled feta cheese
- 3 Tbsp. lemon juice
  Assorted fresh vegetables

In a food processor, combine the first 5 ingredients; cover and pulse until finely chopped. Add cheese and lemon juice; process until creamy. Serve with vegetables.

¼ CUP 176 cal., 15g fat (5g sat. fat), 20mg chol., 361mg sod., 2g carb. (0 sugars, 1g fiber), 7g pro.

WINE TASTING PARTY GAME IDEAS TO PLAY AS YOU SIP

Hosting a wine tasting party is a great way to bring all your friends together. To keep everyone entertained, try planning one (or more) of these activities, all guaranteed to keep your guests laughing.

DRAW THE WINE LABEL
See who's the most artistic by playing an easy drawing game—no skills necessary. Hide the labels on the wine bottles, and after each tasting, have everyone draw what they think would be an appropriate label. The wilder, the better.

DESCRIBE THIS WINE
People often use flowery language to describe wines, but you can make it a little more lively with some silly prompts. Make up cards that say things like, "If this wine was a celebrity, who would it be?" or "Use a word that begins with R to describe this wine."

HOW MANY CORKS?
Have you ever had to guess how many jelly beans are in a jar? Do the same thing with wine corks! Save up corks for a month or so before the party, then put them all in a jar and have guests guess how many there are.

WINE BOTTLE RING TOSS
Don't send your guests home empty-handed! Have everyone bring a bottle of wine, and set them up in a triangular formation. As people leave, have them toss a ring at the bottles from a few feet away. Whichever bottle they hook is the one they get to take home.

PICKLED SHRIMP WITH BASIL

Red wine vinegar plus the freshness of citrus and basil perk up marinated shrimp with hardly any prep. Serve with garlic toast or over greens for a salad.
—*James Schend, Pleasant Prairie, WI*

PREP: 15 min. + marinating
MAKES: 20 servings

- ½ cup red wine vinegar
- ½ cup olive oil
- 2 tsp. seafood seasoning
- 2 tsp. stone-ground mustard
- 1 garlic clove, minced
- 2 lbs. peeled and deveined cooked shrimp (31-40 per lb.)
- 1 medium lemon, thinly sliced
- 1 medium lime, thinly sliced
- ½ medium red onion, thinly sliced
- ¼ cup thinly sliced fresh basil
- 2 Tbsp. capers, drained
- ¼ cup minced fresh basil
- ½ tsp. kosher salt
- ¼ tsp. coarsely ground pepper

1. In a large bowl, whisk the first 5 ingredients. Add shrimp, lemon, lime, onion, sliced basil and capers; toss gently to coat. Refrigerate, covered, up to 8 hours, stirring occasionally.
2. Just before serving, stir minced basil, salt and pepper into shrimp mixture. Serve with a slotted spoon.

½ CUP 64 cal., 2g fat (0 sat. fat), 69mg chol., 111mg sod., 1g carb. (0 sugars, 0 fiber), 9g pro. **DIABETIC EXCHANGES** 1 lean meat, ½ fat.

TEST KITCHEN TIPS
- Pickled shrimp is delicious as an appetizer, but it also makes a great garnish for a Bloody Mary!
- The acid in vinegar can make shrimp tough, so 8 hours is the maximum marinade time—play it safe with a shorter time.

SPANAKOPITA SPRING ROLLS

SPANAKOPITA SPRING ROLLS

I was inspired to turn original spanakopita into a hand-held hors d'oeuvre. I use egg roll wrappers in place of phyllo dough, and now these are the biggest hit among my friends.
—*Jade Randall, Las Vegas, NV*

PREP: 15 min. • **COOK:** 5 min./batch
MAKES: 14 spring rolls

- 2 pkg. (10 oz. each) frozen chopped spinach, thawed and squeezed dry
- 2 cups crumbled feta cheese
- 4 garlic cloves, minced
- 2 tsp. dill weed
- ¼ tsp. salt
- ¼ tsp. pepper
- 14 refrigerated egg roll wrappers
  Oil for deep-fat frying

1. Mix first 6 ingredients. With a corner of an egg roll wrapper facing you, place about ⅓ cup filling just below center of wrapper. (Cover remaining wrappers with a damp paper towel until ready to use.) Fold bottom corner over filling; moisten remaining wrapper edges with water. Fold side corners toward center over filling. Roll up tightly, pressing at tip to seal. Repeat.
2. In an electric skillet or deep-fat fryer, heat oil to 375°. Fry spring rolls, a few at a time, until golden brown, 3-4 minutes, turning occasionally. Drain on paper towels.

FREEZE OPTION Freeze uncooked spring rolls in freezer containers, spacing them so they don't touch and separating the layers with waxed paper. To use, fry frozen spring rolls as directed, increasing time as necessary.

1 SPRING ROLL 245 cal., 12g fat (4g sat. fat), 20mg chol., 568mg sod., 22g carb. (0 sugars, 3g fiber), 10g pro.

GOUDA TURKEY FRITTATA

ONION BRIE APPETIZERS

Guests will think you spent hours preparing these cute appetizers, but they're really easy to assemble, using purchased puff pastry. The tasty combination of Brie, caramelized onions and caraway is terrific.
—*Carole Resnick, Cleveland, OH*

PREP: 25 min. + chilling • **BAKE:** 15 min.
MAKES: 1½ dozen

- 2 medium onions, thinly sliced
- 3 Tbsp. butter
- 2 Tbsp. brown sugar
- ½ tsp. white wine vinegar
- 1 sheet frozen puff pastry, thawed
- 4 oz. Brie cheese, rind removed, softened
- 1 to 2 tsp. caraway seeds
- 1 large egg
- 2 tsp. water

1. In a large skillet, cook onions, butter, brown sugar and vinegar over medium-low heat until the onions are golden brown, stirring frequently. Remove with a slotted spoon; cool to room temperature.
2. On a lightly floured surface, roll the puff pastry into an 11x8-in. rectangle. Cut Brie into thin slices; distribute evenly over the pastry. Cover with the onions; sprinkle with caraway seeds.
3. Roll up 1 long side to the middle of the dough; roll up the other side so the 2 rolls meet in the center. Using a serrated knife, cut into ½-in. slices. Place on parchment-lined baking sheets; flatten to ¼-in. thickness. Refrigerate for 15 minutes. Preheat oven to 375°.
4. In a small bowl, whisk egg and water; brush over slices. Bake until puffed and golden brown, 12-14 minutes. Serve appetizers warm.
1 APPETIZER 121 cal., 8g fat (3g sat. fat), 23mg chol., 109mg sod., 11g carb. (3g sugars, 1g fiber), 3g pro.

GOUDA TURKEY FRITTATA

This cheesy, filling egg skillet isn't just for breakfast—it makes a fantastic dinner or, cut into smaller servings, appetizer. It's a great way to use up turkey leftovers.
—*Nella Parker, hersey, MI*

PREP: 30 min. • **BROIL:** 5 min.
MAKES: 6 servings

- 1 cup diced zucchini
- 2 shallots, finely chopped
- 1 Tbsp. olive oil
- 1 Tbsp. butter
- 4 large eggs, room temperature
- 2 Tbsp. water
- 1 cup finely chopped cooked turkey
- 1½ tsp. minced fresh tarragon
- ¼ tsp. salt
- ¼ tsp. pepper
- ½ cup shredded Gouda cheese

1. In a 10-in. ovenproof skillet, saute zucchini and shallots in oil and butter until tender.
2. In a small bowl, whisk eggs and water; stir in turkey and seasonings. Pour egg mixture into skillet; cover and cook over medium-low heat until eggs are nearly set, 8-10 minutes.
3. Uncover skillet; sprinkle with cheese. Broil 6 in. from the heat for 2-3 minutes or until eggs are completely set. Cut into wedges.
1 PIECE 171 cal., 11g fat (5g sat. fat), 175mg chol., 256mg sod., 3g carb. (1g sugars, 0 fiber), 14g pro.

ZESTY MEDITERRANEAN POTATO SALAD

SPICY BEEF SATAY

The fragrant spices and full flavors of North African cuisine make these appetizers a tasty party food.
—*Roxanne Chan, Albany, CA*

PREP: 35 min. • **BROIL:** 5 min.
MAKES: 2 dozen (½ cup sauce)

- 1 cup white wine vinegar
- ¾ cup sugar
- ½ cup water
- 1 Tbsp. orange marmalade
- ¼ tsp. grated orange zest
- ¼ tsp. crushed red pepper flakes
- ½ cup finely chopped salted roasted almonds
- 2 Tbsp. minced fresh mint
- 1 green onion, finely chopped
- 1 Tbsp. lemon juice
- 1 garlic clove, minced
- ¼ tsp. each ground cinnamon, cumin and coriander
- 1 lb. lean ground beef (90% lean)
  Minced fresh parsley

1. In a small saucepan, combine the first 6 ingredients. Bring to a boil. Reduce heat; simmer, uncovered, for 25 minutes or until reduced to ½ cup.
2. Meanwhile, in a large bowl, combine almonds, mint, onion, lemon juice, garlic and spices. Crumble beef over mixture and mix lightly but thoroughly. Divide into 24 pieces. Shape each piece into a 3x1-in. rectangle; insert a soaked wooden appetizer skewer into each piece.
3. Broil 6 in. from the heat 2-4 minutes on each side or until a thermometer reads 160°. Arrange on a serving platter. Drizzle with sauce mixture and sprinkle with parsley.
1 APPETIZER WITH 1 TSP. SAUCE 74 cal., 3g fat (1g sat. fat), 12mg chol., 25mg sod., 8g carb. (7g sugars, 0 fiber), 4g pro.

ZESTY MEDITERRANEAN POTATO SALAD

I love this recipe that incorporates many of the vegetables I plant in my garden. The dressing is light and fresh—perfect for a picnic or barbecue.
—*Terri Crandall, Gardnerville, NV*

PREP: 25 min. • **COOK:** 15 min. + chilling
MAKES: 8 servings

- 4 large Yukon Gold potatoes, peeled and cubed
- 1½ tsp. salt, divided
- ½ cup olive oil
- ¼ cup lemon juice
- ½ tsp. pepper
- ⅛ tsp. crushed red pepper flakes
- 1 medium sweet red pepper, finely chopped
- ½ small red onion, finely chopped
- ⅓ cup Greek olives, pitted and chopped
- 4 bacon strips, cooked and crumbled
- ½ cup crumbled feta cheese
- ¼ cup loosely packed basil leaves, torn

1. Place potatoes in a large saucepan; add water to cover. Add 1 tsp. salt. Bring to a boil. Reduce heat; cook, uncovered, until tender, 8-10 minutes. Drain and place in a large bowl.
2. In a small bowl, whisk olive oil, lemon juice, the remaining ½ tsp. salt, pepper and red pepper flakes until blended. Spoon over potato mixture; toss to coat. Refrigerate, covered, about 1 hour.
3. Just before serving, add sweet red pepper, onion, olives and bacon to potatoes. Sprinkle with feta and basil.
¾ CUP 341 cal., 18g fat (3g sat. fat), 8mg chol., 685mg sod., 40g carb. (4g sugars, 3g fiber), 6g pro.

PAIRS
WITH

MOSCATO D'ASTI

SPICY
BEEF SATAY

CASSETTE
COOKIES
P. 297

NACHO
SNACK MIX
P. 295

SLOW-COOKED
TURKEY
SLOPPY JOES
P. 298

TOTALLY AWESOME '80s PARTY

There's no better way to celebrate the era of big hair, leg warmers and boomboxes than with a super rad '80s-themed party. Look to these totally tubular '80s-inspired recipes and ideas to create a bash that's sure to go down in history.

NACHO
SNACK MIX

NACHO SNACK MIX

This colorful mixture of bite-sized snack foods, cereal and crackers gets its south-of-the-border accent from taco seasoning. The recipe makes a big batch, but it always goes fast.
—Lizz (Elizabeth) Loder, Fox Point, WI

- -

PREP: 10 min. • **BAKE:** 2 hours + cooling
MAKES: 4 qt.

- 4 cups Crispix
- 1 can (4½ oz.) crisp cheese ball snacks
- 3 cups corn chips
- 2 cups pretzel sticks
- 1 cup cheddar-flavored snack crackers
- 2 Tbsp. taco seasoning
- ½ cup canola oil
- ½ cup butter, melted

1. Preheat oven to 200°. In a large bowl, combine the first 5 ingredients. Spread in 2 ungreased 15x10x1-in. baking pans. Combine taco seasoning, oil and butter; pour over the cereal mixture and toss to coat.
2. Bake for 2 hours, stirring every 30 minutes. Cool in pans on wire racks. Store in airtight containers.
1 CUP 270 cal., 19g fat (6g sat. fat), 16mg chol., 434mg sod., 22g carb. (2g sugars, 1g fiber), 2g pro.

ARTICHOKE SPINACH DIP IN A BREAD BOWL

Baking the dip in the actual bread shell makes this a very attractive dish, and it's very easy to clean up. Every time I serve this, people can't believe how healthy and veggie-filled it is.
—Ella Homel, Chicago, IL

- -

PREP: 25 min. • **BAKE:** 20 min.
MAKES: 4 cups

- 3 jars (7½ oz. each) marinated quartered artichoke hearts, drained and chopped
- 1 cup grated Parmesan cheese
- ¾ cup mayonnaise
- 3 green onions, sliced
- 1 can (4 oz.) chopped green chiles, drained
- 1 pkg. (10 oz.) frozen chopped spinach, thawed and squeezed dry
- 1 cup shredded Swiss cheese
- 1 round loaf (1 lb.) rye or pumpernickel bread

1. Preheat oven to 350°. In a large bowl, combine the first 7 ingredients. Cut a thin slice off the top of bread. Hollow out the bottom half, leaving a ½-in. shell. Cut removed bread into 1-in. cubes.
2. Place bread cubes on an ungreased baking sheet. Broil 6 in. from the heat until golden, 2-3 minutes, stirring once.
3. Place bread shell on an ungreased baking sheet. Spoon dip into bread shell. Bake, uncovered, until heated through, 20-25 minutes. Serve with bread cubes.
NOTES Reduced-fat or fat-free mayonnaise is not recommended for this recipe. If any of the dip does not fit in bread shell, bake, uncovered, in a greased small baking dish until heated through.
¼ CUP 263 cal., 19g fat (5g sat. fat), 15mg chol., 520mg sod., 18g carb. (1g sugars, 3g fiber), 7g pro.

TRI-COLOR PASTA CRAB SALAD

When it comes to cooking, I believe the simpler the better. A few years ago, a co-worker told me about this tasty, simple salad and it's been a favorite ever since.
—Carol Blauw, Holland, MI

- -

PREP: 20 min. + chilling
MAKES: 10 servings

- 4½ cups uncooked tricolor spiral pasta
- 1 pkg. (16 oz.) imitation crabmeat, flaked
- ⅓ cup chopped celery
- ⅓ cup chopped green pepper
- ⅓ cup chopped onion
- ½ cup reduced-fat mayonnaise
- ½ cup reduced-fat ranch salad dressing
- 1 tsp. dill weed

Cook pasta according to the package directions; drain and rinse in cold water. Toss with crab and vegetables. Combine remaining ingredients. Pour over pasta mixture; toss to coat. Cover and refrigerate at least 2 hours before serving.
¾ CUP 242 cal., 7g fat (1g sat. fat), 15mg chol., 579mg sod., 33g carb. (0 sugars, 1g fiber), 10g pro. **DIABETIC EXCHANGES** 2 starch, 1 lean meat, ½ fat.

FRENCH BREAD PIZZA

I often take these French bread pizzas to church picnics or potluck suppers and there are never any left afterward. When I fix them at home, just for the two of us, I freeze two halves in foil to enjoy later.
—Lou Stasny, Poplarville, MS

PREP: 20 min. • **BAKE:** 10 min.
MAKES: 12 servings

- 1½ lbs. ground beef
- ½ tsp. garlic powder
- ½ tsp. salt
- 2 loaves (8 oz. each) French bread, halved lengthwise
- 1 cup cheese dip
- 1 can (4 oz.) mushroom stems and pieces, drained
- 1 cup chopped green onions
- 1 can (4 oz.) sliced jalapenos, drained
- 1 can (8 oz.) tomato sauce
- ½ cup grated Parmesan cheese
- 4 cups shredded part-skim mozzarella cheese

1. Preheat oven to 350°. In a large skillet, cook beef over medium heat until no longer pink, breaking into crumbles; drain. Stir in garlic powder and salt.
2. Arrange bread on a baking sheet, cut side up. Spread with cheese dip. Top with beef mixture, mushrooms, onions and jalapenos. Drizzle with tomato sauce. Top with Parmesan and mozzarella cheeses.
3. Bake until golden brown, 10-15 minutes. Serve warm.

FREEZE OPTION Wrap and freeze loaves. To use, unwrap loaves and thaw on baking sheets in the refrigerator. Bake at 350° for 18 minutes or until cheese is melted. May be frozen for up to 3 months.

1 PIECE 323 cal., 19g fat (11g sat. fat), 71mg chol., 907mg sod., 15g carb. (2g sugars, 1g fiber), 23g pro.

FRENCH BREAD PIZZA

PAIRS WITH

WHITE OR RED ZINFANDEL

CASSETTE
COOKIES

CASSETTE COOKIES

Serve these cassette-shaped cutout cookies while rocking out to your favorite '80s tunes!
—*Lynn Burgess, Rolla, MO*

- -

PREP: 1 hour + standing
BAKE: 15 min./batch + cooling
MAKES: 2 dozen

- ¾   cup butter, softened
- 1   cup sugar
- 2   large eggs, room temperature
- 1   tsp. vanilla extract
- 3   cups all-purpose flour
- 1   tsp. baking powder
- ½   tsp. salt

ROYAL ICING

- 3¾ to 4 cups confectioners' sugar
- 5   to 6 Tbsp. warm water
- 3   Tbsp. meringue powder
- 2   to 3 tsp. water
- 12 drops neon green food coloring
- 12 drops neon pink food coloring
- 10 drops neon blue food coloring
- ⅛   tsp. black paste food coloring

1. In a large mixing bowl, cream butter and sugar until light and fluffy, 5-7 minutes. Add eggs and vanilla; mix well. Combine flour, baking powder and salt; gradually add to the creamed mixture and mix well. Chill for 1 hour or until firm.
2. Preheat oven to 375°. On a lightly floured surface, roll out dough to ¼-in. thickness. Cut into 3x2-in. rectangles. Using a floured spatula, transfer cookies to parchment-lined baking sheets. Chill on baking sheets for 30 minutes or until firm. Bake until lightly browned, about 15 minutes. Cool completely on wire racks.

3. For icing, in a large bowl, combine confectioners' sugar, water and meringue powder; beat on low speed just until blended. Beat on high until stiff peaks form, 4-5 minutes. Keep unused icing covered at all times with a damp cloth. If necessary, beat again on high speed to restore texture.
4. Place ½ cup icing into each of 3 bowls. Tint 1 green, 1 pink, and 1 blue. Keep covered and set aside. Place ¼ cup icing into a bowl; tint black. Keep remaining icing white. Add additional water as needed to reach desired consistency. Frost cookies as desired to look like cassette tapes. Let dry at room temperature for several hours or until icing is firm.

1 COOKIE 222 cal., 6g fat (4g sat. fat), 31mg chol., 130mg sod., 39g carb. (27g sugars, 0 fiber), 3g pro.

LEMON-ORANGE ICED TEA

I finally hit on a recipe for iced tea that doesn't have the aftertaste of artificial sweetener. This tangy drink is perfect for folks who need to monitor their sugar intake.
—*Dawn Lowenstein, Huntingdon Valley, PA*

- -

PREP: 20 min. + chilling
MAKES: 10 servings

- 2   qt. cold water, divided
- 6   tea bags
- 2   sprigs fresh mint
- 3½ tsp. Crystal Light lemonade drink mix
- 2   cups orange juice

1. In a saucepan, bring 1 qt. water to a boil. Remove from the heat. Add tea bags and mint; let stand for 10 minutes.
2. Discard tea bags and mint. Pour tea into a large pitcher. Add the drink mix, orange juice and remaining water; stir well. Refrigerate until chilled. Serve over ice.

1 CUP 27 cal., 0 fat (0 sat. fat), 0 chol., 1mg sod., 5g carb. (5g sugars, 0 fiber), 0 pro.

SAUSAGE
QUICHE
SQUARES

2. Bake, uncovered, until a knife inserted in the center comes out clean, 18-22 minutes. Cool for 10 minutes; cut into 1-in. squares.

NOTE Wear disposable gloves when cutting hot peppers; the oils can burn skin. Avoid touching your face.

1 PIECE 29 cal., 2g fat (1g sat. fat), 24mg chol., 81mg sod., 0 carb. (0 sugars, 0 fiber), 2g pro.

SLOW-COOKED TURKEY SLOPPY JOES

This tangy sandwich filling is so easy to prepare in the slow cooker, and it goes over well at gatherings large and small. I frequently take it to potlucks, and I'm always asked for my secret ingredient.
—Marylou LaRue, Freeland, MI

PREP: 15 min. • **COOK:** 4 hours
MAKES: 8 servings

- 1   lb. lean ground turkey
- 1   small onion, chopped
- ½   cup chopped celery
- ¼   cup chopped green pepper
- 1   can (10¾ oz.) reduced-sodium condensed tomato soup, undiluted
- ½   cup ketchup
- 2   Tbsp. prepared mustard
- 1   Tbsp. brown sugar
- ¼   tsp. pepper
- 8   hamburger buns, split
     Pickle slices, optional

1. In a large skillet coated with cooking spray, cook turkey, onion, celery and green pepper over medium heat until meat is no longer pink, breaking it into crumbles; drain. Stir in soup, ketchup, mustard, brown sugar and pepper.
2. Transfer to a 3-qt. slow cooker. Cover and cook on low about 4 hours to allow flavors to blend. Serve on buns, with pickles if desired.

1 SANDWICH 264 cal., 7g fat (2g sat. fat), 39mg chol., 614mg sod., 34g carb. (13g sugars, 2g fiber), 16g pro. **DIABETIC EXCHANGES** 2 starch, 1½ lean meat.

SAUSAGE QUICHE SQUARES

Having worked in catering, I appreciate all kinds of interesting finger foods that serve a crowd. I'm often asked to bring this appetizer to parties. Each square is like a zippy, crustless quiche.
—Linda Wheeler, Middleburg, FL

PREP: 15 min. • **BAKE:** 20 min. + cooling
MAKES: about 8 dozen

- 1   lb. bulk pork sausage
- 1   cup shredded cheddar cheese
- 1   cup shredded Monterey Jack cheese
- ½   cup finely chopped onion
- 1   can (4 oz.) chopped green chiles
- 1   Tbsp. minced jalapeno pepper, optional
- 10 large eggs
- 1   tsp. chili powder
- 1   tsp. ground cumin
- 1   tsp. salt
- ½   tsp. garlic powder
- ½   tsp. pepper

1. Preheat oven to 375°. In a large skillet, cook and crumble sausage until no longer pink; drain. Place in a greased 13x9-in. baking dish. Layer with cheeses, onion, green chiles and, if desired, jalapeno. In a bowl, beat eggs and seasonings. Pour over the cheese layer.

SLOW-COOKED
TURKEY
SLOPPY JOES

FUDGE PUDDING POPS

This chocolate frozen dessert is the perfect summer treat!
—*Ruth Ann Stelfox, Raymond, AB*

PREP: 10 min. + freezing
COOK: 10 min. + cooling
MAKES: about 1 dozen

- 1   pkg. (3.4 oz.) cook-and-serve chocolate pudding mix
- 3   cups whole milk
- ¼   cup sugar
- ½   cup heavy whipping cream, whipped
      Freezer pop molds or paper cups (3 oz. each) and wooden pop sticks

In a large saucepan over medium heat, combine pudding, milk and sugar; bring to a boil. Cook and stir for 2 minutes. Cool 30 minutes, stirring often. Fold in whipped cream. Pour into pop molds or 3-oz. paper cups; attach lids to molds. Or, if using cups, top with foil and insert pop sticks through foil. Freeze until firm, 3-4 hours.
1 POP 107 cal., 5g fat (3g sat. fat), 16mg chol., 58mg sod., 12g carb. (11g sugars, 0 fiber), 2g pro.

CHERRY POKE CAKE

CHERRY POKE CAKE

I serve this because it's so festive and easy. No one will know your secret is adding a package of gelatin to a boxed cake mix!
—*Margaret McNeil, Germantown, TN*

PREP: 15 min. + chilling
BAKE: 30 min. + cooling
MAKES: 20 servings

- 1   pkg. white cake mix (regular size)
- 1   pkg. (3 oz.) cherry gelatin
- 1½ cups boiling water
- 1   pkg. (8 oz.) cream cheese, softened
- 2   cups frozen whipped topping
- 1   can (21 oz.) cherry pie filling

1. Prepare cake mix according to package directions, using a greased 13x9-in. baking pan. Bake at 350° for 30-35 minutes or until a toothpick comes out clean.
2. Dissolve gelatin in boiling water. Cool cake on a wire rack for 3-5 minutes. Poke holes in cake with a meat fork or wooden skewer; gradually pour gelatin over cake. Cool for 15 minutes. Cover and refrigerate for 30 minutes.
3. In a large bowl, beat cream cheese until fluffy. Fold in whipped topping. Carefully spread over cake. Top with pie filling. Cover and refrigerate for at least 2 hours before serving.
1 PIECE 245 cal., 11g fat (5g sat. fat), 39mg chol., 242mg sod., 34g carb. (22g sugars, 1g fiber), 3g pro.

CREATE A SNOW CONE BAR

The heat is on! Make your '80s party extra chill with a snow cone bar. Guests can choose between boozy and alcohol-free versions of the classic syrups.

Create shaved ice using a blender with a "crush" setting. Slowly add water for a slushy effect; add more ice as needed. Add one of following syrups to each snow cone.

BLUE RASPBERRY SYRUP

Simmer 1 cup sugar and ¾ cup water until sugar is dissolved; remove from heat. Add 1 envelope unsweetened blue raspberry Kool-Aid and 1 tsp. lemon juice; cool completely.
—AMANDA KIPPERT, TUCSON, AZ

FUZZY NAVEL SYRUP

Simmer 1 cup sugar and ½ cup water until the sugar is dissolved; remove from the heat. Stir in 1 envelope unsweetened orange Kool-Aid mix and 1 tsp. lemon juice. Cool completely; stir in ½ cup peach schnapps liqueur.
—MATTHEW CROSS, DOWNERS GROVE, IL

SHIRLEY TEMPLE SYRUP

Simmer 1 cup sugar and 1 cup pomegranate juice until sugar is dissolved; remove from heat. If desired, stir in 1 tsp. fresh lemon juice; cool completely.
—*TASTE OF HOME* TEST KITCHEN

PINA COLADA SYRUP

Combine 1 cup cream of coconut, ¾ cup rum and ¾ cup unsweetened pineapple juice.
—LAUREN EBELING, DOWNERS GROVE, IL

MARGARITA SYRUP

Simmer 1 cup sugar, ½ cup water and 2 tsp. grated lime zest until sugar is dissolved; remove from heat. Let the mixture cool completely. Strain through a fine-mesh strainer into a bowl; discard lime zest. Stir in ¼ cup tequila, 2 Tbsp. fresh lime juice and 2 Tbsp. Triple Sec.
—MONIQUE PEREZ, CHICAGO, IL

PARTY INSPIRATIONS

Need an idea for a get-together? Any excuse for a party with friends is a good one, but here are 10 great ideas to get you started—with menus to match.

BEACH PARTY

Grab your beach towel, flip-flops and shades—it's time for a beach bash! To bring a seaside vibe to your summer gathering, turn to these refreshing, easy-to-eat recipes.

• • • • •

ON THE MENU:

COOL POOL

Here's a party-perfect way to chill drinks. First, fill water balloons with water, tie them off and place them in the freezer until frozen solid. Then add the frozen balloons to a kiddie pool, nestle in the beverages and invite your guests to grab and sip as they please.

BEER TASTING

Take guests on a flavorful tour of craft beers by hosting a tasting party. You don't have to be a savvy beer connoisseur to pull off this fun and casual shindig. Just have a variety of brews—lagers, stouts, ales, porters—for guests to taste and rate. Pub-inspired snacks, hot bites and other hearty eats will round out your menu. Cheers!

• • • • •

ON THE MENU:

Grilled Shrimp-Stuffed Mushrooms, p. 15

Mustard Pretzel Dip, p. 36

Buffalo Wing Dip, p. 40

Sour Cherry Shandy, p. 45

Refreshing Beer Margaritas, p. 55

Beer & Pretzel Caramels, p. 133

BEER SCORECARDS

Design and print scorecards (or buy some from Etsy or party stores) and have your guests rate different types of beer according to aroma, appearance, taste and finish. Have a few beer novices in the crowd? Remind them that anyone can enjoy the array of flavors—it's all for fun!

BRUNCH & BUBBLY

Celebrate a promotion, an engagement, or just the weekend— it's time to break out the bubbly! There's no better way to spend a morning than to gather with your favorite gal pals for an upscale brunch of sunny specialties and fabulous drinks.

● ● ● ● ●

ON THE MENU:

HOW TO OPEN A BOTTLE OF CHAMPAGNE

Want to know how to open a bottle of champagne without sending the cork flying? Popping the bubbly is easier than you think. Learn how on page 46.

FAN FUN

The dog days of summer might be over, but it can still get quite toasty outside. Put colorful, collapsible fans at every place setting for when guests need a quick cooldown.

END OF SUMMER

As September rolls around and the final days of summer slip away, celebrate the last of the sunshine with a colorful spread of drinks, snacks and desserts meant to delight.

• • • • •

ON THE MENU:

Terrific Tomato Tart, p. 24

Tomatillo Salsa, p. 25

Marinated Pork Kabobs, p. 40

Quick White Sangria, p. 45

Berry Nectarine Salad, p. 85

Fresh Plum Kuchen, p. 127

KEEPING COOL

Set a metal strainer with ice and a scoop for serving on top of a glass bowl to catch whatever melts—and spare your guests from watery sangria.

KENTUCKY DERBY DAY

You can bet on a good time at this Kentucky Derby soiree. Kick off racing's greatest day with gorgeous spring blossoms, food inspired by the South and, of course, homemade mint juleps.

● ● ● ● ●

ON THE MENU:

Sweet Onion Pimiento Cheese Deviled Eggs, p. 14

Benedictine Spread, p. 25

Mint Julep, p. 59

Kentucky Hot Brown Sliders, p. 111

Pecan Tarts, p. 127

Grandma's Strawberry Shortcake, p. 143

LUCK OF THE DRAW

Have guests pick—from a fedora or bowler hat—a numbered piece of paper randomly assigned to a racehorse. Whoever selects the winning horse's number wins a prize at the party's end.

SET THE SCENE

Miniature figurines and other horse-racing toys make great decorations as well as party favors.

CUTE CUTLERY
For a fun presentation, wrap green plastic utensils in orange paper napkins to look like garden-fresh carrots.

GARDEN PARTY
Welcome warm weather and budding blooms with a spring social in the garden. Choose a low-effort menu that's full of fresh herbs, fruits and vegetables and celebrate spring!

• • • • •

ON THE MENU:
Gorgonzola Tomatoes on Endive, p. 22

Asparagus with Fresh Basil Sauce, p. 38

Cherry Limeade, p. 48

Nutty Chicken Sandwiches, p. 103

Lavender Shortbread, p. 119

RADISH CENTERPIECE
Cut radish leaves off at the base of the stem. Arrange the radishes in a clear glass hurricane vase. Make a mixture of cold water and a couple of drops of dish soap, then pour it over the radishes to fill the vase (the soap will help keep the radish leaves from wilting). Arrange the radish leaves at the top of the vase to desired fullness.

TEA PARTY

Put some spring in your steep with this sunny spread that's perfect for Mother's Day, bridal showers or just a weekend get-together. Your teacup will runneth over with a splash of cream, a spoonful of sugar and a smattering of your closest friends.

• • • • •

ON THE MENU:

Traditional Scones, p. 16

Cucumber Canapes, p. 17

Mini Blueberry Bundt Cakes, p. 118

CHINA SHOP

If you don't own a full set of crockery, that's no cause for concern! The more patterns, shapes and colors on your table, the merrier. Head to your neighborhood secondhand store to stock up on an eclectic mix of cups, saucers and plates. Or crowdsource from friends and family ahead of the event for a sentimental selection of dishes.

CADDY HACK

Instead of setting up a fixed tea station, create a tea caddy you can pass around. Load up a pretty tray with honey, lemon wedges, sugar cubes, napkins, teaspoons, milk or cream, a whole slew of tea sachets and whatever else might tickle your friends' fancies. When seated around the table, all your guests can steep, sip and enjoy with ease.

MY FAVORITE THINGS

We all have a few favorite things—a handmade porcelain mug, comfy slippers, shiny lip gloss—that bring a small spark of joy to an otherwise ordinary day. What are yours? At the holidays, gather your favorite people for a gift swap that celebrates life's little treasures. You may find that the time spent with good friends is your favorite thing of all.

● ● ● ● ●

ON THE MENU:

Marinated Almond-Stuffed Olives, p. 31

Walnut & Fig Goat Cheese Log, p. 36

Italian Sausage Bruschetta, p. 39

Perfect Lemon Martini, p. 49

SANTA BELT NAPKIN RINGS

Bright red napkins that resemble Santa's suit—how jolly! Just cinch them up with handcrafted napkin rings made from black ribbon and gold glitter card stock. To make each ring, cut a square from the card stock. Mark two vertical lines in the center of the square that match the width of the ribbon. Use a craft knife to cut a slit at each line, then thread the ribbon through the slits and tie it around a napkin.

COFFEE TABLE CHRISTMAS
SMALL-SPACE SOIREE If you have a coffee table, nibble-and-pass snacks, and—of course—a bottle (or two) of wine, you can cuddle in close and make any Christmas gathering feel like the most welcoming celebration ever.

WARM IT UP Make any room feel instantly cozier by adding fuzzy textures throughout the space. A fluffy rug, soft blankets, plush pillows and a chunky sweater-weave floor pouf invite guests to hunker down.

WINTER WARMERS

The snow is blowing and the wind is howling. Come in from the cold, and indulge in a hot drink or appetizer to chase away the chill. These celebratory sips and bites have a cozy factor that is unmatched, and they're so simple to make for a group.

• • • • •

ON THE MENU:

Lemony Bacon-Artichoke Dip, p. 18

Smoked Gouda & Roast Beef Pinwheels, p. 31

Sausage Wonton Stars, p. 37

Fireside Glogg, p. 52

Hot Buttered Rum, p. 52

PAPER UMBRELLA BACKDROP

Cut fishing line roughly the length of your wall. With a glue gun, attach a cocktail umbrella to the line by the cardboard knob on top. Add umbrellas to the line at 8-inch intervals, gluing so that they lie in varying directions. Repeat steps as many times as needed to make the desired number of garlands. Hang with clear tape. Voila! Perfect photo op.

DIY PINEAPPLE CENTERPIECE

It's easy to make a tropical centerpiece using a hollow pineapple as a vase. Use a sharp knife to remove the top of the pineapple just below the base of the crown. Use a pineapple corer or a sharp knife to remove the fruit. Insert a small vase or Mason jar filled with fresh water into the pineapple. Add flowers, palm fronds or other florals.

TROPICAL PARADISE PARTY

Why go out when you can stay in? Invite your friends over to enjoy good company and good eats with this tropical collection of fruity cocktails, bite-sized snacks and delectably sweet treats.

● ● ● ● ●

ON THE MENU:

Hawaiian Egg Rolls, p. 16

Pineapple Salsa, p. 22

Easy Coconut Shrimp, p. 38

Nutty Hawaiian, p. 49

LEARN **HOW TO MAKE A PINEAPPLE BOWL**, P. 22

INDEX